FOURTH EDITION

2

W9-AOB-002

Series Director: **Diane Larsen-Freeman**

Grammar Dimensions

Form • Meaning • Use

Ingrid Wisniewska
Heidi Riggenbach
Virginia Samuda

THOMSON
HEINLE

Australia • Canada • Mexico • Singapore • Spain • United Kingdom • United States

THOMSON
HEINLE

Series Director: Diane Larsen-Freeman
Grammar Dimensions 2: Form, Meaning, and Use
Ingrid Wisniewska, Heidi Riggenbach, Virginia Samuda

Publisher, Academic ESL: *James W. Brown*
Director of Content Development: *Anita Raducanu*
Director of Product Marketing: *Amy Mabley*
Executive Marketing Manager: *Jim McDonough*
Senior Field Marketing Manager: *Donna Lee Kennedy*
Editorial Assistant: *Katherine Reilly*
Senior Production Editor: *Maryellen Eschmann-Killeen*

Cover Image: © Rubberball Productions/Getty/RF

Copyright © 2007, by Thomson Heinle, a part of The Thomson Corporation. Thomson, the Star logo, and Heinle are trademarks used herein under license.

All rights reserved. No part of this work covered by the copyright hereon may be reproduced or used in any form or by any means—graphic, electronic, or mechanical, including photocopying, recording, taping, Web distribution or information storage and retrieval systems—without the written permission of the publisher.

Printed in the United States of America.
1 2 3 4 5 6 7 8 9 10 — 10 09 08 07 06

For more information contact Thomson Heinle, 25 Thomson Place, Boston, Massachusetts 02210 USA, or you can visit our Internet site at http://elt.thomson.com

Credits appear on pages C1–C2, which constitutes a continuation of the copyright page.

Senior Print Buyer: *Mary Beth Hennebury*
Development Editors: *Amy Lawler, Sarah Barnicle*
Production Project Manager: *Chrystie Hopkins*
Production Services: *Pre-Press Company, Inc.*
Interior Designer: *Lori Stuart*
Cover Designer: *Studio Montage*
Printer: *R.R. Donnelley*

For permission to use material from this text or product, submit a request online at http://www.thomsonrights.com

Any additional questions about permissions can be submitted by email to thomsonrights@thomson.com

ISBN 10: 1-4130-2741-5
ISBN 13: 978-1-4130-2741-9

International Student Edition
ISBN 10: 1-4130-2754-7
ISBN 13: 978-1-4130-2754-9

Library of Congress Control Number:
2006932088

CONTENTS

A Word from Diane Larsen-Freeman xii
Welcome to *Grammar Dimensions*, Fourth Edition xiii
Empirical and Experiential Support for the *Grammar Dimensions* Approach xviii
Acknowledgments from the Series Director xix
A Special Thanks xx

Unit 1 Simple Present 1

Opening Task 1

Focus 1 Verbs in the Simple Present Tense (Use) 2
Focus 2 Simple Present Tense (Form) 2
Focus 3 Showing How Often Something Happens (Form/Meaning) 4
Focus 4 Talking About Facts (Use) 11

***Use Your English* Activities 13**

Unit 2 Present Progressive and Simple Present 18

Opening Task 18

Focus 1 Present Progressive: Actions in Progress (Use) 20
Focus 2 Present Progressive (Form) 21
Focus 3 Simple Present or Present Progressive? (Use) 22
Focus 4 Verbs Not Usually Used in the Progressive (Meaning) 26
Focus 5 States and Actions (Use) 27

***Use Your English* Activities 30**

Unit 3 Talking About the Future 34

Opening Task 34

Focus 1 Talking about the Future with *Will* and *Be Going To* (Meaning) 36
Focus 2 *Will* and *Be Going To* (Form) 37

Focus 3 Making Predictions: *Will* or *Be Going To?* (Use) 38
Focus 4 Future Plans and Intentions: *Be Going To* (Use) 39
Focus 5 Two More Uses of *Will*: Making Quick Decisions and Serious Promises (Use) 41

***Use Your English* Activities 44**

Unit 4 Asking Questions 48

Opening Task 48

Focus 1 Review of *Yes/No* Questions (Form/Meaning) 50
Focus 2 Review of *Wh*-Questions (Form/Meaning) 52
Focus 3 *Wh*-Questions That Focus on the Subject (Form/Meaning) 54
Focus 4 *Wh*-Questions with Rising Intonation: Checking Information (Use) 57
Focus 5 Choice Questions (Form/Meaning/Use) 58
Focus 6 Tag Questions (Form/Meaning) 60
Focus 7 Tag Question Intonation (Use) 63

***Use Your English* Activities 66**

Unit 5 Modals of Probability and Possibility 70

Opening Task 70

Focus 1 Using *Could, May, Might, Must, Couldn't* and *Can't* to Show How Certain You Are about the Present (Meaning) 72
Focus 2 Modals of Probability and Possibility (Form) 74
Focus 3 Modals of Probability and Possibility in the Past (Form) 77
Focus 4 Modals of Probability and Possibility with the Progressive (Form) 79
Focus 5 Future Probability and Possibility with Modals (Meaning) 81

***Use Your English* Activities 84**

Unit 6 Past Progressive and Simple Past with Time Clauses 88

Opening Task 88

Focus 1 Past Progressive and Simple Past (Use) 90

Focus 2 Past Progressive (Form) 91
Focus 3 *When, While,* and *As Soon As* (Meaning) 92
Focus 4 Time Clauses with *When, While, As Soon As, Before,* and *After* (Form) 94
***Use Your English* Activities 99**

Unit 7 Similarities and Differences 104

Opening Task 104

Focus 1 Expressing Difference: Comparatives and Superlatives (Form/Meaning) 106
Focus 2 Similarity and Difference: *As . . . As* and *Not As . . . As* (Meaning) 108
Focus 3 Using *As . . . As* and *Not As . . . As* (Form) 110
Focus 4 Making Tactful Comparisons with *As . . . As* and *Not As. . .As* (Use) 113
***Use Your English* Activities 116**

Unit 8 Measure Words and Quantifiers 120

Opening Task 120

Focus 1 Measure Words with Food (Meaning) 122
Focus 2 Measure Words with Count and Noncount Nouns (Form) 125
Focus 3 Common Quantifiers (Form/Meaning/Use) 129
***Use Your English* Activities 133**

Unit 9 Degree Complements 136

Opening Task 136

Focus 1 *Enough, Not Enough, Too* (Meaning) 138
Focus 2 *Enough, Not Enough, Too* (Form) 140
Focus 3 *Too Much* and *Too Many*; *Too Little* and *Too Few* (Form/Meaning) 142
Focus 4 *Too* versus *Very* (Meaning) 143
***Use Your English* Activities 146**

Unit 10 Giving Advice and Expressing Opinions 150

Opening Task 150

Focus 1 Giving Advice with *Should*, *Ought To*, *Shouldn't* (Meaning) 152
Focus 2 Using *Need To* and Imperatives to Give Advice (Use) 153
Focus 3 *Should* and *Ought To* versus *Must* (Use) 154
Focus 4 *Should* and *Ought To* versus *Had Better* (Use) 155
Focus 5 *Should* versus *Could* and *Might* (Use) 157
Focus 6 *Should* and *Ought To* versus *Might, Could, Need To, Had Better,* and *Must* (Use) 160
Focus 7 Expressing Opinions with *Should, Ought To,* and *Should Not* (Meaning) 161

***Use Your English* Activities 162**

Unit 11 Modals of Necessity and Prohibition 166

Opening Task 166

Focus 1 Modals of Necessity, Prohibition, and Permission (Meaning) 168
Focus 2 Modals and Phrasal Modals: *Must*, *Have To*, and *Have Got To* (Form) 169
Focus 3 *Have To* versus *Have Got To* (Use) 172
Focus 4 Using *Cannot (Can't)* and *Must Not (Mustn't)* to Show Something Is Prohibited or Not Permitted (Meaning/Use) 173
Focus 5 *Must* and *Have To* versus *Must Not*, *Cannot*, and *Do Not Have To* (Meaning/Use) 175
Focus 6 Talking about the Present, Past, and Future with *Have To* and *Must* (Form) 178

***Use Your English* Activities 181**

Unit 12 Expressing Likes and Dislikes 184

Opening Task 184

Focus 1 Expressing Similarity with *Too* and *Either* (Form/Meaning) 186
Focus 2 Expressing Similarity with *So* and *Neither* (Form/Meaning) 186
Focus 3 Expressing Similarity with *So* (Use) 187
Focus 4 Showing Agreement with Short Phrases (Use) 188

Focus 5 Short Phrases or Hedges and Emphatic *Do* (Use) 190
Focus 6 Likes and Dislikes with Gerunds and Infinitives (Use) 192
***Use Your English* Activities 193**

Unit 13 Present Perfect with *Since* and *For* 196

Opening Task 196

Focus 1 Present Perfect: Connecting Past and Present (Use) 198
Focus 2 Forming the Present Perfect (Form) 200
Focus 3 *For* and *Since* (Meaning) 202
Focus 4 *For* and *Since* (Form) 203
Focus 5 Verbs Not Used with Present Perfect and *For* (Meaning) 204
***Use Your English* Activities 206**

Unit 14 Present Perfect and Simple Past 212

Opening Task 212

Focus 1 Present Perfect versus Simple Past (Use) 214
Focus 2 *Ever* and *Never* in Questions and Statements (Meaning) 217
Focus 3 Present Perfect in Questions (Use) 218
Focus 4 *Already* and *Yet* (Meaning) 219
***Use Your English* Activities 221**

Unit 15 Present Perfect Progressive 226

Opening Task 226

Focus 1 Present Perfect Progressive and *Just*: Recent Activities (Use) 228
Focus 2 Present Perfect Progressive (Form/Meaning) 229
Focus 3 Perfect Progressive: Unfinished Actions (Use) 230
Focus 4 Present Perfect Progressive for New Habits (Use) 231
Focus 5 Present Perfect versus Present Perfect Progressive (Use) 232
***Use Your English* Activities 235**

Unit 16 Making Offers with *Would You Like* 238

Opening Task 238

Focus 1 Offers with *Would You Like* (Form) 240
Focus 2 *Would You Like . . . ?* or *Do You Want . . . ?* (Use) 240
Focus 3 Accepting and Refusing Offers (Use) 242

***Use Your English* Activities 245**

Unit 17 Requests and Permission 248

Opening Task 248

Focus 1 Making Polite Requests (Use) 250
Focus 2 Politely Refusing Requests (Use) 251
Focus 3 Responding to Requests (Form) 252
Focus 4 Asking for Permission (Use) 255
Focus 5 Responding to Requests for Permission (Use) 256

***Use Your English* Activities 257**

Unit 18 *Used To* with *Still* and *Anymore* 262

Opening Task 262

Focus 1 Comparing Past and Present with *Used To* (Meaning) 264
Focus 2 *Used To* (Form) 265
Focus 3 *Anymore* (Use) 265
Focus 4 *Still* (Form/Meaning) 266
Focus 5 Adverbs of Frequency (Form) 268

***Use Your English* Activities 269**

Unit 19 Past Perfect 272

Opening Task 272

Focus 1 Past Perfect and Simple Past (Meaning) 274
Focus 2 Past Perfect (Meaning) 274

Focus 3 *Before*, *After*, *By the Time*, *By* (Meaning) 277
Focus 4 Past Perfect versus Present Perfect (Use) 278

***Use Your English* Activities 280**

Unit 20 Articles 284

Opening Task 284

Focus 1 Definite and Indefinite Articles: *The*, *A/An*, Ø (no article), and *Some* (Form/Meaning) 286
Focus 2 Using Articles: First and Second Mention (Use) 287
Focus 3 Indefinite Articles with Singular, Plural, and Noncount Nouns (Form) 289
Focus 4 *Some* Instead of Ø (No Article) (Meaning) 290
Focus 5 *The* with Singular, Plural, and Noncount Nouns (Form) 291
Focus 6 Making General Statements with Ø (No Article) (Meaning) 292
Focus 7 *The* with Unique/Easily Identified Nouns (Meaning) 293
Focus 8 Using *The*: Second Mention, Related Mention, and Certain Adjectives (Meaning/Use) 295

***Use Your English* Activities 299**

Unit 21 Articles with Names of Places 302

Opening Task 302

Focus 1 Articles with Names of Places (Form) 304
Focus 2 Articles with Names of Institutions (Form) 307

***Use Your English* Activities 309**

Unit 22 The Passive 312

Opening Task 312

Focus 1 Active and Passive (Meaning) 314
Focus 2 Forming the *Be* Passive (Form) 315
Focus 3 The Passive (Use) 317

Focus 4 Including the Agent in Passive Sentences (Use) 318
Focus 5 Forming the *Get*-Passive (Form) 319
Focus 6 *Be*-Passive versus *Get*-Passive (Use) 322
***Use Your English* Activities 324**

Unit 23 Phrasal Verbs 328

Opening Task 328

Focus 1 Phrasal Verbs (Form) 330
Focus 2 When to Use Phrasal Verbs and How to Learn Them (Meaning/Use) 331
Focus 3 Phrasal Verbs That Take Objects (Form/Meaning) 333
Focus 4 Separating Verbs and Particles (Use) 335
Focus 5 Inseparable Phrasal Verbs (Form/Meaning) 336
Focus 6 When and When Not to Separate Phrasal Verbs (Use) 339
Focus 7 Phrasal Verbs That Do Not Take Objects (Form/Meaning) 341
***Use Your English* Activities 344**

Unit 24 Adjective Clauses and Participles as Adjectives 348

Opening Task 348

Focus 1 Adjective Clauses: Using *Who* and *That* to Describe People (Form/Meaning) 350
Focus 2 *Which* and *That* (Form/Use) 352
Focus 3 Participles as Adjectives (Form/Meaning) 355
***Use Your English* Activities 359**

Unit 25 Conditionals 362

Opening Task 362

Focus 1 Hypothetical Conditionals (Form/Meaning) 364
Focus 2 Word Order in Conditionals (Form) 366
Focus 3 Past Hypothetical Conditionals (Form/Meaning) 367

Focus 4 Future Conditionals (Form/Meaning) 371
Focus 5 Future Conditionals or Hypothetical Conditions? (Meaning) 373
Focus 6 Factual Conditionals (Form/Meaning) 375
Focus 7 *Would*, *Might*, *May*, and *Will* in Conditionals (Meaning) 377
***Use Your English* Activities 378**

Appendices A-1

Answer Key (Puzzles and Problems Only) A-14

Credits C-1

Index I-1

A Word from Diane Larsen-Freeman, Series Editor

Before ***Grammar Dimensions*** was published, teachers would ask me, "What is the role of grammar in a communicative approach?" These teachers recognized the importance of teaching grammar, but they associated grammar with form and communication with meaning, and thus could not see how the two easily fit together. ***Grammar Dimensions*** was created to help teachers and students appreciate the fact that grammar is not just about form. While grammar does indeed involve form, in order to communicate, language users also need to know the meaning of the forms and when to use them appropriately. In fact, it is sometimes not the form, but the *meaning* or *appropriate use* of a grammatical structure that represents the greatest long-term learning challenge for students. For instance, learning when it is appropriate to use the present perfect tense instead of the past tense, or being able to use two-word or phrasal verbs meaningfully, represent formidable challenges for English language learners.

The three dimensions of *form*, *meaning*, and *use* can be depicted in a pie chart with their interrelationship illustrated by the three arrows:

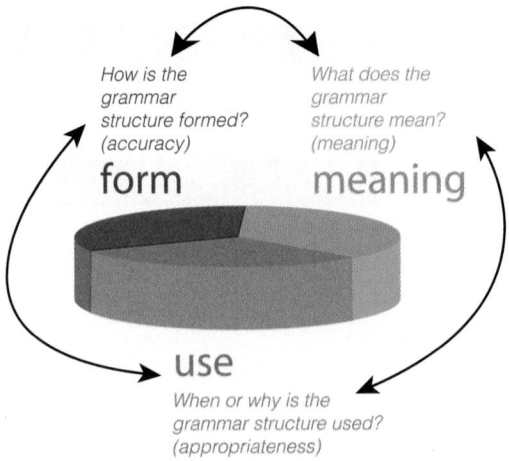

Helping students learn to use grammatical structures accurately, meaningfully, and appropriately is the fundamental goal of ***Grammar Dimensions.*** It is consistent with the goal of helping students to communicate meaningfully in English, and one that recognizes the undeniable interdependence of grammar and communication.

To learn more about form, meaning, and use, read ***The Grammar Book: An ESL/EFL Teacher's Course,*** Second Edition, by Marianne Celce-Murcia and Diane Larsen-Freeman. ISBN: 0-8384-4725-2. Enjoy the Fourth Edition!

Welcome to *Grammar Dimensions*, Fourth Edition!

The **clearest**, most **comprehensive** and **communicative** grammar series available! The fourth edition of ***Grammar Dimensions*** is more **user-friendly** and makes teaching grammar more **effective** than ever.

GRAMMAR DIMENSIONS IS COMPREHENSIVE AND CLEAR.

Grammar Dimensions systematically addresses the three dimensions of language—form, meaning, and use—through clear and comprehensive grammar explanations and extensive practice exercises. Each unit methodically focuses on each students' dimension and then integrates what they have learned in end-of-unit activities. In addition, grammatical structures are recycled throughout the series allowing students to practice and build upon their existing knowledge.

GRAMMAR DIMENSIONS IS COMMUNICATIVE.

Grammar Dimensions includes a large variety of lively communicative and personalized activities throughout each unit, eliciting self-expression and personalized practice. Interactive activities at the start of each unit serve as diagnostic tools directing student learning towards the most challenging dimensions of language structure. Integrated activities at the end of each unit include reading, writing, listening, and speaking activities allowing students to practice grammar and communication in tandem. New research activities encourage students to use authentic Internet resources and to reflect on their own learning.

GRAMMAR DIMENSIONS IS USER-FRIENDLY AND FLEXIBLE.

Grammar Dimensions has been designed to be flexible. Instructors can use the units in order or as set by their curriculum. Exercises can be used in order or as needed by the students. In addition, a tight integration between the Student Book, the Workbook, and the Lesson Planner makes teaching easier and makes the series more user-friendly.

GRAMMAR DIMENSIONS IS EFFECTIVE.

Students who learn the form, meaning, and use of each grammar structure will be able to communicate more accurately, meaningfully, and appropriately.

New to the Fourth Edition

- **NEW and revised grammar explanations** and examples help students and teachers easily understand and comprehend each language structure.
- **NEW and revised grammar charts and exercises** provide a wealth of opportunities for students to practice and master their new language.
- **NEW thematically and grammatically related Internet and *InfoTrac®College Edition activities*** in every unit of books 2, 3, and 4 develop student research using current technologies.
- **NEW Reflection activities** encourage students to create personal language goals and to develop learning strategies.
- **NEW design, art, and photos** make each activity and exercise more engaging.
- **NEW Lesson Planners** assist both beginning and experienced teachers in giving their students the practice and skills they need to communicate accurately, meaningfully, and appropriately. All activities and exercises in the Lesson Planner are organized into step-by-step lessons so that no instructor feel overwhelmed.

SEQUENCING OF *GRAMMAR DIMENSIONS*

In *Grammar Dimensions* students progress from the sentence level to the discourse level, and learn to communicate appropriately at all levels.

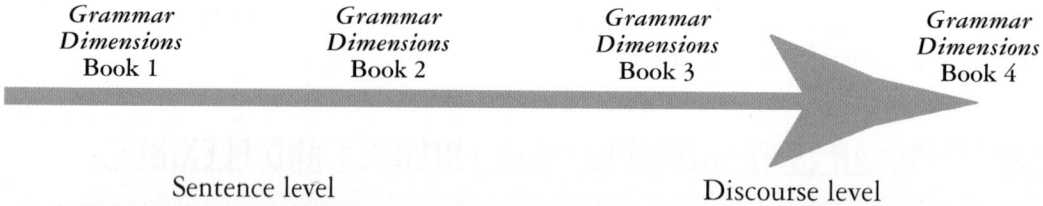

	Book 1	Book 2	Book 3	Book 4
Level	High-beginning	Intermediate	High-Intermediate	Advanced
Grammar level	Sentence and sub-sentence level	Sentence and sub-sentence level	Discourse level	Discourse level
Primary language and communication focus	Semantic notions such as *time* and *place*	Social functions, such as *making requests* and *seeking* permission	Cohesion and coherence at the discourse level	Academic and technical discourse
Major skill focus	Listening and speaking	Listening and speaking	Reading and writing	Reading and writing

Guided Tour of *Grammar Dimensions*

Unit goals **provide a roadmap** for the grammar points students will work on.

"**Opening Task**" can be used as a **diagnostic warm-up** exercise to explore students' knowledge of each structure.

UNIT 4

ASKING QUESTIONS

Yes/No, Wh-, Tag, and Choice Questions

UNIT GOALS

- Understand formation of different types of questions
- Understand meaning of different types of questions
- Recognize the uses of different intonation patterns for various question types

OPENING TASK

Any Questions?

STEP 1

What kinds of questions do you ask in class? Work with a partner to make a list of useful questions for learning English.

STEP 2

What questions could you ask the teacher in the newspaper article? Work alone or with other students to complete the questions on the facing page.

48 UNIT 4

FOCUS 4 *Wh*-Questions with Rising Intonation: Checking Information

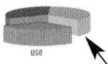

EXAMPLES	EXPLANATIONS
(a) A: Where are you from? ↗ B: Vanuatu.	Most *Wh*-questions end with falling intonation.
(b) A: Where are you from? ↗ B: Vanuatu. It's in the south Pacific. (c) A: Jennifer Lopez was here last night. B: Who was here last night? ↗ A: Jennifer Lopez.	A *Wh*-question with rising intonation shows that you are not sure about what you heard or that you want to check that you heard something correctly. The *Wh*-word is also stressed (said strongly).
(d) A: Jennifer Lopez was here last night. B: Who? ↗	Sometimes, just the *Wh*-word (with rising intonation) is used.

EXERCISE 6

Complete the conversation with appropriate *Wh*-questions. For each question, draw an arrow ↗ or ↘ to show if the question ends with falling or rising intonation.

Example: **Albert:** So, what did you think of the new Eisentraut movie?
Leslie: It was O.K., I guess, but I expected something more from a movie that cost $200 million to make.

Albert: (1) _____?
Leslie: $200 million. Amazing, isn't it? It's hard to imagine that amount of money.
Albert: (2) _____?
Leslie: It's an action movie set in the future, but I thought it was rather slow-moving. In fact, I almost fell asleep a couple of times.
Albert: (3) _____?
Leslie: It's about two hours, maybe a little longer. Luckily the seats were really comfortable.
Albert: (4) _____?
Leslie: At that new movie theater on Fourth Street, across from the parking garage. It only opened a couple of weeks ago, so it's got a state-of-the-art sound system, thick carpets, terrific popcorn. . . .
Albert: (5) _____?
Leslie: Twelve dollars.
Albert: (6) _____?
Leslie: Twelve dollars . . . I'm not kidding! I can't believe I spent twelve bucks on a movie that really wasn't very good.

ASKING QUESTIONS *Yes/No, Wh-*, Tag, and Choice Questions 57

"**Focus**" **sections** present the **form, meaning,** and/or **use** of a particular structure helping students develop the skill of "**grammaring**"—the ability to use structures accurately, meaningfully, and appropriately.

Clear grammar charts present rules and explanation preceded by examples, so teachers can have students work inductively to try to discover the rule on their own.

EXERCISE 8

Guess where each of the choice questions on the left was probably asked. Choose from the places or situations listed on the right.

QUESTIONS	PLACES/SITUATIONS
1. Paper or plastic?	A. a cash register in a department store
2. Would you like coleslaw or french fries with that?	B. a job interview
3. Do you want premium grade or regular?	C. a gas station
4. Will that be cash or charge?	D. a small shop selling hats and T-shirts
5. First class or economy?	E. an airline office
6. Do you say "large" or "extra large"?	F. a fast-food restaurant
7. Do you prefer mornings or evenings?	G. a check-out counter in a supermarket

Practice asking and answering the questions with a partner. Imagine yourself in each place or situation. Use more than one way of answering.

ASKING QUESTIONS *Yes/No, Wh-*, Tag, and Choice Questions 59

Purposeful exercises provide a wealth of opportunity for students to practice and personalize the grammar.

Use Your English

ACTIVITY 1 speaking/listening

- STEP 1 Your teacher is going to stick a piece of paper on your back and on the backs of your classmates. Get up and walk around the class, looking at what is written on your classmates' backs.
- STEP 2 Your job is to guess what is written on your back. You can find this out by asking questions. You can also answer the questions that your classmates ask you about what is written on their backs. For the first five minutes, you can only ask *Yes/No* questions. Refuse to answer any question that is not a *Yes/No* question. When your teacher gives you a signal, you can ask any kind of question that you like. Here are some possible *Yes/No* questions to ask: Is this a person? Is this person male or female? Is this an object? Is it expensive? Is this an animal? Is this food? Here are some possible *Wh*-questions: How big is this? Where was he or she born? What color is this?

ACTIVITY 2 speaking/writing

The international student office at your school is preparing a short guide for students who have just arrived in this country. The purpose of this guide is to give new students a clear idea of what to expect when they arrive here. You have been asked to write a chapter called "Frequently asked questions."

Get together with two or three other students and make a list of all the questions that people in this country frequently ask you. Compare your lists with those of other students in the class. Use the information from your classmates to make a list of the questions that people here frequently ask international students and that new students should be ready to answer.

66 UNIT 4

"Use Your English" (fondly known as the purple pages) offer communicative activities that **integrate grammar with reading, writing, listening, and speaking skills.** Communicative activities consolidate grammar instruction with enjoyable and meaningful tasks.

ACTIVITY 5 speaking/listening

Your English teacher has just quit her job and is now relaxing on a beach in Tahiti. Your school is desperately searching for a new teacher. Your classmates have decided to take matters into their own hands and you have decided to interview teachers yourselves. Pretend one of your classmates is an applicant for the position. Ask him or her some questions about his or her experience, interests, and future goals. Listen to your classmate's answers. They may help you ask other questions.

ACTIVITY 6 listening/writing

CD Tracks 6,7

A friend of yours has applied for a job teaching English in Latvia. She cannot travel to Latvia for a job interview, so the school has to interview her by phone. You are at her house when the school calls. You can hear her half of the conversation (the answers that she gives), but you can't hear the questions that the interviewer asked.

Listen to your friend's half of the conversation. In the first column, write the questions that you think the interviewer **probably** asked. Then listen to the complete interview to compare your questions with the ones the interviewer **actually** asked. Use the second column to write any questions that are different from the ones in the first column.

PROBABLE QUESTIONS	ACTUAL QUESTIONS

Engaging listening activities on audio cassette and audio CD further reinforce the target structure.

Research activity using ***InfoTrac®College Edition*** and the Internet encourages students to read articles on carefully selected topics and use this information to reflect on a theme or on information studied in each unit. ***InfoTrac® College Edition***, an Online Research and Learning Center, appears in Grammar Dimensions 2, 3, and 4 and offers over 20 million full-text articles from nearly 6,000 scholarly and popular periodicals. Articles cover a broad spectrum of disciplines and topics—ideal for every type of researcher. Instructors and students can gain access to the online database 24/7 on any computer with Internet access.

ACTIVITY 7 speaking/writing

Imagine you are going to write an essay on one of these topics: (1) Learning a foreign language, (2) Applying for a job, or (3) Using the Internet for research.

What three main questions will your essay answer? Compare your questions with another student. Write your questions on the board and choose the best three for each title.

ACTIVITY 8 speaking/listening

Bring in a photograph and give it to your teacher. Your teacher will mix up the pictures and distribute them randomly. Look at your photograph for thirty seconds and then give it back to the teacher. The teacher will put all the photographs on a table or hang them up. Students will take turns being questioned by the class. When it is your turn, your classmates will ask you questions about the picture you looked at. They will try to guess which picture it was. Try to use all types of questions: *Yes/No*, *Wh-*, statement form, choice, and tag.

ACTIVITY 9 research on the web

InfoTrac® College Edition: Go to InfoTrac to find information about a country you are interested in. Type in the name of the country and *Fact File*, for example, *France Fact File*. Make a list of questions using information in the article. Ask your classmates if they know the answers.

ACTIVITY 10 reflection

Work in a group. Choose one aspect of learning English, for example, writing or vocabulary. Write a questionnaire about how students in your class learn and practice this skill. Interview other students in your class using your questionnaire. Report the results to the class. What general patterns did you find?

ASKING QUESTIONS *Yes/No, Wh-*, Tag, and Choice Questions 69

Reflection activities help students understand their learning style and create learning strategies.

Supplements

These additional components help teachers teach and student learn to use English grammar structures accurately.

The Lesson Planner

The lesson planner facilitates teaching by providing detailed lesson plans and examples, answer keys to the Student Book and Workbook, references to all of the components, and the tapescript for the audiocassette activities. The Lesson Planner minimizes teacher preparation time by providing:

- Summary of main grammar points for the teacher
- Information for the teacher on typical student errors
- Step-by-step guidelines for every focus box, exercise, and activity
- Suggested correlations between exercises and activities in the Use Your English pages
- Suggested timing for each exercise and each lesson
- Lead-in suggestions and examples for focus boxes
- Suggestions for expansion work follow most exercises
- Balance of cognitive and communicative activities
- Explanation for the teacher of the purpose of each activity, in order to differentiate cognitive from communicative emphasis
- Occasional methodology notes to anticipate possible procedural problems.

ExamView Test Generator

Assessment CD-ROM with ExamView Pro Test Generator

The Assessment CD-ROM allows instructors to **create customized quizzes and tests** quickly and easily from a test bank of questions. Monitoring student understanding and progress has never been easier! The answer key appears with instructor copies of each quiz or test created.

Audio Program

Audio cassettes and CDs **provide listening activities for** each unit so students can practice listening to **grammar structures.**

Workbook

Workbooks **provide additional exercises** for each grammar point presented in the student text. Also offers editing practice and questions types found on many language exams.

Web site

Features additional grammar practice activities: elt.thomson.com/grammardimensions.

Empirical and Experiential Support for the *Grammar Dimensions* Approach

Opening Task Activities

The approach to teaching grammar used in the *Grammar Dimensions* series is well-grounded empirically and experientially. The Opening Task in each unit situates the learning challenge and allows students to participate in and learn from activity right from the beginning (Greeno 2006). In addition, students don't enter the classroom as empty vessels, waiting to be filled (Sawyer 2006). By observing how students perform on the Opening Task, teachers can analyze for themselves what students know and are able to do and what they don't know or are not able to do. Teachers can thus select from each unit what is necessary for students to build on from what they already bring with them.

Consciousness-Raising Exercises and Focus Boxes

Many of the exercises in *Grammar Dimensions* are of the consciousness-raising sort, where students are invited to make observations about some aspect of the target structure. This type of activity promotes students' noticing (Schmidt 1990), an important step in acquiring the grammar structure. The Focus Boxes further encourage this noticing, this time very explicitly. Explicit formulations of the sort found in the Focus Boxes can lead to implicit acquisition with practice (DeKeyser 1998). Moreover, certain learners (those with analytic learning styles) benefit greatly from explicit treatment of grammar structures (Larsen-Freeman and Long 1991).

Productive Practice and Communicative Activities

However, noticing by itself is insufficient. In order to be able to use the grammar structure, students need productive practice (Gatbonton and Segalowitz 1988; Larsen-Freeman 2003). Therefore, many of the exercises in ***Grammar Dimensions*** are of the output practice sort. Furthermore, each unit ends with communicative activities, where attention to the grammar is once again implicit, but where students can use the grammar structure in "psychologically authentic" or meaningful ways. Psychological authenticity is very important in order for students to be able to transfer what they know to new situations so that they can use it for their own purposes (Blaxton 1989) and so they are not left to contend with the "inert knowledge problem," (Whitehead 1929) where they know about the grammar, but can't use it.

The Three Dimensions of Grammar: Form, Meaning, and Use

Finally, applied linguistics research (Celce-Murcia and Larsen-Freeman 1999) supports the fundamental premise underlying ***Grammar Dimensions:*** that knowing a grammar structure means being able to use it accurately, meaningfully, and appropriately. Form focus or meaning focus by itself is insufficient (Larsen-Freeman 2001); all three dimensions—form, meaning, and use—need to be learned.

References

Blaxton, T. (1989). Investigating dissociations among memory measures: Support for a transfer-appropriate processing framework. *Journal of Experimental Psychology: Learning, Memory, and Cognition 15 (4): 657-668.*

Celce-Murcia, M. and D. Larsen-Freeman. (1999). *The grammar bbook: An ESL/EFL teacher's course.* Second Edition. Boston: Heinle & Heinle.

De Keyser, R. (1998). Beyond focus on form: Cognitive perspectives on learning and practicing second language grammar. n C. Doughty and J. Williams (eds.), *Focus on Classroom Second Language Acquisition.* Cambridge: Cambridge University Press, 42–63.

Gatbonton, E. and N. Segalowitz. (1988). Creative automatization: Principles for promoting fluency within a communicative framework. *TESOL Quarterly* 22 (3): 473–492.

Greeno, J. (2006). Learning in activity. In R. K. Sawyer (ed.), *The Cambridge handbook of learning sciences.* Cambridge: Cambridge University Press, 79–96.

Larsen-Freeman, D. (2001). Teaching grammar. In M. Celce-Murcia (ed.), *Teaching English as a Second or Foreign Language.* Third edition. Boston: Heinle & Heinle, 251–266.

Larsen-Freeman, D. (2003). *Teaching language: From grammar to grammaring.* Boston: Heinle & Heinle.

Larsen-Freeman, D. and M. Long. (1991). *An introduction to second language qcquisition research.* London: Longman.

Sawyer, R. K. (2006). Introduction: The new science of learning. In R. K. Sawyer (ed.), *The Cambridge handbook of learning sciences.* Cambridge: Cambridge University Press, 1–16.

Schmidt, R. (1990). The role of consciousness in second language learning. *Applied Linguistics* 11 (2), 129–158.

Whitehead, A. N. 1929. *The aims of education.* New York: MacMillan.

Acknowledgments from the Series Director

This fourth edition would not have come about if it had not been for the enthusiastic response of teachers and students using all the previous editions. I am very grateful for the reception ***Grammar Dimensions*** has been given.

I am also grateful for all the authors' efforts. To be a teacher, and at the same time a writer, is a difficult balance to achieve . . . so is being an innovative creator of materials, and yet, a team player. They have met these challenges exceedingly well in my opinion. Then, too, the Thomson Heinle team has been impressive. I am grateful for the leadership exercised by Jim Brown and Sherrise Roehr. I also appreciate all the support from Anita Raducanu, Amy Mabley, Sarah Barnicle, Laura Needham, Chrystie Hopkins, Mary Beth Hennebury, and Abigail Greshik of Pre-Press Company. Deserving special mention are Amy Lawler and Yeny Kim, who never lost the vision while they attended to the detail with good humor and professionalism.

I have also benefited from the counsel of Marianne Celce-Murcia, consultant for the first edition of this project, and my friend. Finally, I wish to thank my family members, Elliott, Brent, and Gavin, for not once asking the (negative yes-no) question that must have occurred to them countless times: "Haven't you finished yet?" As we all have discovered, this project has a life of its own and is never really finished! And, for this, I am exceedingly grateful.
Happy Grammaring all!

A Special Thanks

The series director, authors, and publisher would like to thank the following reviewers whose experienced observations and thoughtful suggestions have assisted us in creating and revising ***Grammar Dimensions***.

Michelle Alvarez
University of Miami
Coral Gables, Florida

Edina Pingleton Bagley
Nassau Community College
Garden City, New York

Jane Berger
Solano Community College,
California

Mary Bottega
San Jose State University

Mary Brooks
Eastern Washington University

Christina Broucqsault
California State Polytechnic University

José Carmona
Hudson Community College

Susan Carnell
University of Texas at Arlington

Susana Christie
San Diego State University

Diana Christopher
Georgetown University

Gwendolyn Cooper
Rutgers University

Julia Correia
Henderson State University
Arkadelphia, Arkansas

Sue Cozzarelli
EF International, San Diego

Catherine Crystal
Laney College, California

Kevin Ccross
University of San Francisco

Julie Damron
Interlink at Valparaiso University, Indiana

Glen Deckert
Eastern Michigan University

Eric Dwyer
University of Texas at Austin

Nikki Ellman
Laney College
Oakland, California

Ann Eubank
Jefferson Community College

Alice Fine
UCLA Extension

Alicia Going
The English Language Study Center, Oregon

Molly Gould
University of Delaware

Maren M. Hargis
San Diego Mesa College

Penny Harrold
Universidad de Monterrey
Monterrey, Mexico

Robin Hendrickson
Riverside City College
Riverside, California

Mary Herbert
University of California, Davis Extension

Jane Hilbert
ELS Language Center, Florida International University

Eli Hinkel
Xavier University

Kathy Hitchcox
International English Institute, Fresno

Abeer Hubi
Altarbia Alislamia Schools
Riyadh, Saudi Arabia

Joyce Hutchings
Georgetown University

Heather Jeddy
Northern Virginia Community College

Judi Keen
University of California, Davis, and *Sacramento City College*

Karli Kelber
American Language Institute, New York University

Anne Kornfield
LaGuardia Community College

Kay Longmire
Interlink at Valparaiso University, Indiana

Robin Longshaw
Rhode Island School of Design

Robert Ludwiczak
Texas A&M University
College Station, Texas

Bernadette McGlynn
ELS Language Center, St. Joseph's University

Billy McGowan
Aspect International, Boston

Margaret Mehran
Queens College

Richard Moore
University of Washington

Karen Moreno
Teikyo Post University, Connecticut

Gino Muzzetti
Santa Rosa Junior College, California

Mary Nance-Tager
LaGuardia Community College, City University of New York

So Nguyen
Orange Coast College
Costa Mesa, California

Karen O'Neill
San Jose State University

Mary O'Neal
Northern Virginia Community College

Nancy Pagliara
Northern Virginia Community College

Keith Pharis
Southern Illinois University

Amy Parker
ELS Language Center, San Francisco

Margene Petersen
ELS Language Center, Philadelphia

Nancy Pfingstag
University of North Carolina, Charlotte

Sally Prieto
Grand Rapids Community College

India Plough
Michigan State University

Mostafa Rahbar
University of Tennessee at Knoxville

Dudley Reynolds
Indiana University

Dzidra Rodins
DePaul University
Chicago, Illinois

Ann Salzman
University of Illinois at Urbana-Champaign

Jennifer Schmidt
San Francisco State University

Cynthia Schuemann
Miami-Dade Community College

Jennifer Schultz
Golden Gate University, California

Mary Beth Selbo
Wright College, City Colleges of Chicago

Mary Selseleh
American River College
Sacramento, California

Stephen Sheeran
Bishop's University, Lenoxville, Quebec

Kathy Sherak
San Francisco State University

Sandra E. Sklarew
Merritt Community College
Oakland, California

Keith Smith
ELS Language Center, San Francisco

Helen Solorzano
Northeastern University

Jorge Vazquez Solorzano
Bachillerato de la Reina de Mexico
S. C., Mexico, D. F., Mexico

Christina Valdez
Pasadena City College
Pasadena, California

Danielle Valentini
Oakland Community College
Farmington Hills, Michigan

Amelia Yongue
Howard Community College
Columbia, Maryland

UNIT 1

SIMPLE PRESENT

Habits, Routines, and Facts

UNIT GOALS

- Know when to use simple present tense
- Form simple present tense correctly
- Understand the meanings of various adverbs of frequency
- Place adverbs of frequency in correct sentence position

OPENING TASK

How Do You Learn Grammar?

STEP 1

How do you prefer to study grammar—in a group with other students, or individually at home?

STEP 2

What do you usually do to learn grammar? Read each statement and say how often you do each of these things. 1 = never 2 = rarely 3 = sometimes 4 = often 5 = always

1. If I don't understand a new grammar point, I . . .
   a. look it up in a grammar book. 1 2 3 4 5
   b. look it up on the Internet. 1 2 3 4 5
   c. ask my teacher. 1 2 3 4 5
2. If I want to practice a new grammar point, I . . .
   a. write some example sentences. 1 2 3 4 5
   b. try to use it in conversation. 1 2 3 4 5
   c. look for examples in a book or a newspaper. 1 2 3 4 5
3. In order to improve my grammar, I . . .
   a. ask my teacher to correct my mistakes. 1 2 3 4 5
   b. ask my friends to correct my mistakes. 1 2 3 4 5
   c. don't worry about mistakes. 1 2 3 4 5
4. I prefer to practice new grammar by . . .
   a. working in a group with classmates. 1 2 3 4 5
   b. listening to and reading grammar explanations. 1 2 3 4 5
   c. making my own examples. 1 2 3 4 5

STEP 3

Compare your answers with another student. Explain the reasons for your answers. Do you like to learn English grammar in the same ways? In what ways are you similar and in what ways are you different? Write a few sentences about how you learn grammar.

Example: *I use the Internet to look up grammar rules, but my partner goes to the library.*

STEP 4

Tell the rest of the class how you and your partner learn English grammar.

FOCUS 1 Verbs in the Simple Present Tense

Habits and Routines

EXAMPLES	EXPLANATIONS
(a) I **ask** questions when I **do not understand**. (b) Elzbieta **uses** English as much as possible.	*Ask, do not understand*, and *uses* are simple present verbs. Use the simple present to talk about habits (things you do again and again).
(c) Our classes **start** at 9:00 A.M. (d) Daniela **goes** to school five days a week.	Use the simple present to talk about everyday routines (things you do regularly).

EXERCISE 1

Go back to Step 2 of the Opening Task on page 1. Underline all the simple present verbs you can find. Compare your answers with a partner.

FOCUS 2 Simple Present Tense

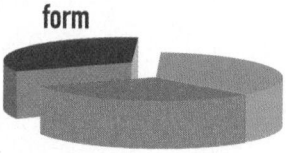

STATEMENT	NEGATIVE	QUESTION	SHORT ANSWER
I / You / We / They work.	I / You / We / They do not/don't work.	Do I / you / we / they work?	Yes, I / you / we / they do.
He / She / It works.	He / She / It does not/doesn't work.	Does he / she / it work?	Yes, he / she / it does.
			No, I / you / we / they don't.
			No, he / she / it doesn't.

EXERCISE 2

Look at what you wrote in Step 3 of the Opening Task on page 1. Underline all the simple present verbs that you used. Did you use them correctly? Check your answers with a partner and then with your teacher.

EXERCISE 3

STEP 1 **What are some *other* things you do and do not do to learn English grammar? Complete the following, using full sentences.**

Some things I do:

1. I usually write an example sentence in my notebook.
2. I _____
3. I _____

Some things I don't do:

1. I _____
2. I _____
3. I _____

STEP 2 **Get together with a partner, and tell each other about things you do and do not do to learn English grammar. Then, without showing your answers to each other, write about what your partner does and doesn't do.**

My partner, (name) _____,
does several different things to learn English grammar. (She/He) _____
_____
_____
_____

STEP 3 **Now get together with a different partner. Ask each other what you do to learn English grammar (*Do you . . .* ?). Together with your new partner, decide on the three most useful ways to learn English grammar. Share your ideas with the rest of the class. Write them here:**

1. We _____
2. We _____
3. We _____

FOCUS 3 Showing How Often Something Happens

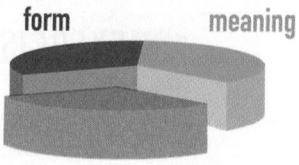

Adverbs of Frequency

EXAMPLES	EXPLANATIONS
(a) Kazue **often** uses a dictionary, but Florian **never** uses one. Most Often (100%) ↑ always usually often sometimes seldom rarely hardly ever ↓ never Least Often (0%)	*Often* and *never* are adverbs of frequency. They show how often something happens. For more information on adverbs of frequency, see Unit 18, Focus 5.
(b) I **usually** get up early. (c) He **never** calls me.	Where to put adverbs of frequency: **before** the main verb (b and c)
(d) She is **always** happy. (e) They are **rarely** late.	**after** the verb *be* (d and e)

EXERCISE 4

Which of these things do you do to practice English? Tell your partner. Add some more ideas of your own. Use an adverb of frequency from the chart.

- Use a dictionary?
- Read a grammar book?
- Use the Internet?
- Write in your journal?
- Read the newspaper?
- Play games?
- Write words in a vocabulary notebook?
- .....
- .....
- .....

Example: Student A: *Do you use a dictionary to help you study?*
Student B: *I **rarely** use my dictionary in class, but I **often** look up new words at home.*

EXERCISE 5

STEP 1 **Describe a typical day for students in each of these photos. Use the words in the box.**

sit in rows	take notes	work in groups
work in pairs	ask questions	raise your hand
answer questions	listen carefully	use computers

1

2

3

4

STEP 2 **Read the descriptions below and match each description to a picture on page 5. Write the number of the picture under each description. Compare your answers with a partner.**

A We sit in rows, and the teacher stands at the front. The teacher explains grammar rules, and the students listen and take notes. Students sometimes practice their writing in class.

_____

B Our English classes are always very relaxed. We usually work in pairs or small groups and often play games in class to practice our English. These games are a lot of fun and we sometimes laugh a lot. We don't feel nervous about speaking English when we play games.

_____

C We often work on special projects in our English class. We use computers to find information about a topic or we interview people to see what they think. Then we make a presentation about our topic to the rest of the class.

_____

D The students in my English class are very enthusiastic. Every time the teacher asks a question, everybody wants to answer it. We always raise our hands and hope that the teacher will choose us.

_____

STEP 3 **How are the classes in the photographs like (or unlike) classes in your country? First, discuss this question with your partner. Then be ready to tell the rest of the class.**

EXERCISE 6

STEP 1 **Complete the chart about students and teachers in your country and in the United States. The first one about teachers in your country has been done for you as an example. If you do not have enough room to write your answers on the chart, copy the chart into your notebook.**

	TEACHERS IN YOUR COUNTRY	STUDENTS IN YOUR COUNTRY	TEACHERS IN THE UNITED STATES	STUDENTS IN THE UNITED STATES
Usually	stand in front of the class			
Sometimes				
Hardly ever	walk around the class			
Never				

STEP 2 **Get together with another student from another country, if possible. Ask this partner questions about teachers and students in his or her country.**

Example: *Tell me about teachers in your country. Do they usually give a lot of homework? Do they sometimes tell jokes in class?*

STEP 3 **Look at the information from your chart and from your partner's chart. Use the information to make as many true sentences as you can.**

Example: *Students in my country usually stand up when the teacher comes into the room.*

EXERCISE 7

STEP 1 **Get together with a partner. Quickly look at the occupations in the box below.**

OCCUPATIONS		
a student	a police officer	a businessperson
an administrative assistant	a flight attendant	a bartender
a mechanic	a teacher	a nurse
an architect	a bus driver	a restaurant server

STEP 2 **Read the job descriptions below. Can you match them with the occupations in the box? Write the occupation on the line next to each description.**

1. He wears a uniform and usually travels many miles a day. He serves food and drinks, but he hardly ever prepares them himself. a flight attendant
2. She works in an office, but she often takes work home with her. She generally earns a high salary, but often feels a lot of stress. She sometimes entertains clients in the evening. _____
3. He usually wears a uniform and always carries a gun. He leads a dangerous life, so his job rarely gets boring. _____
4. He often works at night and meets many different people. He serves drinks and gets tips when people like his service. _____
5. She wears a uniform and drives many miles a day. She never serves food and drinks. _____
6. He spends many hours in the classroom and asks questions. He always has a lot of work to do and sometimes writes on the board. _____
7. She often wears a uniform and walks many miles a day. She works very hard and does not earn very much money, although she sometimes gets generous tips. _____
8. He spends a lot of time in the classroom and likes to ask questions. He often writes on the board. _____

STEP 3 **Now write similar descriptions for the jobs in the box that are not described above. What do these workers do?**

9. _____
10. _____
11. _____
12. _____

STEP 4 **On your own, think of two more jobs and write a short job description for each one.**

13. _____

14. _____

STEP 5 **Get together with another student and read your descriptions to each other. Ask and answer questions until you guess the jobs your partner described in Step 4. For example:** ***Does he or she . . . ? Is he or she a . . . ?***

EXERCISE 8

Sam is looking for a roommate to share his apartment, and Dave is looking for a place to live. They are trying to find out if they will get along as roommates. Complete their conversation, using verbs that fit the meaning of the sentences. Sometimes more than one answer is possible.

Sam: What do you usually do on weekends?

Dave: Well, I usually (1) ___wake up___ early, about 5:30, and then I (2) _____ by the river for an hour or so before breakfast.

Sam: Yeah? And what (3) _____ you _____ next?

Dave: After breakfast, I (4) _____ a cold shower, and then I usually (5) _____ my bike, or I sometimes (6) _____ tennis for a couple of hours. What (7) _____ you _____ on Saturday mornings?

Sam: I like to relax on weekends; I (8) _____ home and (9) _____ the newspaper and (10) _____ TV.

Dave: All weekend?

Sam: No. On Sundays, I often get in my sports car and (11) _____ to the beach.

Dave: Great! I like swimming, too. It's a habit that I learned from my brother. He (12) _____ in the ocean every day of the year, even in the winter.

Sam: Well, I rarely (13) _____ in the ocean. I usually (14) _____ on the beach and try to get a good suntan. Then I (15) _____ some of my friends, and we go to a nightclub and dance.

Dave: Don't you ever exercise?

Sam: Well, I (16) (not) _____ to a health club or gym, but every Saturday night I go to a nightclub, and I (17) _____ for hours. That's my idea of exercise.

Dave: Look, here's the phone number of a friend of mine. He (18) _____ dancing and nightclubs, just like you. Why don't you give him a call and see if he wants to be your roommate?

EXERCISE 9

STEP 1 **Talk to your partner about your daily routines. Complete the chart using adverbs of frequency. Would you make good roommates, or not?**

	YOU	YOUR PARTNER
Wake up early		
Sleep late		
Go to bed early		
Stay up late		
Go running		
Go to a nightclub		
Play tennis		
Relax at home		
Watch TV (not "a lot")		
Have friends over		
Read quietly		

STEP 2 **Change partners. Tell your new partner about your previous partner.**

FOCUS 4 Talking About Facts

EXAMPLES	EXPLANATIONS
(a) The sun **rises** in the east and **sets** in the west. (b) Brazilians **speak** Portuguese. (c) Water **boils** at 100° C.	Use the simple present to talk about facts (things that are true).

EXERCISE 10

STEP 1 **Match the pictures to the animal names in the box.**

horse	elephant	spider	bat
bear	swan	scorpion	antelope

What do you know about these animals? Be ready to tell the rest of the class anything that you know.

STEP 2 **Get together with a partner and draw lines connecting the animals in Column A with appropriate information about them in Column B. Don't worry if you are not sure of all the answers. With your partner, decide what you think is probably the best match for each piece of information.**

A	B
Horses	live for about two years.
Bats	sometimes go for four days without water.
Scorpions	stay with the same mates all their lives.
Elephants	use their ears to "see."
Swans	have twelve eyes.
Antelopes	sleep during the winter months.
Bears	sleep standing up.
Spiders	run at 70 miles per hour.

STEP 3 **Get together with another pair and compare your answers. When you are ready, compare your answers with the rest of the class. As a class, decide on what you think are probably the best answers. Then check your answers on page A-14.**

STEP 4 **Do you know any other unusual facts about these animals or any other animals? Tell the rest of the class about them.**

Use Your English

ACTIVITY 1 speaking/listening

The purpose of this activity is to prove or disprove the following statements about your classmates. Stand up, walk around the room, and ask your classmates questions to see if the following are true (T) or false (F).

1.	Most of the people in this room do not eat breakfast.	T	F
2.	Women drink more coffee than men.	T	F
3.	Fifty percent of the people in this room watch TV at night.	T	F
4.	Somebody in this room wears contact lenses.	T	F
5.	More than three people read a newspaper in English every day.	T	F
6.	More than 50 percent of the people in this room drive a car.	T	F
7.	Nobody likes opera.	T	F
8.	More than two people here come to school by bike.	T	F
9.	Everybody gets more than six hours of sleep a night.	T	F
10.	Most of the people in this room have a sister.	T	F

ACTIVITY 2 speaking/listening/writing

Interview someone about his or her job. Find out three things he or she sometimes does, often does, and never does. Write a description of the job based on your interview. What is your opinion of the job? Is it different from or similar to what you expected?

ACTIVITY 3 speaking/listening

The purpose of this activity is to find out what people usually do on certain special days.

STEP 1 Form a team with one or two other students, and choose one of the special days from the chart below.

STEP 2 Tell the rest of the class which special day your team has chosen. Make sure that there is at least one team for each special day.

STEP 3 With your team, interview three different people (native speakers of English if possible). Find out what they do or what they think usually happens on this special day. Make notes on the chart below or in your notebook. If possible, record your interviews.

STEP 4 After doing your interviews, use your notes to tell the rest of the class what your team found.

New Year's Eve

Valentine's Day

Halloween

Thanksgiving Day

STEP 5 Listen to your recorded interview, or use your notes to identify and write down any sentences that contain the simple present tense or adverbs of frequency.

ACTIVITY 4 listening

CD Tracks 1,2,3

STEP 1

Listen to the audio of people describing what they do on certain special days. Which special days do you think each speaker is talking about? Write your answers under "Special Day" in the chart below.

SPEAKER	SPECIAL DAY	VERBS IN THE SIMPLE PRESENT TENSE
Speaker 1		
Speaker 2		
Speaker 3		

STEP 2

Listen to the audio again. On the right side of the chart, write down as many examples of verbs in the simple present tense as you can.

ACTIVITY 5 speaking/listening

Prepare a short talk for your classmates, describing a special day or holiday that people celebrate in your country, city, or region. Talk about what people usually do on this day and how they celebrate. Don't forget to include an introduction to your talk. For example: *I am going to tell you about a very special holiday in my country. The name of the holiday is. . . .* If possible, record your talk and listen after class.

ACTIVITY 6 speaking/listening/writing

STEP 1 Complete the following with information that is true about yourself. Write complete sentences.

Something I usually do in summer	
Something I often do on weekends	
Something I rarely do in this country	
Something I sometimes do on Fridays	

STEP 2 Memorize these four sentences about yourself.

STEP 3 Walk around the room. When your teacher tells you to stop, find the nearest person. Tell the person your four sentences and listen to that person's sentences. Then memorize each other's sentences.

STEP 4 Walk around the room. When your teacher tells you to stop, find a different person. Tell this new person about the last person you spoke to. Then listen to that person's sentences. Do not talk about yourself. Memorize what he or she tells you.

STEP 5 Find someone different. Tell him or her the information the last person told you. Listen to the new person's sentences. Memorize what he or she tells you.

STEP 6 Now find someone new. Continue the process for as long as possible. Remember, you always pass along the information the last person tells you. Try to speak to as many different people as possible.

STEP 7 At the end, tell the rest of the class the information you heard from the last person. Is all the information true?

ACTIVITY 7 writing

Write a description of a typical high school classroom in your country. For example, what does the room look like? Where do the students sit? Where does the teacher sit? Is there any special equipment in the room? What is on the walls? What do teachers and students usually do when they are in the classroom?

ACTIVITY 8 research on the web

On the Web: Use an Internet search engine such as Google® or Yahoo® to find out about a celebration or holiday in another country. When does it take place? What do people usually wear/eat/do? If you want, you can research one of these examples: Mardi Gras (Brazil), Obon (Japan), Inti Raymi (Peru), Songkran (Thailand).

ACTIVITY 9 reflection

Think of one study skill that you would like to improve. Describe in detail how you usually practice this study skill. Try to break your description down into several different steps. Read your description to your partner.

Example: Writing an essay: First, I get out my notebooks, dictionary, and grammar book. Then I find some sheets of rough paper. I sharpen all my pencils. Then I . . .

UNIT 2

PRESENT PROGRESSIVE AND SIMPLE PRESENT

Actions and States

UNIT GOALS

- Know when to use present progressive
- Form present progressive correctly
- Choose between simple present and present progressive
- Know which verbs are not usually used in the present progressive

OPENING TASK

What's Happening?

STEP 1

A typical day at the office includes short conversations. Look at the picture. Where is this conversation happening? What are they discussing?

STEP 2

Work with a partner. Student A will look at picture A on the next page. Student B will look at picture B on page A-14. There are ten differences between the pictures. What are they?

Example:

Student A: *The woman at the front is opening a letter.*

Student B: *No, she isn't. She's writing a letter.*

Picture A

FOCUS 1 Present Progressive: Actions in Progress

EXAMPLES	EXPLANATIONS
(a) Right now, **I am sitting** on the couch and my brothers **are cooking** dinner. (b) It **is raining** and Oscar **is waiting** for the bus.	*Am sitting* and *are cooking* are present progressive forms. Use the present progressive to describe an action that is in progress and happening at the time of speaking.
(c) This semester, **I am taking** three math classes. (d) Their baby **is waking up** very early these days.	Use the present progressive for an action that is happening **around** the time of speaking, but not happening **exactly** at that time.
At time of speaking: *right now*, *at the moment*, *today*, *at present* Around time of speaking: *this year*, *this semester*, *this week*, *these days*	These time expressions are often used with the present progressive.

EXERCISE 1

STEP 1 **Read the following statements about picture A in the Opening Task. Without looking back at the picture, which statements are true (T) and which ones are false (F)?**

1. Two women are talking on the phone. T F
2. Three men are wearing jackets. T F
3. Two people standing. T F
4. Two men are reading. T F
5. Three people are talking. T F
6. One man is drinking coffee. T F

STEP 2 **Now look at picture A and check your answers. How many of your answers were correct?**

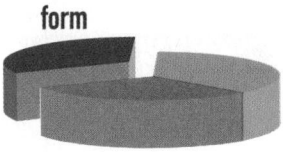

FOCUS 2 Present Progressive

To form the present progressive, use *be* + present participle (*-ing*) of the main verb:

STATEMENT	NEGATIVE	QUESTION	SHORT ANSWER
I am (I'm) working.	I am not (I'm not) working.	Am I working?	Yes, I am. No, I'm not.
You are (you're) working.	You are not (aren't) working.	Are you working?	Yes, you are. No, you aren't. (No, you're not.)
She/He/It is (She's/He's/It's) working.	She/He/It is not (isn't) working.	Is she/he/it working?	Yes, she/he/it is. No, she/he/it isn't. (No, she's/he's/it's not.)
We are (We're) working.	We are not (aren't) working.	Are we working?	Yes, we are. No, we aren't. (No, we're not.)
They are (They're) working	They are not (aren't) working.	Are they working?	Yes, they are. No, they aren't. (No, they're not.)

EXERCISE 2

Study the picture on page 19 for one minute. Close your book and, from memory, write as many sentences as possible to describe what is happening in the picture. Compare your sentences with those of the rest of the class. Who can remember the most?

FOCUS 3 Simple Present or Present Progressive?

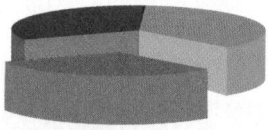

EXAMPLES	EXPLANATIONS	
	Simple Present	**Present Progressive**
(a) Philippe **watches** six TV programs a day.	For an action that happens regularly, again and again. (See Unit 1.)	
(b) A: Where's Philippe? B: In his room. He's **watching** TV. (c) Leanne can't come to the phone right now because she's **taking** a shower.		For an action that is in progress **at** the time of speaking.
(d) Philippe **is watching** more TV than usual these days (e) Audrey **is learning** Greek this semester.		For an action in progress **around** the time of speaking.
(f) Carmina **lives** in Mexico City. (g) The sun **rises** in the east. (h) Mark always **reads** the sports section of the newspaper first.	For facts, situations, and states that we do not expect to change.	
(i) Angela **is living** with her mother for the time being. (Someday she will move into a house of her own.) (j) Matt will start college next year. Until then, he **is working** at Fat Burger.		For situations and actions that are temporary and that we expect to change.
(k) Cell phones **are becoming** more popular these days.		For situations and actions that are changing.

EXERCISE 3

Check (✓) the sentence (*a* or *b*) that is closest in meaning to the first statement. Compare your answers with a partner.

1. I live in New York now.
   a. New York is my home.
   b. I expect to move very soon.

2. I'm staying with a friend.
   a. I'm at my friend's house right now.
   b. I won't stay at my friend's house for long.

3. I start work early in the morning.
   a. I usually start work early every day.
   b. I start work earlier than usual these days.

4. I'm walking to work these days.
   a. I'm walking to work right now.
   b. I started walking to work recently.

5. I'm writing to you on my computer at work.
   a. I am writing at this moment.
   b. I usually write letters on my computer.

6. Oh, no! The boss is coming over to my desk.
   a. The boss is walking towards my desk right now.
   b. The boss visits my desk quite often.

7. Many students are using wireless Internet in cafés.
   a. Many students are using computers in cafés these days.
   b. Many students are using computers in cafés right now.

8. The receptionist makes the coffee at work.
   a. He makes the coffee every day.
   b. He is making the coffee night now.

EXERCISE 4

Complete the following sentences using either the simple present or the present progressive. Use a form of the verb in parentheses. The first one has been done for you.

Melissa: Hello?

Chris: Oh hi! Is Angie there?

Melissa: Hi, Chris. It's Melissa. Angie's here, but she (1) _____is taking_____ (take) a shower at the moment. How are you? What (2) _____ you _____ (do) these days?

Chris: I (3) _____ (study) business management this semester. How about you?

Melissa: I (4) _____ (take) computers and Spanish. I _____ (work) part-time at the computer store for a few weeks.

Chris: I (5) _____ (speak) Spanish, but I'm terrible at computers. In fact, I _____ (have) trouble with my computer right now.

Melissa: I could help you, if you like.

Chris: Sure! (6) _____ you _____ (have) time today? What time (7) _____ you _____ (finish) work?

Melissa: At around 3 P.M. on Saturdays, but I usually (8) _____ (not, get) home till around 4.

Chris: OK, let's meet at 4:30.

EXERCISE 5

When people send text messages by phone, they often use just the first letters of each word to make the messages shorter. Can you translate the following into written English? Write your answers below.

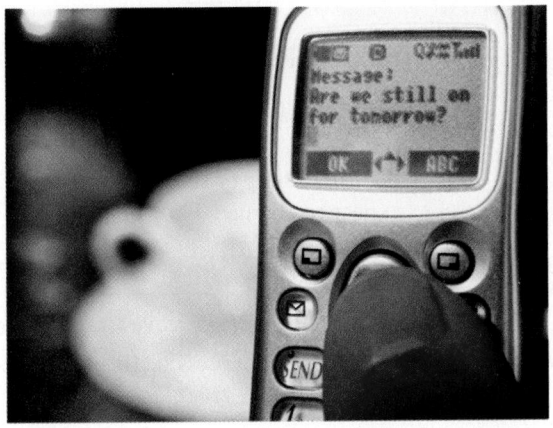

Key:
B = believe, C = see,
D = don't, H = hear,
I = I, it
K = know, L = later, love
M = mean, N = next,
O = or, N = not,
R = are, S = so,
T = think, U = you,
W = what, welcome

1. **CUL** See you later
2. **IHU** _____
3. **KWIM?** _____
4. **ILU** _____
5. **IDTS** _____
6. **IDK** _____
7. **BION** _____
8. **URW** _____

You can find the answers on page A-15.

Now underline all the verbs from your answers. Write them in the appropriate boxes below. The first one has been done for you.

VERBS THAT EXPRESS EMOTIONS AND FEELINGS	VERBS THAT EXPRESS SENSES AND PERCEPTIONS	VERBS THAT EXPRESS COGNITION: KNOWLEDGE THOUGHTS, AND BELIEFS
	See	

Which verb does not fit these categories? _____

FOCUS 4 Verbs Not Usually Used in the Progressive

EXAMPLES	EXPLANATIONS
(a) He **loves** me, but he **hates** my cat. (b) NOT: He is loving me, but he is hating my cat. (c) I **know** your sister. (d) NOT: I am knowing your sister.	Some verbs are not usually used in the progressive. The reason is that they describe states or situations that we do not expect to change. They do not describe actions.
(e) Hugo **likes** opera, but his girlfriend **prefers** ballet. (f) Those flowers **smell** wonderful! (g) I **think** the President has some interesting ideas about health care, but many people **believe** he is wrong. (h) Please be careful with that vase. It **belongs** to my aunt. (i) A: Are you going to buy that radio? B: No, it **costs** too much.	Common nonprogressive (stative) verbs: • Verbs that express feelings and emotions: *love prefer hate like appreciate want dislike* • Verbs that describe the senses: *see hear taste smell* • Verbs that express knowledge, opinions, and beliefs: *think believe know understand* • Verbs that express possession: *have belong own possess* • Other common nonprogressive verbs: *be seem owe exist need appear cost weigh*

EXERCISE 6

Complete the following with the simple present or the present progressive, using the verbs in parentheses.

Technology (1) is changing (change) the way we communicate. Today, more and more people (2) _____ (own) cell phones. Look around you. How many people (3) _____ (use) a cell phone right now? Cell phones (4) _____ (give) us a feeling of safety. We never (5) _____ (feel) lonely. Cell phones (6) _____ (become) popular with teenagers, too. They often (7) _____ (send) hundreds of text messages every day. They (8) _____ (think) they will be unpopular if they (9) _____ (not, have) a cell phone. People (10) _____ (talk) to each other more these days, but (11) _____ they _____ (understand) each other better?

FOCUS 5 States and Actions

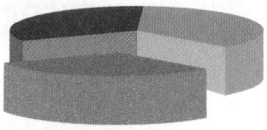

EXAMPLES	EXPLANATIONS
(a) I **love** you. (b) I **hate** my job. (c) She **knows** a lot about the history of her country.	Nonprogressive verbs usually describe a state or quality that we do not expect to change. They do not describe actions.
State / Action (d) I **weigh** 120 pounds. / I **am weighing myself** (to see if I've gained weight). (e) Mmm! Dinner **smells** great! / I'm **smelling** the milk (to see if it smells fresh). (f) This soup **tastes** good. / He **is tasting** the soup (to see if it needs salt).	Some verbs describe both a state **and** an action. If the verb describes a state, use the simple present. If the verb describes an action, use the present progressive.
(g) David **is** very polite. (h) Tanya **is** a little shy.	Do not use *be* in the progressive when it describes a state or quality you do not expect to change.
(i) We **have** two cars. (j) NOT: We are having two cars. (k) We **are having fun.** (l) We always **have fun** on vacation.	Do not use *have* in the progressive to describe possession. However, you can use *have* in the progressive to describe an experience. Use the progressive if the experience is in progress at or around the time of speaking (k). Use the simple present if the experience happens again and again (l). Common expressions using *have* to describe an experience: *have fun* / *have a good time* *have problems* / *have trouble with* *have difficulty with*
(m) I can't talk to you right now because I **have** a really sore throat. (n) NOT: I am having a sore throat. (o) Sandy **has** a headache and a high fever today. Maybe she **has** the flu. (p) NOT: Sandy is having a headache and a high fever today. Maybe she is having the flu.	Do not use *have* in the progressive to describe a medical problem or physical discomfort.

EXERCISE 7

Work with a partner or in a small group. You need a die and a small object (like a coin) to represent each person. Each person will also need a piece of paper and a pen or pencil.

STEP 1 Take turns throwing the die. The person who throws the highest number starts.

STEP 2 Put your coins (or objects) on the square marked "Start" on the following page.

STEP 3 Throw the die and move your coin that number of squares.

STEP 4 Complete the sentence in the square you land on by saying the answer out loud. If everyone agrees with your answer, you may write it on a piece of paper with your name and take another turn. If the class is not sure, the teacher will be the referee. If you make a mistake or do not know the answer, the next person gets a turn. The winner is the first person to reach the final square.

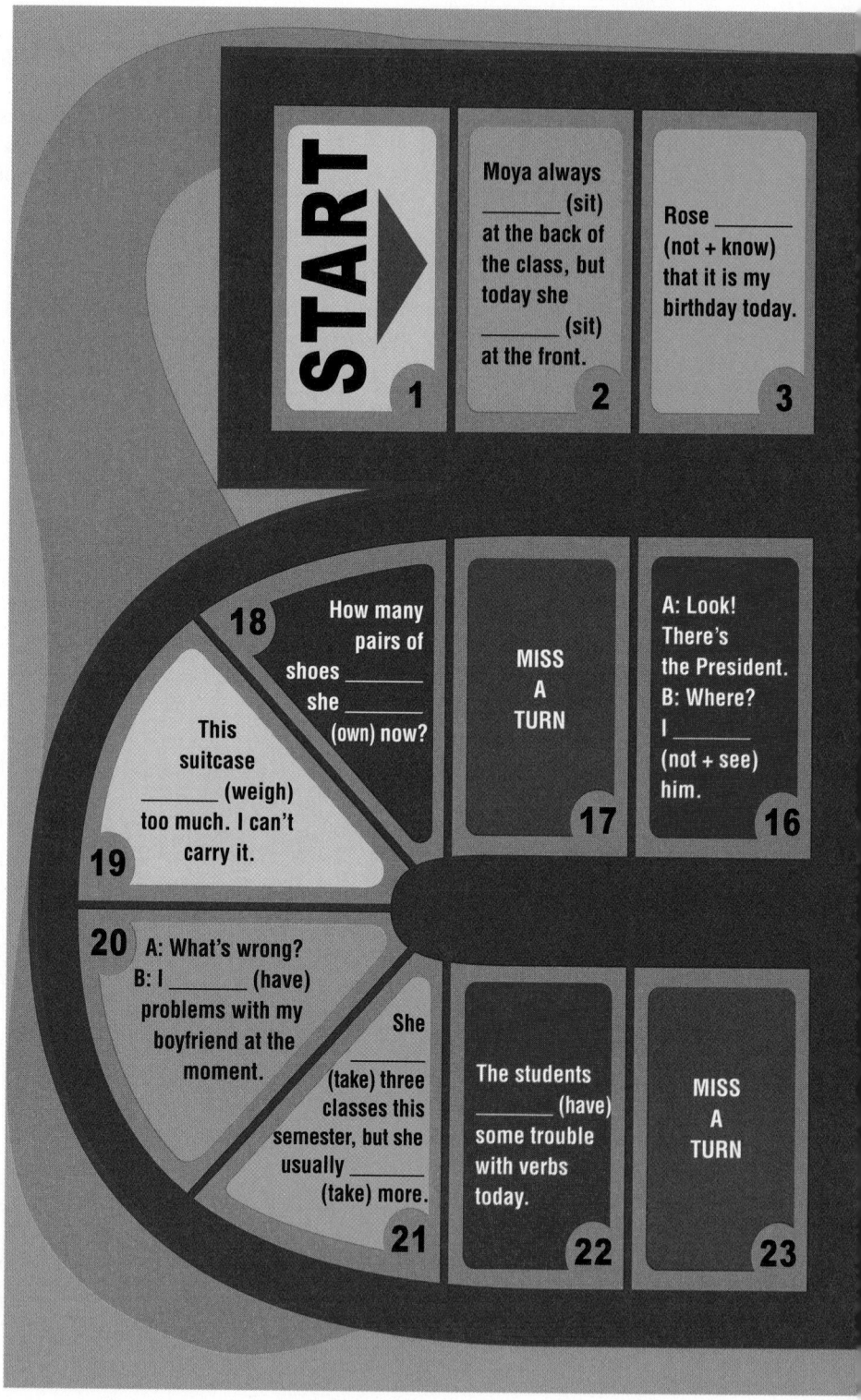

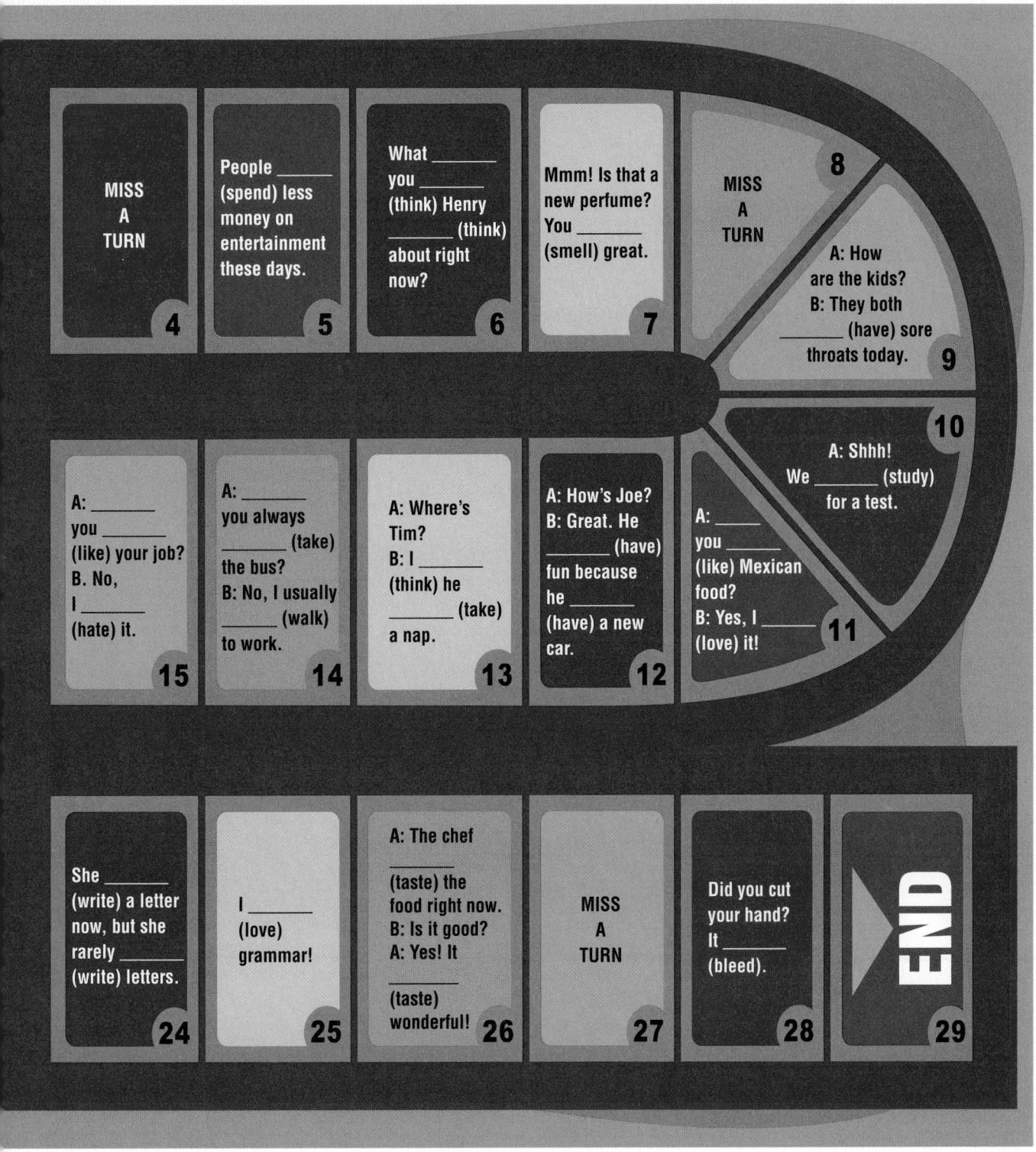
MISS A TURN
4
People _____ (spend) less money on entertainment these days.
5
What _____ you _____ (think) Henry _____ (think) about right now?
6
Mmm! Is that a new perfume? You _____ (smell) great.
7
MISS A TURN
8
A: How are the kids? B: They both _____ (have) sore throats today.
9
10
A: Shhh! We _____ (study) for a test.
A: _____ you _____ (like) Mexican food? B: Yes, I _____ (love) it!
11
A: How's Joe? B: Great. He _____ (have) fun because he _____ (have) a new car.
12
A: Where's Tim? B: I _____ (think) he _____ (take) a nap.
13
A: _____ you always _____ (take) the bus? B: No, I usually _____ (walk) to work.
14
A: _____ you _____ (like) your job? B. No, I _____ (hate) it.
15
She _____ (write) a letter now, but she rarely _____ (write) letters.
24
I _____ (love) grammar!
25
A: The chef _____ (taste) the food right now. B: Is it good? A: Yes! It _____ (taste) wonderful!
26
MISS A TURN
27
Did you cut your hand? It _____ (bleed).
28
END
29

Use Your English

ACTIVITY 1 listening/writing

In this activity, you will hear a teacher describe a Resource Center.

CD Track 4

STEP 1 Before you listen, write down three things that you expect students to be doing in the Resource Center.

STEP 2 Listen to the audio again. Write down examples of simple present and present progressive verbs in the chart below.

SIMPLE PRESENT	PRESENT PROGRESSIVE

ACTIVITY 2 writing/listening

Go to a crowded place where you can sit, watch, and listen to what is happening around you. Look carefully at everything that is happening. Pretend you are a journalist or a radio or television reporter. Describe in writing everything that you see. Do not forget to include everything you hear as well.

ACTIVITY 3 speaking/listening

Do you know how to play tic-tac-toe? In this activity, you will be playing a version of this well-known game. Work with a partner or in teams.

STEP 1 Copy each of the following onto separate cards or different pieces of paper.

she/speak	she/dance (?)*	you/live
we/hear	we/sing	I/see
I/understand	they/work (?)*	
they/eat	he/believe	
they/think about	you/write (?)*	(?)* = make a question

STEP 2 Place the cards face down on the table in front of you.

STEP 3 Player or Team X chooses a square from the box below and picks up a card from the pile. The player must make a meaningful statement that includes the word(s) in the square and the word(s) on the card. If the card has a "?" on it, the player must ask a question. Each statement or question must contain at least four words, not including the words in the square. Use the simple present or present progressive.

every day	today	usually
this week	occasionally	right now
often	at the moment	sometimes

STEP 4 If everyone accepts the statement, Player or Team X marks the square with an X.

STEP 5 Player or Team O then chooses a different square and takes a new card. The Player or Team O makes a statement. If the statement is correct, Player or Team O marks the square with an O.

STEP 6 The first person or team to have three Xs or three Os in a straight line wins. You can play this game again and again by erasing the Xs and Os at the end of each round, or by writing them on small pieces of paper and covering the squares with these. Good luck!

ACTIVITY 4 speaking/listening/writing

STEP 1

Go around the classroom and try to find a different person for each of the situations in the chart below. Write the person's name in the box marked *Name* and add more information in the box marked *Information.* We have given some suggestions here, but you probably have more ideas of your own.

SITUATION	NAME	INFORMATION
. . . is reading a book in English		*Title? His/her opinion?*
. . . regularly reads a newspaper from his/her country		*Why?*
. . . reads more than one book a month (in any language)		*Favorite books?*
. . . usually goes to the movies several times a month		*How often? Favorite movie?*
. . . is wearing an article of clothing made in the U.S.A.		*Describe it.*
. . . regularly plays a musical instrument		*What kind? How often?*
. . . is wearing perfume or cologne at the moment		*What kind? Describe it.*
. . . has a pet		*What kind? How old?*

STEP 2

Look at all the information that you collected. Choose three or four of the most interesting or surprising things that you learned about your classmates and write about this information. Remember to include an introduction. For example: *I interviewed some of my classmates and I learned several new things about them. First, I learned that Maria likes to read. In fact, she is reading a book in English that she is enjoying very much. . . .*

Read your report to a partner. Ask your partner to listen first to count the examples of the **simple present** and then listen again, doing the same for the **present progressive.**

ACTIVITY 5 writing

Journal Entry: What things are changing in your country? What things are getting more popular? What things are disappearing? How do you feel about it?

ACTIVITY 6 research on the web

On the Web: Use an Internet search engine such as Google® or Yahoo® to find out about events that are happening right now in your town or neighborhood. Type the name of your city or town and "current events." Choose one event that you like and tell your class or a partner about it.

ACTIVITY 7 reflection

How do you use technology in your studies? How are your study habits changing because of technology? Write a journal entry about how you feel about these changes.

UNIT 3

TALKING ABOUT THE FUTURE

Be Going To and *Will*

UNIT GOALS

- Form statements and questions about the future using *be going to* and *will*
- Know the uses of *be going* to and *will*
- Choose between *be going to* and *will*

OPENING TASK

Telling Your Future

Some people believe that you can see your future in the lines of your palm. Palm reading is the art of telling your future by looking at your palm. What is your opinion of palm reading?

STEP 1

Read the meanings connected with each line on page 35.

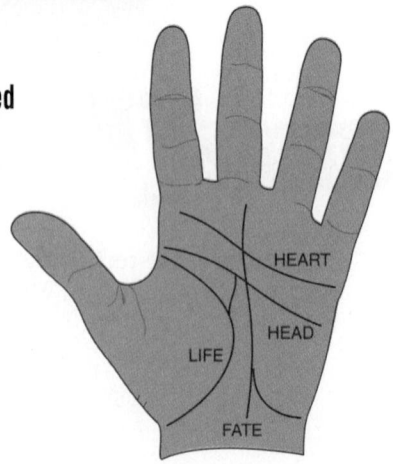

Life Line:

Does a line cross your life line? You will have a big change in your life. You are going to move, change schools or jobs, or marry.

Does your life line split into two branches? Your life will be full of adventure.

Does it bend towards your little finger? You are going to have a pleasant and quiet life.

Head Line:

Does it go straight across? You will be a lawyer, a doctor, or a scientist.

Does it curve down? You will be an artist, a musician, or a dancer.

Heart Line:

Is it close to your head line? You will have a few close friends.

Is there a wide space between your heart and head lines? You will be friends with many different people.

Fate Line:

Is it a straight downward line? You will achieve all your goals.

Does it bend towards your first finger? You are going to be successful.

STEP 2

Use the information to make predictions about each person's future.

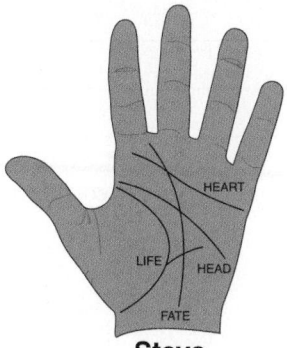

Steve

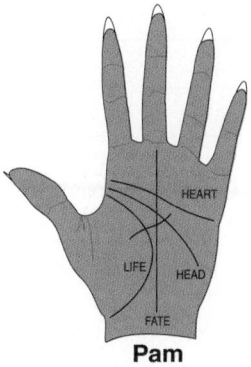

Pam

STEP 3

Look at your partner's palm. Make predictions about your partner's future.

FOCUS 1 Talking About the Future with *Will* and *Be Going To*

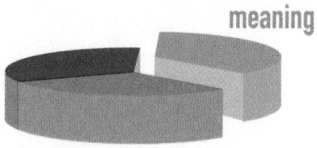

EXAMPLES	EXPLANATIONS
(a) Your life **is going to** be full of adventure. OR (b) Your life **will** be full of adventure. (c) You **are going to** be sucessful. OR (d) You **will** be sucessful.	Use either *be going to* or *will* to make a prediction or talk about the future.

EXERCISE 1

Write predictions about yourself and your partner using the information from the Opening Task.

Example: *My partner's life will be full of adventure.*

1. _____

_____

2. _____

_____

3. _____

_____

4. _____

_____

5. _____

_____

6. _____

_____

Check your sentences. Did you use *will* and *be going to* correctly?

FOCUS 2 *Will* and *Be Going To*

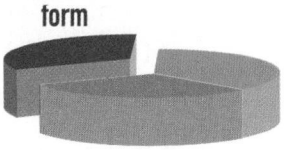

Will does not change to agree with the subject:

STATEMENT	NEGATIVE	QUESTION
I / You / We / They / She / He / It — will leave. / 'll	I / You / We / They / She / He / It — will not / won't leave.	Will — I / you / we / they / she / he / it — leave?

Be going to changes to agree with the subject:

STATEMENT	NEGATIVE	QUESTION
I — am going to leave. / 'm	I — am not / 'm not going to leave.	Am — I — going to leave?
You / We / They — are going to leave. / 're	You / We / They — are not / aren't going to leave. /'re not	Are — you / we / they — going to leave?
She / He / It — is going to leave. / 's	He / She / It — is not / isn't going to leave. / 's not	Is — he / she / it — going to leave?

EXERCISE 2

STEP 1 **Imagine our world 100 years from now. Write yes/no questions about what life will be like.**

Example: Will we live in houses with solar energy for electricity?

1. _____
2. _____
3. _____
4. _____

STEP 2 **Ask your partner the questions from Step 1 and write down his or her answers. Think of what things we are going to have and also things we are *not* going to have.**

Example: No. We aren't going to live in houses with solar electricity. We will live in houses under the sea.

1. _____
2. _____
3. _____
4. _____

FOCUS 3 Making Predictions: *Will* or *Be Going To*?

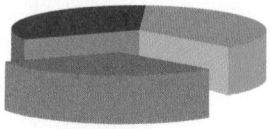

EXAMPLES	EXPLANATIONS
(a) Be careful! That chair **is going to** break. (b) NOT: Be careful! That chair will break! (c) Oh no!! That little boy **is going to** fall off the bridge (d) NOT: Oh no!! That little boy will fall off the bridge.	It is better to use *be going to* for actions or events that you think will happen very soon or immediately
(e) *Babysitter to child:* Your mommy's **going to** be very angry about this. (f) *Student to professor*: **Will** the test be difficult? *Professor*: It **will** be tough, but I don't think you **will** have too many problems with it.	When the future event or action will not happen immediately: It is better to use *be going to* in informal situations (relaxed and friendly situations, with family or friends). In informal speech, *going to* is usually pronounced *gonna*. It is better to use *will* in more formal situations.

EXERCISE 3

For each of the following, decide on the best form to use: *be going to* or *will*. In some sentences, it is possible to use both. The first one has been done for you.

1. Quick! Catch the baby! I think he ___is going to___ roll off the bed.
2. Excuse me, Mr. President. Do you think unemployment _____ decrease in the foreseeable future?
3. Oh, no! Look at those clouds. It _____ rain.
4. I predict that you _____ meet a tall, dark, and handsome stranger, and you _____ fall in love and get married.
5. One day we _____ look back at all this and laugh.
6. I don't believe it. Look at Paula! I think she _____ ask that guy to dance with her.
7. A: What do you think about my son's chances of getting into Harvard, Dr. Heath?

   B: I don't think he _____ have any problems at all, Mrs. Lee.
8. Meteorologists predict that the drought _____ end sometime this fall.

FOCUS 4 Future Plans and Intentions: *Be Going To*

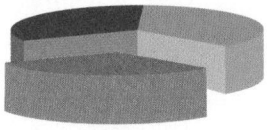

EXAMPLES	EXPLANATIONS
(a) What **are** you **going to** do this summer? (b) We'**re going to** spend the month of August in Italy. We bought the tickets last week, and we'**re going to** leave on August 2nd.	It is better to use *be going to* to talk about a future plan or an intention (something you want to do in the future). This shows that you made the decision to do this **before** speaking.

EXERCISE 4

In this exercise, you need to get information from one of your classmates. Use *be going to* or *will* in your answers, as appropriate.

1. Get together with a partner and find out three things he or she intends to do after class:

   My partner _____
2. Now find out three things he or she does not intend to do after class:

   My partner _____

3. Now find out three possible plans that he or she has for this weekend:

   My partner _____

   Finally, look back at what you have written in this exercise. Where did you choose *be going to* and where did you choose *will?* Why did you make these choices?

EXERCISE 5

Read the following conversation between two friends carefully and decide if the use of *be going to* or *will* is more appropriate. Check (✓) the sentences you think are acceptable. Correct the sentences you think are unacceptable.

A: (1) ✓ What are you going to do next year? (2) ___ Are you going to go to college?

B: (3) ___ Yes! I'm going to go to college in California. I sent in my application six months ago. (4) ___ I'll study nursing.

A: (5) ___ Fantastic! You'll be a very good nurse.

B: Thanks. What are your plans?

A: I'm not sure. (6) ___ I'm going to wait until I get my exam results. (7) ___ I'll work during my vacation. I already have a part-time job at the sports center.

B: That sounds good. Did you hear the news about Stan? (8) ___ He's going to get married!

A: That's wonderful news! (9) ___ Is he going to invite us?

FOCUS 5 Two More Uses of *Will*: Making Quick Decisions and Serious Promises

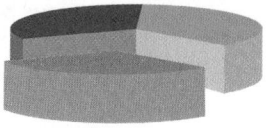

EXAMPLES	EXPLANATIONS
(a) A: I think there's someone at the front door. B: I'll go and check (b) A: Telephone! B: OK. I'll get it. (c) A: I need someone to help out at the recycling center. B: Oh, I **will**!	Use *will* for quick decisions or for something you have decided to do at that moment. The contracted *'ll* is usually used in these situations. Do not use *'ll* in short answers.
(d) I **will** always love you. (e) I'll give you my homework tomorrow, I promise! (f) A: Remember, this is top secret. B: I **won't** tell anybody. You can count on me.	Use *will* to make a serious promise. *Will + not = won't*

EXERCISE 6

Complete the following, using a form of *be going to* or *will,* as appropriate. The first is an example.

A: What (1) are you going to (you) do tonight?

B: The World Cup Final (2) _____ be on TV at 6:30. Julie (3) _____ come over and watch it with me.

A: Oh really? Who do you think (4) _____ win?

B: The newspapers say Brazil (5) _____ win. But I think Mexico (6) _____ give them a good match. What (7) _____ (you) do tonight?

A: I (8) _____ go to the movies with Fran. I (9) _____ be home around 11.

B: You'd better take your umbrella. It looks like it (10) _____ rain any minute.

A: Thanks. Can I take yours? I promise I (11) _____ lose it!

B: Sure. I (12) _____ go look for it in the closet.

EXERCISE 7

With a partner, look at these situations and decide on ways to respond using *will* or *be going to*.

1. You look out of the window and notice there are a lot of stormy, black clouds in the sky. What do you say?

   Example: We are going to need an umbrella.

   _____

2. Your friend Oscar is interested in music and in physics, but he can't decide which one to major in next year. After a lot of thought and discussion, he has finally decided to major in music. What does he say to his family?

   _____

   _____

3. Your friend is organizing an international potluck. She needs people to bring food from different countries. You want to help. What will you promise to do? What are you going to bring or cook?

   _____

   _____

4. It's 6:30 A.M. You have to drive to the airport to pick up your uncle at 7:30 A.M., but your car won't start. Your roommate offers to lend you hers, but she needs to have it back by 9:00 A.M. to get to work. What do you tell her?

   _____

   _____

5. You are standing in line in the campus cafeteria. You notice that the backpack of the student in front of you is open and all her books are about to fall out. What do you tell her?

   _____

   _____

6. One of your classmates is sick and has to go to the doctor's office. He is very worried about missing his history class. You are also in that class. What can you say to reassure him?

   _____

   _____

7. Your friend is giving you a ride home. Suddenly you notice a little boy who is about to run into the road. Your friend hasn't seen him. What do you say?

_____

_____

8. Your friend Frank loves ballet. He has just bought the last ticket for a special gala performance of *Swan Lake* next Saturday night. You ask him about his plans for the weekend. What does he say?

_____

_____

9. You have promised to do the dishes and clean up the kitchen after dinner. Just before you get started, you receive an unexpected phone call from a friend whose car has broken down, and he urgently needs your help. As you are leaving, your roommate comes into the room and asks, "What about the dishes?" What do you say?

_____

_____

10. Madame Cassandra is a fortune-teller who makes exciting predictions about the future. Your teacher is consulting Madame Cassandra. What does Madame Cassandra tell your teacher?

_____

_____

Use Your English

ACTIVITY 1 speaking/listening/writing

The purpose of this activity is to collect as much information as possible about the future plans and intentions of your classmates. Look at the chart below. Complete as many squares as you can by finding the required information. *Maybe* and *I don't know* are not acceptable answers! Write the information in the appropriate square as well as the name or names of the people who gave you the information. The first person to get information for three squares in a row in any direction is the winner. Good luck!

Find someone who is going to take the TOEFL® test* soon. When is she or he going to take it?	Find three people who are going to cook dinner tonight. What are they going to cook?	Find two people who are going to go to the library after this class. What are they going to do there?
Find two people who are going to play the same sport this week. What sport are they going to play?	Find someone who is going to move to another city within a year. What city is she or he going to move to?	Find someone who is going to go to the movies today. What movie is she or he going to see?
Find someone who is going to get his or her hair cut in the next two weeks. Where is she or he going to get it cut?	Find two people who are going to watch TV tonight. What are they going to watch?	Find two people who are going to celebrate their birthdays next month. What are their birth dates?

*TOEFL is a registered trademark of the Educational Testing Service (ETS). This publication is not endorsed or approved by ETS.

ACTIVITY 2 writing/speaking

STEP 1 Write predictions about the future for your teacher and five of your classmates. Write each prediction on a small slip of paper, and give each one to the appropriate person.

STEP 2 The people who receive predictions will read them aloud, and the rest of the class will decide if they think the predictions will come true.

ACTIVITY 3 writing

What are your predictions for the next ten years? What do you think will happen in the world? What do you think will happen in your country?

STEP 1 Write a brief report on your predictions. Your report should include a short introduction to your topic. It is not necessary to use *will* and *be going to* in every sentence you write!

STEP 2 When you finish writing, read your report carefully and check your use of *will* and *be going to*. Remember, it is often possible to use either one.

We have written the beginning of a report to give you some ideas, but you probably have better ideas of your own.

Life in the Future

Nobody knows exactly what will happen in the future, but in my opinion, there will be many important changes in the world in the next ten years. Some of them will be good and some of them will be bad. In this short report, I am going to talk about some of my predictions for the future of the world, as well as the future of my country.

First, let me tell you about my predictions for the world ...

ACTIVITY 4 speaking/listening

CD Track 5

STEP 1

Listen to the audio of an interviewer and three students talking about their goals and future plans. About how old do you think each speaker is? Take a guess. Take notes on what each speaker says in the chart below

SPEAKER	AGE	FUTURE PLANS AND GOALS
Student 1		
Student 2		
Student 3		

STEP 2

Think about your own goals and future plans. Are they similar to those of any of the three speakers? Explain to a partner.

STEP 3

Listen to the audio again. Write down all the examples you hear of the future with *will* and *be going to*.

ACTIVITY 5 speaking/listening

STEP 1

In this activity, you will interview several people about their goals and future plans. Interview at least three young people who are at different stages of their lives: college students, high school students, and children. Find out what they are going to do when they leave school. Take notes about their goals and plans or, if possible, record your interviews.

STEP 2

Make a list of the most interesting plans and share them with the rest of the class. Report your findings to the class.

STEP 3

(Optional) If you recorded the interviews, listen to the recording and take note of the different ways these native speakers talk about the future. What verb forms do they use to express the future?

ACTIVITY 6 listening/speaking

In this activity, you will create a chain story about your teacher's next vacation.

STEP 1 Your teacher will start by telling you where he or she is going to go for his or her next vacation and one thing he or she is going to do:

Teacher: *I'm going to go to Hawaii for my vacation, and I am going to climb a mountain.*

STEP 2 The next person repeats the first part and adds another statement about the teacher's vacation until everyone in the room has added to the description.

Student 1: Ms. O'Neill is going to Hawaii. She is going to climb a mountain. She is going to swim in the ocean, too.

ACTIVITY 7 research on the web

On the Web: Choose one type of technology that you are interested in: for example, cameras, cars, computers, music players, or video games. Use an Internet search engine such as Google® or Yahoo® to research new developments. How will this type of technology be different in the future? How will it affect our lives?

ACTIVITY 8 reflection

Think of three ways you would like to improve your study skills. Write an action plan. What skills are you going to improve? How are you going to work on them?

UNIT 4

ASKING QUESTIONS

Yes/No, Wh-, Tag, and Choice Questions

UNIT GOALS

- Understand formation of different types of questions
- Understand meaning of different types of questions
- Recognize the uses of different intonation patterns for various question types

OPENING TASK

Any Questions?

STEP 1

What kinds of questions do you ask in class? Work with a partner to make a list of useful questions for learning English.

STEP 2

What questions could you ask the teacher in the newspaper article? Work alone or with other students to complete the questions on the facing page.

South City College 2006 Teacher of the Year!

Teacher of the Year

Congratulations to Elena Dominguez, who was named Teacher of the Year. Elena was born in Venezuela and now lives in South City. She came to South City College five years ago to complete her Masters in Education. She started teaching Spanish here three years ago. Elena is married and has one daughter. She speaks Spanish and is planning a study trip to Mexico with her students next spring. She likes jogging and cycling. Her favorite food is pineapple. She loves teaching because she learns something new every day.

STEP 3

With a partner, role-play the conversation between you and Elena Dominguez.

FOCUS 1 Review of *Yes/No* Questions

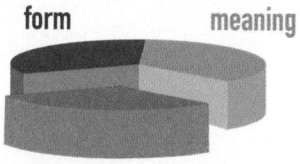

EXAMPLES	EXPLANATIONS
(a) *Question*: Are you Brazilian? *Answer*: Yes, I am./No, I'm not. (b) *Question*: Do you understand? ↗ *Answer*: Yes, I do./No, I don't.	When you ask a *Yes/No* question, you expect the answer *yes* or *no*. *Yes/No* questions end with rising intonation.
subject ***be*** (c) *Statement*: He is tired. ***be*** *subject* *Question*: **Is** he tired? (d) **Are** you ready to go? (e) **Am** I too late for dinner? (f) **Was** the plane on time? (g) **Were** they mad at me?	***Yes/No* questions with *be*:** Invert the subject and the verb (move the verb **in front of** the subject).
subject verb (h) *Statement*: They speak Turkish. *do subject base verb* *Question*: **Do** they **speak** Turkish? (i) NOT: Speak they Turkish? (j) **Does** the bus **stop** here? (k) **Do** you **take** credit cards? (l) **Did** the President **know** about this?	***Yes/No* questions with other verbs:** Put the appropriate form of *do* **in front of** the subject. Put the base form of the verb **after** the subject.
subject *be verb + -ing* (m) *Statement*: They are leaving. *be* *subject* *verb + -ing* *Question*: **Are** they **leaving**? (n) **Is** your computer **working** today? (o) **Am I meeting** you tomorrow? (p) **Was** it **raining** there? (q) **Were** her parents **visiting**?	***Yes/No* questions with verbs in the progressive:** Invert the subject and *be* (move the *be* verb **in front of** the subject). Put the -ing form of the verb **after** the subject. For information on *Yes/No* questions with present perfect and past perfect, see Units 13–14, and 19.

EXAMPLES	EXPLANATIONS
subject *modal* *base verb* (r) *Statement*: It will rain. *modal* *subject* *base verb* *Question:* **Will** it **rain**? (s) Would you repeat that? (t) Can you help me?	***Yes/No* questions with modals:** Invert the subject and the modal (put the modal **in front of** the subject). Put the base form of the verb **after** the subject.
(u) *Statement*: She asked him out. ↘ *Question*: She asked him out? ↗ (v) You're from England? (w) Sasha can come? (x) He's 40 years old? Yes, he is.	**Statement form of *Yes/No* questions:** A statement said with rising intonation is also a type of *Yes/No* question. This type of question is common in informal conversation. When a statement form question is used, the speaker usually expects the listener to agree.

EXERCISE 1

Get together with a partner and make a list of five *Yes/No* questions you could ask your teacher. Write them here or in a notebook. You will have an opportunity to ask these questions later in the unit.

1. _____
_____
_____

2. _____
_____
_____

3. _____
_____
_____

4. _____
_____
_____

5. _____
_____
_____

FOCUS 2 Review of *Wh*-Questions

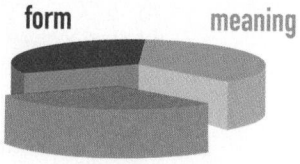

EXAMPLES	EXPLANATIONS
(a) Q: What is your name? A: Elena. *Who* *What* *When* *Where* *Why* *Whose* *Which* *How*	A *Wh*-question usually begins with a *Wh*-word and expects the speaker to give information rather than *yes* or *no* in the answer.
(b) Where do you come from? ↗ (c) When did you arrive? ↗ (d) How many languages do you speak? ↗	*Wh*-questions usually end in falling intonation.
(e) Q: Why are you late? A: Because I missed the bus. *Wh-word* *be* *subject*	**_Wh_-questions with _be_:**
(f) **Where** **is** the restroom? (g) **What** **was** her name? (h) Who **are** his friends? (i) What's the time? (j) Where's my car?	Choose a *Wh*-word. Invert the subject and the verb. In informal speech, *is* is often contracted to *'s* in *Wh*-questions.
(k) Q: When did she get here? A: Just a few minutes ago. *Wh-word* *do* *subject* *base verb*	**_Wh_-questions with other verbs:**
(l) Who(m) do you love? (m) What does a judge do? (n) Where did Nicole live?	Choose a *Wh*-word. To form a question, follow the *Wh*-word with a form of *do*. In informal speech, use *who* instead of *whom*.
(o) Q: What time can you leave? A: As soon as this class is over. *Wh-word* *modal* *subject* *base verb*	**_Wh_-questions with modals:**
(p) How long can I stay? (q) When will she come?	Choose a *Wh*-word. To form a question, put the modal directly after the *Wh*-word and before the subject.

EXERCISE 2

Get together with a partner and write down five *Wh*-questions you could ask your teacher. Write them on a piece of paper or in your notebook. You will have an opportunity to ask them later in the unit.

EXERCISE 3

Bruno and Ken are friends. Bruno has just introduced Ken to his cousin, Marta. Ken is very interested in getting to know more about her, so now he is asking Bruno all about her.

Get together with a partner and look at the answers that Bruno gave. What questions do you think Ken probably asked? Write them in the appropriate place.

Ken: (1) _____?
Bruno: Yes, I think she does.
Ken: (2) _____?
Bruno: No, she doesn't.
Ken: (3) _____?
Bruno: Usually around midnight.
Ken: (4) _____?
Bruno: Not usually.
Ken: (5) _____?
Bruno: In Buenos Aires.
Ken: (6) _____?
Bruno: Three times a week, I think.
Ken: (7) _____?
Bruno: No, she isn't.
Ken: (8) _____?
Bruno: Yes, I'm pretty sure she was.
Ken: (9) _____?
Bruno: Last year, or maybe the year before. I can't remember exactly.
Ken: (10) _____?
Bruno: I have no idea. You'll have to ask her that question yourself.

Now change partners. Read the questions that you wrote while your new partner reads Bruno's answers. When you finish, change roles to read your partner's dialogue. Compare your questions with a partner's questions. Does Marta seem like a different person? In what ways?

FOCUS 3 *Wh*-Questions That Focus on the Subject

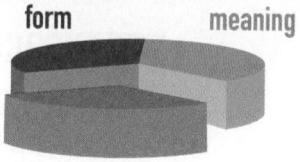

EXAMPLES	EXPLANATIONS
(a) Q: **Who(m)** did you call? A: I called Tony. *object*	This question asks about the object. *Who* is more common in informal speech. *Whom* is very formal.
(b) Q: **Who** called you? A: Martin called me. *subject*	This question asks about the subject.
Wh-word Verb (c) Q: **Who** lives here? A: Shan lives here. (d) Q: **Who** told you? A: Herb did.	For *Wh*-questions about the subject, put the appropriate *Wh*-word in front of the verb. Do not use *do* in the question.
(e) Q: **What** annoys her? A: Everything. (f) Q: **What** music annoys her? A: Rock music. (g) Q: **What** bands annoy her? A: Aerosmith and Bon Jovi.	Use *what* to ask a general question about something. Use *what* + a noun when you want a more specific answer. Make the verb singular or plural to agree with the noun.

EXERCISE 4

Get together with another student or someone in your class for this exercise. First read the report on the next page. Next, think of the questions you need to ask your friend in order to complete the report. Write the questions in the "Question Box." Ask your partner all of the questions without showing them to him or her. Finally, use the answers that your friend gives you to complete the report.

Report:

My friend (1) _____ is from (2) _____ and speaks (3) _____ languages: (4) _____. He/she was born in (5) _____ and he/she has (6) _____ brothers and sisters. His/her favorite subjects in school were (7) _____. He/she is taking this class because (8) _____. In his/her free time, he/she likes to (9) _____. His/her favorite (10) _____ is/are (11) _____. When he/she first came here, (12) _____ surprised him/her. After he/she finishes school, he/she hopes to (13) _____. (14) _____ make(s) him/her happy, but (15) _____ make(s) him/her angry. Finally, there is one more thing I'd like to tell you about my friend: (16) _____.

QUESTION BOX

1. _____?
2. _____?
3. _____?
4. _____?
5. _____?
6. _____?
7. _____?
8. _____?
9. _____?
10. _____?
11. _____?
12. _____?
13. _____?
14. _____?
15. _____?
16. _____?

EXERCISE 5

Chris is talking to Robin about his next vacation. Read their conversation below and write a question to go with each of Chris's answers. When you're finished, compare your questions with other students' questions in class.

Robin: (1) _____?
Chris: I'm going to Borneo for two weeks.

Robin: (2) _____?
Chris: No, it'll be my first trip to Borneo.

Robin: (3) _____?
Chris: The unique wildlife really interests me.

Robin: (4) _____?
Chris: I'm going with two environmentalists on a study trip.

Robin: (5) _____?
Chris: I met them on a summer course last year.

Robin: (6) _____?
Chris: We're taking backpacks and camping equipment.

Robin: (7) _____?
Chris: They have some poisonous snakes there, which worries me a little.

Robin: (8) _____?
Chris: We're leaving on Sunday morning.

Robin: (9) _____?
Chris: It takes twenty hours by plane.

Robin: (10) _____?
Chris: The flight is at 4 P.M.

FOCUS 4 *Wh*-Questions with Rising Intonation: Checking Information

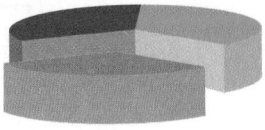

EXAMPLES	EXPLANATIONS
(a) A: Where are you from? ↗ B: Vanuatu.	Most *Wh*-questions end with falling intonation.
(b) A: **Where** are you from? ↗ B: Vanuatu. It's in the south Pacific. (c) A: Jennifer Lopez was here last night. B: **Who** was here last night? ↗ A: Jennifer Lopez.	A *Wh*-question with rising intonation shows that you are not sure about what you heard or that you want to check that you heard something correctly. The *Wh*-word is also stressed (said strongly).
(d) A: Jennifer Lopez was here last night. B: **Who**? ↗	Sometimes, just the *Wh*-word (with rising intonation) is used.

EXERCISE 6

Complete the conversation with appropriate *Wh*-questions. For each question, draw an arrow ↗ or ↘ to show if the question ends with falling or rising intonation

Example: **Albert:** So, what did you think of the new Eisentraut movie? ↘
Leslie: It was O.K., I guess, but I expected something more from a movie that cost $200 million to make.

Albert: (1) _____?
Leslie: $200 million. Amazing, isn't it? It's hard to imagine that amount of money.

Albert: (2) _____?
Leslie: It's an action movie set in the future, but I thought it was rather slow-moving. In fact, I almost fell asleep a couple of times.

Albert: (3) _____?
Leslie: It's about two hours, maybe a little longer. Luckily the seats were really comfortable.

Albert: (4) _____?
Leslie: At that new movie theater on Fourth Street, across from the parking garage. It only opened a couple of weeks ago, so it's got a state-of-the-art sound system, thick carpets, terrific popcorn. . . .

Albert: (5) _____?
Leslie: Twelve dollars.

Albert: (6) _____?
Leslie: Twelve dollars . . . I'm not kidding! I can't believe I spent twelve bucks on a movie that really wasn't very good.

FOCUS 5 Choice Questions

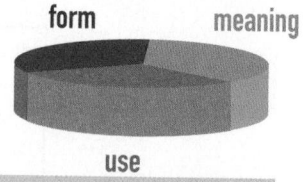

EXAMPLES	EXPLANATIONS
(a) A: Are you a **graduate student or a professor?** B: I'm a graduate student. (b) A: Do you live **in a dorm or an apartment?** B: I live off campus, in an apartment.	A choice question has two or more possibilities, or options. The speaker expects you to choose one of these options in your answer. You can add more information in your answer if you want.
(c) Does Tina walk ↗ to school or take ↘ the bus? (d) A: Are you from Malaysia or from Indonesia? B: Neither. I'm from Singapore.	Choice questions have a different intonation pattern from *Yes/No* questions. *Yes/No* questions have rising intonation at the end; choice questions have rising intonation in the middle and falling intonation at the end.
(e) A: Would you like coffee or tea? B: I'll have some tea, please.	Choice questions are often used to get information quickly or to make offers (please see Unit 16 for more information on making offers with *Would . . . like*).
(f) A: (Do you want) paper or plastic? B: Paper, please.	In informal conversation, the first part of the question is sometimes dropped. Answers to choice questions are often very short. Adding *please* to your answer makes it more polite.

EXERCISE 7

Thongchai is a new student from Asia. You want to find out some information about him. Complete the following choice questions with options that are similar in meaning and form.

1. Are you from Thailand or _____?
2. Do you speak Chinese or _____?
3. Do you eat noodles or _____ for breakfast?
4. Do you live _____ or _____?
5. Are you going to study _____ or _____?
6. Do you walk to class or _____?
7. Do you like to play tennis or _____?

Practice asking and answering the questions you completed with a partner.

EXERCISE 8

Guess where each of the choice questions on the left was probably asked. Choose from the places or situations listed on the right.

QUESTIONS	PLACES/SITUATIONS
1. Paper or plastic?	A. a cash register in a department store
2. Would you like coleslaw or french fries with that?	B. a job interview
3. Do you want premium grade or regular?	C. a gas station
4. Will that be cash or charge?	D. a small shop selling hats and T-shirts
5. First class or economy?	E. an airline office
6. Do you say "large" or "extra large"?	F. a fast-food restaurant
7. Do you prefer mornings or evenings?	G. a check-out counter in a supermarket

Practice asking and answering the questions with a partner. Imagine yourself in each place or situation. Use more than one way of answering.

FOCUS 6 Tag Questions

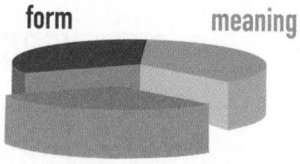

EXAMPLES	EXPLANATIONS
statement *tag* (a) He is nice, **isn't he**? (b) She isn't here, **is she**? (c) We're late, **aren't we**? (d) They like it, **don't they**? (e) NOT: They like it, like they? (f) You didn't go, **did you**?	A tag question is a statement, followed by a short question (a tag). Tag questions are often used in conversation. The speaker expects a *yes* or *no* answer. The verb in the tag agrees with the subject.
statement *tag* *affirmative + negative* (g) They play tennis, **don't they**? (h) The car was hot, **wasn't it**? (i) NOT: The car was hot, was not it? (j) Our teacher will help, **won't** he? (k) She is sleeping, **isn't she**? (l) We can wait, **can't we**? (m) I am right, **aren't I**? (n) NOT: I am right, amn't I?	An affirmative statement has a negative tag. The speaker thinks that the answer will probably be *yes*. The verbs in negative tags are contracted.
statement *tag* *negative + affirmative* (o) Your friends don't drive, **do they**? (p) It wasn't hot, **was it**? (q) You won't help, **will you**? (r) The baby isn't sleeping, **is she**? (s) We can't wait, **can we**?	A negative statement has an affirmative tag. The speaker thinks that the answer will probably be *no*. The verbs in affirmative tags are not contracted.
(t) Q: You're not cold, **are you**? A: No, I'm not. (u) NOT: Yes, I'm not. (v) Q: You're cold, **aren't you**? (w) A: Yes, I am. (x) NOT: No, I am.	When you answer a tag question, respond to the statement, not to the tag. If you agree with the statement: Answer *no* to a negative statement. Answer *yes* to an affirmative statement.

EXAMPLES	EXPLANATIONS
(y) Q: She left, **didn't she**? A: (Yes,) she did. OR Right. OR I think so.	It's not always necessary to use the words *yes* or *no* in your answers.
(z) Q: They won't call, **will they**? A: (No,) they won't. OR I doubt it. OR Probably not. OR I don't think so. OR No way.	*No way* is very informal.

EXERCISE 9

Ivana is talking with her school's career counselor. Complete the counselor's questions with an appropriate tag.

1. You are studying business and computers, _____?
2. Computer skills are very important nowadays, _____?
3. You won't finish until next June, _____?
4. Your grades aren't final yet, _____?
5. You also speak Russian, _____?
6. That's a difficult language, _____?
7. And you worked as a store manager in your vacations, _____?
8. You don't want to work in a large company, _____?
9. Those jobs can be very stressful, _____?
10. But you want a job with good career opportunities, _____?
11. There are a lot of different possibilities, _____?
12. We'll meet again and talk some more about it next week, _____?

EXERCISE 10

Deb and Sylvie are talking on the phone and making plans for their friend Bouzid's birthday.

Work with a partner. Fill in the blanks with an appropriate tag question and then put the conversation in order. Write the order of the conversation on the next page. We have done some of them for you.

DEB

B) Yes, it is, but we took him to Greens last year, _____ _____?

D) No, I won't. Maybe you should call him right away.

F) Great! I guess you don't have time to go shopping on Thursday, _____ _____?

H) Of course I will. But we'd better make sure he's free before we make any more plans.

J) Yes, he loves it. Why don't we take him to the Taj Mahal?

L) That's a great idea! And you took a class in vegetarian cooking last semester, _____ _____?

N) No, he doesn't.

P) You're right, it is. Let's take him out to a really nice restaurant.

R) No, it isn't, I forgot about that. Do you have any ideas about where to take him?

SYLVIE

A) It's Bouzid's birthday next Thursday. _____?

C) No, I don't think so. Thursdays are always so busy. But you'll be able to help me,

E) So what about Greens? Their food is all vegetarian, _____?

G) That's a good idea. He likes indian food, _____?

I) Oh my goodness, you're right, we did. So why don't we cook for him instead?

K) OK. You won't see him until the day after tomorrow, _____ _____?

M) But the Taj Mahal isn't open on Thursdays, _____?

O) I certainly did. And I've got lots of new recipes that I want to try out.

Q) Let me think... He doesn't eat meat, _____?

S) OK. I'll call him and then let you know what he says.

1. A	4. ____	7. ____	10. ____	13. ____	16. ____	18. ____
2. P	5. ____	8. ____	11. ____	14. ____	17. ____	19. S
3. G	6. ____	9. E	12. ____	15. ____		

You can find the answers to this exercise on page A-15.

FOCUS 7 Tag Question Intonation

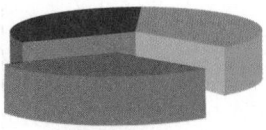

EXAMPLES	EXPLANATIONS
(a) Q: His name is Tom, isn't it? ↗ A: Yes, it is. (b) Q: It's not going to rain today, is it? ↗ A: No, it isn't. (c) Q: His name is Tom, isn't it? ↗ (d) Q: It's not going to rain today, is it? ↗	Falling intonation in tag questions shows that the speaker is fairly sure that the information in the statement is true. The speaker is also sure that the listener will agree. A person making an affirmative statement with falling intonation (a) expects the answer *yes*. A person making a negative statement with falling intonation (b) expects the answer *no*. Rising intonation in tag questions shows that the speaker is not sure if the information in the statement is true.

EXERCISE 11

Go back to the conversation in Exercise 10. With a partner, draw arrows ↗ or ↘ to show falling or rising intonation in the tags. One of you will take Sylvie's part and the other will take Deb's. Read the exercise aloud to practice intonation. Finally, get together with another pair and listen to each other's performances.

EXERCISE 12

Your teacher will ask some tag questions. Circle **Y** if you think the expected answer is **yes** and **N** if you think the expected answer is **no**.

1. Y N	4. Y N	7. Y N
2. Y N	5. Y N	8. Y N
3. Y N	6. Y N	9. Y N

EXERCISE 13

Read each tag question aloud, using the intonation as marked. For each question, tell whether the speaker expects a certain answer, and if so, what the speaker expects the answer to be, *yes* or *no*. Answer the question the way you think the speaker expects it to be answered.

	(a) Is the speaker fairly sure what the answer will be?	(b) If *yes* to (a), answer the question.
1. It's going to rain today, isn't it? ↗		
2. You don't know where my umbrella is, do you? ↗		
3. You're driving today, aren't you? ↗		
4. It's not my turn to drive, is it? ↗		
5. You made lunch for me, didn't you? ↗		
6. I didn't forget to thank you, did I? ↗		
7. I'm pretty forgetful, aren't I? ↗		

EXERCISE 14

Your teacher has been nominated for a "Teacher-of-the-Year Award" and will appear at a press conference to answer questions from journalists and reporters. You and your classmates are all newspaper reporters. You need to write a profile of your teacher for your paper and want to get as much information from him or her as possible.

STEP 1 **Get together with two or three other students. As a group, choose eight questions that you would most like to ask your teacher at the press conference. You can use some of the questions you wrote in Exercise 1, Exercise 2, and the Opening Task if you want to, or you can make completely new questions. Important note:**

- Two questions must be *Yes/No* questions.
- Two questions must be *Wh*-questions.
- Two questions must be *tag* questions.
- Two questions must be choice questions.

STEP 2 When you have decided on your questions, your teacher will hold the press conference, but he or she will only answer your questions if they are correctly formed and if the intonation is appropriate. If another group asks a question that your group wanted to ask, you must ask a different question (your teacher will not answer the same question twice). Write your questions and the answers below. If possible, record the "press conference" and listen to the recording to check your intonation and your teacher's answers.

QUESTIONS	ANSWERS

Use Your English

ACTIVITY 1 speaking/listening

STEP 1 Your teacher is going to stick a piece of paper on your back and on the backs of your classmates. Get up and walk around the class, looking at what is written on your classmates' backs.

STEP 2 Your job is to guess what is written on your back. You can find this out by asking questions. You can also answer the questions that your classmates ask you about what is written on their backs. For the first five minutes, you can only ask *Yes/No* questions. Refuse to answer any question that is not a *Yes/No* question. When your teacher gives you a signal, you can ask any kind of question that you like. Here are some possible *Yes/No* questions to ask: Is this a person? Is this person male or female? Is this an object? Is it expensive? Is this an animal? Is this food? Here are some possible *Wh*-questions: How big is this? Where was he or she born? What color is this?

ACTIVITY 2 speaking/writing

The international student office at your school is preparing a short guide for students who have just arrived in this country. The purpose of this guide is to give new students a clear idea of what to expect when they arrive here. You have been asked to write a chapter called "Frequently asked questions."

Get together with two or three other students and make a list of all the questions that people in this country frequently ask you. Compare your lists with those of other students in the class. Use the information from your classmates to make a list of the questions that people here frequently ask international students and that new students should be ready to answer.

ACTIVITY 3 speaking/writing

Work in a group. You are going to play the role of career counselor to one person in your group. Make a list of 10–15 questions that would help that person decide what kind of career to choose. Write the questions on a sheet of paper. When you are ready, choose one person to answer your questions (you can add further questions during the interview!). Then change roles.

ACTIVITY 4 writing/reading

STEP 1

In this activity you cannot speak, but you can write. Sit down next to a student that you do not know very well. Spend a couple of minutes thinking about some of the things you would like to know about this person. Take a piece of paper and write **one** question for your partner to answer. Pass the question to your partner. Read the question that your partner gives you. Without speaking, write your answer to the question and write another question for your partner to answer. **Do not speak at all.**

STEP 2

Exchange papers with your partner. Read your partner's answer to your question and answer his or her question to you. Continue writing questions and answers to each other until your teacher tells you to stop. Now you can speak!

Optional: With your partner's permission, share some of the information from your silent interview with the rest of the class.

STEP 3

Look back over the questions that you and your partner wrote. Were you able to use any of the kinds of questions discussed in this unit?

ACTIVITY 5 speaking/listening

Your English teacher has just quit her job and is now relaxing on a beach in Tahiti. Your school is desperately searching for a new teacher. Your classmates have decided to take matters into their own hands and you have decided to interview teachers yourselves. Pretend one of your classmates is an applicant for the position. Ask him or her some questions about his or her experience, interests, and future goals. Listen to your classmate's answers. They may help you ask other questions.

ACTIVITY 6 listening/writing

CD Tracks 6,7

A friend of yours has applied for a job teaching English in Latvia. She cannot travel to Latvia for a job interview, so the school has to interview her by phone. You are at her house when the school calls. You can hear her half of the conversation (the answers that she gives), but you can't hear the questions that the interviewer asked.

Listen to your friend's half of the conversation. In the first column, write the questions that you think the interviewer **probably** asked. Then listen to the complete interview to compare your questions with the ones the interviewer **actually** asked. Use the second column to write any questions that are different from the ones in the first column.

PROBABLE QUESTIONS	ACTUAL QUESTIONS

ACTIVITY 7 speaking/writing

Imagine you are going to write an essay on one of these topics: (1) Learning a foreign language, (2) Applying for a job, or (3) Using the Internet for research.

What three main questions will your essay answer? Compare your questions with another student. Write your questions on the board and choose the best three for each title.

ACTIVITY 8 speaking/listening

Bring in a photograph and give it to your teacher. Your teacher will mix up the pictures and distribute them randomly. Look at your photograph for thirty seconds and then give it back to the teacher. The teacher will put all the photographs on a table or hang them up. Students will take turns being questioned by the class. When it is your turn, your classmates will ask you questions about the picture you looked at. They will try to guess which picture it was. Try to use all types of questions: *Yes/No*, *Wh-*, statement form, choice, and tag.

ACTIVITY 9 research on the web

InfoTrac® College Edition: Go to *InfoTrac* to find information about a country you are interested in. Type in the name of the country and *Fact File*, for example, *France Fact File*. Make a list of questions using information in the article. Ask your classmates if they know the answers.

ACTIVITY 10 reflection

Work in a group. Choose one aspect of learning English, for example, writing or vocabulary. Write a questionnaire about how students in your class learn and practice this skill. Interview other students in your class using your questionnaire. Report the results to the class. What general patterns did you find?

UNIT 5

MODALS OF PROBABILITY AND POSSIBILITY

Could, May, Might, Must, Couldn't, and *Can't*

UNIT GOALS

- Use *could, may, might, must, couldn't,* and *can't* to show how certain you are about a present situation
- Form statements and questions to describe probability and possibility in the present and past
- Use the progressive with modals of probability and possibility
- Use *could, may, might, will/be (probably) going to, may not,* and *might not* to talk about future probability and possibility

OPENING TASK

Identify the Mystery Person

One evening toward the end of March, a New York taxi driver found that someone had left a briefcase on the back seat of his cab. When he opened it, he found that the briefcase was empty, except for the things you can see on the next page.

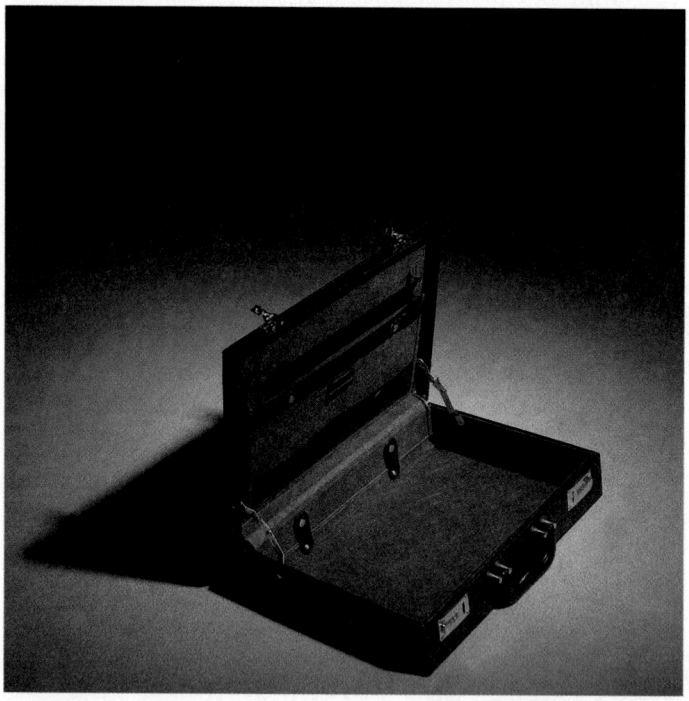

STEP 1

With a partner, examine everything on the next page carefully. Can you find any clues about the identity of the owner of the briefcase? Use the chart to write down your ideas and to show how certain you are about them.

HOW CERTAIN ARE YOU?	GUESSES										
	Name	Sex	Age	Marital Status	Occupation	Likes and Interests	Family and Friends	Habits	Recent Activities	Future Plans	Anything else?
Less than 50% certain (it's possible)											
90% certain (it's probable)											
100% certain (it's certain)											

MARCH

SUNDAY	MONDAY	TUESDAY	WEDNESDAY	THURSDAY	FRIDAY	SATURDAY
1	2 Board meeting 10:30 send papers to Washington	3 meeting 8 lunch Sally leave for NYC 7:00	4 Ash Wednesday NYC EXECUTIVE MEETING	5	6 return from NYC meeting 10:30 drinks Bob Theatre 8:30	7 wedding anniversary dinner 8
8 golf 9:30	9 report on NYC meeting due	10 Sally's Birthday meeting with Vice president 2p.m. movie 8	11 Paris arrive 14.50	12 meeting	13	14 Call Sally
15 Purim	16 Accountant Lunch Robert Haywood Call Paris Office	17 St. Patrick's Day Opera 9:30	18 Visitors from Tokyo office Dinner Japanese restaurant 7p.m.	19	20 Export meeting	21 Spring Begins tennis 2p.m. Mike Kids home from school
22 golf 9:30	23 Japanese Class	24 Doctor: 8 sales meeting 10:30	25 9:00 Accountant tennis Mike	26 Lunch SALLY	27 Doctor: 9 10:00 sales meeting Japanese Class	28 check passport
29 TOKYO?	30	31				

STEP 2

Now get together with a group and share your ideas about the identity of this mystery person, showing how certain you feel about each one.

Example: *He might be a businessman.*

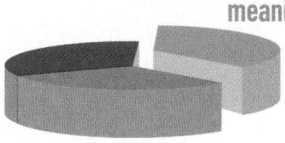

FOCUS 1 Using *Could, Might, May, Must, Couldn't,* and *Can't* to Show How Certain You Are about the Present

EXAMPLES	EXPLANATIONS
	Could, might, may, and *must* show how certain or not you are about a present situation.
Situation: He's got a baseball hat on. *Less Certain* (a) He could play baseball. (b) He might play baseball. (c) He may play baseball. *More Certain* Situation: She is wearing a white coat. *Less Certain* (d) She **could** be a doctor. (e) She **might** be a doctor. (f) She **may** be a doctor. *More Certain*	**Possible (less than 50% certain)** Use *could, might,* or *may* to express possibility (to show that you believe something is possible, but you are not very certain if it is true or not). You are making a guess. *May* shows that you are a little more certain that something is true.
Situation: He's wearing a baseball hat. He's carrying a baseball glove. (g) He **must** play baseball. Situation: She is carrying a stethoscope. (h) She **must** be a doctor.	**Probable (about 90% certain)** Use *must* to express probability (to show that you believe something is probably true). You are **almost** certain that this is true. You are drawing a conclusion, based on what you know.
(i) He **couldn't** be a soccer player. (j) She **can't** be a teacher.	Use *couldn't* and *can't* to show that you are almost certain that something is **not** true.
Situation: It's the middle of a baseball game. He is throwing a ball to his teammate. (k) He **plays** baseball. Situation: She performed heart surgery on my mother in the hospital and saved her life. (l) She **is** a doctor. (m) She **isn't** a nurse.	**Certain (100% certain)** These are facts. You are completely certain about these situations. Do not use *could, might, may,* or *must.* For information on other ways of using *could, might, may,* and *must*, see Units 10, 11, and 17.

EXERCISE 1

Look at the situations below and complete the sentences to show how certain the speaker is about each one.

SITUATION	POSSIBLE
She always wears a purple hat.	***Less Certain*** 1. She _____ like purple. 2. She _____ like purple. 3. She _____ like purple. ***More Certain***
Situation	Probable
She always wears a purple hat and a purple coat.	4. She _____ like purple.
Situation	Certain
She always wears purple clothes, she drives a purple car, and lives in a purple house surrounded by purple flowers.	5. She _____ purple.
Situation	Possible
He's carrying a French newspaper.	***Less Certain*** 6. He _____ be French. 7. He _____ be French. 8. He _____ be French. ***More Certain***
Situation	Probable
He's carrying a French newspaper and he's speaking French to the people with him.	9. He _____ be French.
Situation	Certain
He's carrying a French newspaper and he's speaking French to the people with him. He was born in France and has a French passport.	10. He _____ be British. 11. He _____ be French.

Compare your answers with a partner's and then check what you have written with the information in Focus 1.

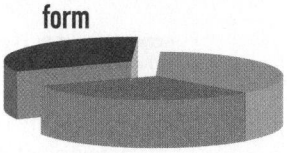

FOCUS 2 Modals of Probability and Possibility

EXAMPLES	EXPLANATIONS
subject + modal + verb (a) Jack **could** live here. (b) NOT: Jack could lives here. (c) Alex **might** know him. (d) NOT: Alex mights know him. (e) Shirley **may** be at home. (f) NOT: Shirley maybe at home.	**Affirmative Statements** Modals come before the base form of the verb. Modals have only one form. They do not take *s*. *Maybe* is not a modal.
subject + modal + not + verb (g) She **must not** like cats. (h) Bo **might not** know that. (i) That's impossible! Ron **couldn't** be in Las Vegas. I saw him just a few minutes ago. He **can't** be there.	**Negative Statements** *May not, might not,* and *must not* are not usually contracted when they express possibility or probability. *Couldn't/can't* show that you strongly believe that something is impossible. *Couldn't/can't* are usually contracted. However, *could* expresses very weak certainty. It shows that you are not very certain if something is possible.
modal + subject + verb (k) **Could** Sid be in Reno? (l) **Might** Cathy know about this?	**Questions** *May* and *must* are not used in questions about possibility and probability.
Question: / *Answer:* (m) Does he take the train? / I'm not sure. He **might**. (n) Does Sue like Thai food? / She **may not**. She doesn't like spicy food very much. (o) Is Jay at home? / He **might be**. He's not in his office. (p) Is Tom busy right now? / He **might not be**. I'll ask him.	**Short Answers** Use the modal by itself in short answers. Use the modal + *be* in short answers to questions with *be*. Use the modal + *not* for negative short answers.

EXERCISE 2

Turn back to the Opening Task on pages 70–71. Make statements about the owner of the briefcase. Use *must, may, could, might, couldn't,* or *can't* to show how certain you feel. Share your opinions with your classmates and be ready to justify them as necessary.

Example: Name: *In my opinion, the owner of the briefcase might be called Chris Murray because this name is on the boarding pass. However, this boarding pass could belong to somebody else.*

1. SEX: In my opinion, the owner of the briefcase _____
   because _____
   _____
2. OCCUPATION: I believe he or she _____
   because _____
   _____
3. MARITAL STATUS: This person _____
   I think this because _____
   _____
4. LIKES AND INTERESTS: _____
   _____
5. HABITS: _____
   _____
6. AGE: _____
   _____

EXERCISE 3

Add an appropriate short answer to the questions in these conversations. The first one has been done for you. Several responses are possible.

A: Where's Mike? Is he at lunch?

B: I don't know. He (1) ___might be.___

A: Do you know if he speaks Turkish?

B: Yes, he (2) _____. He lived in Turkey for ten years.

A: Do you think he has time to help me translate this letter?

B: I'm not sure. He (3) _____ (not). He'll be in meetings all day today.

A: Do you know if he'll come back here later?

B: He (4) _____, but I don't really know.

A: Will he be here tomorrow?

B: He (5) _____ (not). I think he is planning to work at home tomorrow.

A: If I leave message, will he call me? It's very urgent.

B: Well, he (6) _____, but I can't say for sure.

form

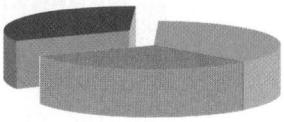

FOCUS 3 Modals of Probability and Possibility in the Past

EXAMPLES	EXPLANATIONS
subject + modal + have + past participle (a) Vi **may have left.** (b) I'm not sure how Liz went home last night. She **could have taken** a cab. (c) There's nobody here; everyone **must have gone** out.	**Affirmative Statements** Choose the appropriate modal + *have* + past participle to show how certain you are about something that happened in the past.
subject + modal + not + have + past participle (d) I **may not have seen** him. (e) Selena **might not have been** in town last week. (f) Darius **couldn't have robbed** the store. He was at home with me all evening.	**Negative Statements:** Choose the appropriate modal + *not* + *have* + past participle to show how certain you are that something did **not** happen in the past.
modal + subject + have + past participle? (g) **Could** she **have known?** (h) **Might** the police **have followed** the stolen car?	**Questions:** Choose the appropriate modal + subject + *have* + past participle to ask about possibility and probability in the past. Remember that *must* and *may* are not usually used in questions about possibility or probability.
(i) Q: Did Jerry talk to Kramer last night? A: I'm not sure. He **may have.** (j) Q: Did Bernadette remember to go to the store? A: She **must have.** The refrigerator is full of food.	**Short Answers:** Use the appropriate modal + *have* in short answers.
(k) Q: Was Vinny depressed? A: It's hard to say. He **might have been.** (l) NOT: He might have.	Remember to use the appropriate modal + *have been* in short answers to questions using *be.*

EXERCISE 4

Turn back to the Opening Task. Make statements showing how certain you are about the person's past activities. Use *must, may, could, might, couldn't,* or *can't* + *have* + past participle to show how certain you feel. Be ready to share and justify your opinions.

EXERCISE 5

Read the following situations. Can you figure out what happened? Think of as many possible explanations as you can. Then compare your ideas with a partner.

Example: You are walking along the street when you see a $20 bill on the ground. *Someone must have dropped it. Someone might have put it there as a trick.*

1. A boy is crawling on the ground looking for something. He is crying.

   _____

2. A car has stopped in the middle of the road. A bicycle is on the ground next to the car.

   _____

3. There is a big hole in the front window of the bank.

   _____

4. Your train is twenty minutes late.

   _____

5. A man and a woman are sitting in a restaurant. The woman is holding a diamond ring. She looks surprised.

   _____

6. A man is standing outside a house. He is wearing pajamas and slippers. He is holding a newspaper and ringing the front door bell.

   _____

7. A man is standing in line at the bus stop. His coat is completely wet.

   _____

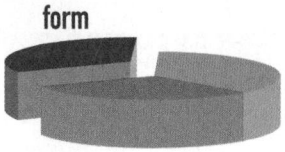

FOCUS 4 Modals of Probability and Possibility with the Progressive

EXAMPLES	EXPLANATIONS
subject + modal + be + verb + -ing (a) He **might be sleeping.** (b) Q: What's Lisa doing these days? A: I'm really not sure. She **may be working** in Latvia. (c) Something smells good! Albert **must be cooking** dinner.	Use modals with the progressive to make a guess or draw a conclusion about something in progress at or around the time of speaking.
(d) You **must know** the Van Billiard family. They live in Amherst. (e) NOT: You must be knowing the Van Billiard family.	Remember that some verbs cannot be used in the progressive. For more information, see Unit 2.
subject + modal + have been + verb + -ing (f) He **may have been sleeping.** (g) Mo **must have been working** on his car; his hands are really dirty.	Use this form to make a guess or draw a conclusion about something that was in progress before the time of speaking.

EXERCISE 6

Look back at the situations in Exercise 5. Can you make any statements about the people in these situations using *must, may, might*, or *could* with a progressive form? Use present forms (to talk about what you think they might be doing now) or past forms (to talk about what you think they might have been doing before now). For example: *Someone may be watching to see how many people try to pick up the $20 bill.* Compare your ideas with a partner's.

EXERCISE 7

The police are investigating a murder. What might Sherlock Holmes conclude about the following pieces of evidence? Get together with a partner to come up with a theory about what happened. After that, share your conclusions with the rest of the class, using *must, may, could, might*, or *couldn't/can't* to show how certain you feel. Finally, take a vote to decide who has the most interesting theory. How probable do you think this theory is?

Police Report:

The victim was found in her bedroom on the second floor of her house. The front door and her bedroom door were locked from inside. There were two wine glasses on the table in her room; one was empty, the other was full. There was an ashtray with several cigarette butts in it. The victim had a small white button in her hand and several long, blond hairs. Her watch was found on the floor; it had stopped at 11:30. The drawers of the victim's desk were open, and there were papers all over the floor. Nothing appeared to be missing.

EXERCISE 8

You are a reporter for your local newspaper. The editor has asked you to report on the murder described in Exercise 7. Explain what you think happened and why you believe this to be so. Make a headline for your report. Display your headline and your report so that your classmates can compare the different theories about the murder.

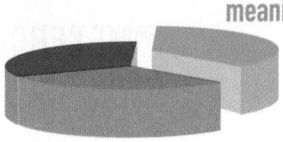

FOCUS 5 Future Probability and Possibility with Modals

EXAMPLES	EXPLANATIONS
(a) There are a few clouds in the sky; it **could** / **might** / **may** rain later. (b) Cheer up! She **might** call tomorrow. (c) We **may** see them next month.	Use *could, might*, or *may* to express future possibility. *May* shows that you are a little more certain that something will happen.
(d) Q: Where's Anna? A: She'**ll probably** get here soon. (e) NOT: She must get here soon. (f) Q: What's Jim going to do after he graduates next year? A: He'**s probably going to** travel around the world on a motorcycle. (g) NOT: He must travel round the world on a motorcycle.	Use *will* or *be going to* with *probably* to show that you are almost certain that something will happen in the future. Do not use *must.*
(h) Look! The sun's coming out. It **may not** rain after all. (i) NOT: It could not rain after all. (j) Fran **might not** come to the airport with us tomorrow. (k) NOT: Fran could not come to the airport with us tomorrow.	Use *may not* or *might not* to show that it is possible that something will **not** happen. Do not use *could not.*

EXERCISE 9

Work with a partner and turn back to the Opening Task. From the evidence given, what can you say about the person's future plans? Use *probably will/be going to, may, could, must,* or *may not/might not* as necessary. Be prepared to share and justify your answers.

EXERCISE 10

Work with a partner and choose the best way to complete each sentence. Bubble in the correct answer. Discuss the reasons for your choice. Share your reasons with the rest of the class.

1. **A:** Where's Rose?
   B: I'm not sure. She _____ in the library.
   ○ *is* ○ *might be* ○ *must be*

2. **A:** My daughter just got a scholarship to Stanford!
   B: You _____ be very proud of her.
   ○ *could* ○ *must* ○ *might*

3. **A:** How does Sheila get to school?
   B: I don't really know. She _____ the bus.
   ○ *might take* ○ *takes* ○ *must take*

4. **A:** It's really cold in here today
   B: Yes. Somebody _____ the window open.
   ○ *must leave* ○ *might leave* ○ *must have left*

5. **A:** I wonder why Zelda always wears gloves.
   B: I don't know. She _____ some kind of allergy.
   ○ *may have had* ○ *has* ○ *may have*

6. **A:** Have you heard the weather forecast?
   B: No, but look at all those dark clouds in the sky. I think it _____ rain.
   ○ *could* ○ *must* ○ *is probably going to*

7. **A:** Did my mother call while I was out?
   B: I'm not sure. She _____.
   ○ *might have* ○ *might* ○ *did*

8. **A:** Ellen gave a violin recital in front of five hundred people yesterday. It was her first public performance.
   B: Really? She _____ very nervous.
   ○ *could have been* ○ *must be* ○ *must have been*

9. **A:** Are you coming to Jeff's party?
   B: I'm not sure. I _____ go to the concert instead.
   ○ *must* ○ *will* ○ *might*

10. **A:** Can I speak to Professor Carroll?
    B: She's not in her office, and she doesn't have any more classes today, so she _____ home.
    ○ *might go* ○ *must have gone* ○ *will probably go*

11. **A:** Jenny's sneezing again.
    B: Yes, she _____ a terrible cold.
    ○ ***must have*** ○ ***must be having*** ○ ***must have had***

12. **A:** Look, Maynard's sitting outside his own apartment. Isn't that weird?
    B: Not really. He _____ his keys, and now he's waiting for his wife to come home.
    ○ ***may be losing*** ○ ***may have lost*** ○ ***may have been losing***

13. **A:** Is Myrna working in the city today?
    B: She _____. I'm not sure.
    ○ ***could*** ○ ***could have*** ○ ***could be***

14. **A:** I can hear the water running in the bathroom.
    B: Yes, Bira _____ another shower.
    ○ ***must take*** ○ ***must have taken*** ○ ***must be taking***

15. **A:** What's up? You look worried.
    B: I am. My dog's sick. I think he _____ eaten some poison.
    ○ ***may be*** ○ ***may have been*** ○ ***may have***

16. **A:** Have you heard? Mel's father died last night.
    B: Poor Mel. He _____ feeling terrible. They were very close.
    ○ ***must*** ○ ***must be*** ○ ***must have been***

17. **A:** Dean has just won a million dollars in the lottery.
    B: He _____. He never buys lottery tickets.
    ○ ***must not have*** ○ ***could not*** ○ ***couldn't have***

18. **A:** Does Isaiah still share a house with his sister?
    B: I don't know. He _____.
    ○ ***might be*** ○ ***might*** ○ ***might have***

EXERCISE 11

Look back at the Opening Task. Who do you think the "Mystery Person" is? What do you think happened to him or her? Complete the following newspaper article with your ideas about what might have happened. Remember to use *must, may, could, might*, or *couldn't/can't* to show how certain you feel.

MISSING MYSTERY PERSON

It has been a week since New York taxi driver Ricardo Oliveiro found a briefcase on the back seat of his cab. It has been a week of guessing and speculation: Who is the owner of this briefcase and where is he or she now? Several different theories have been proposed, but so far the most interesting is the one which follows . . .

Use Your English

ACTIVITY 1 speaking/listening

Can you guess these objects? Get together with a partner and see how many different possibilities you can come up with for each picture. Classify your interpretations as "Possible," "Probable," and "Certain." Compare your answers with the rest of the class. (You can find the answers on page A-15.)

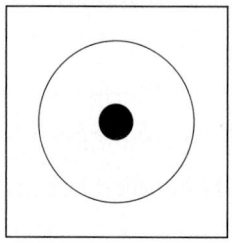

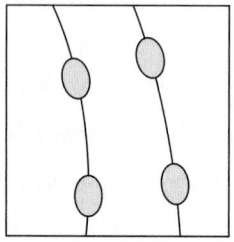

ACTIVITY 2 speaking/listening

STEP 1 The purpose of this activity is to confuse your classmates. Form teams and create five different drawings of familiar things seen from an unusual point of view. One example is shown below.

STEP 2 Exchange papers with another team. As a team, see how many different interpretations you can make of each drawing. Write each guess beside the appropriate drawing, showing how probable you think your interpretation is.

STEP 3 When you have made your guesses, exchange papers with another team until all teams have had a chance to "interpret" all the drawings.

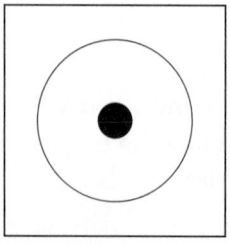

It could be a donut.
It might be a hat from above.
It could be an eyeball.

Which team got the most "correct" interpretations? Which team had the most interesting or unusual interpretations?

ACTIVITY 3 speaking/listening

Get together with a partner and examine the pictures below. What's going on? Who are the people? Imagine this story happened yesterday. Create a newspaper story telling what you think might have happened. You can use the photographs in any order that you like. Compare your story with those of your classmates. In what ways do their interpretations differ from yours?

ACTIVITY 4 listening

CD Track 8

STEP 1

Listen to the audio of two different people talking about the pictures on page 85. As you listen to their stories, number each picture to show which one comes first, second, and so on. Which story is the most likely, in your opinion? Speaker 1's story or Speaker 2's story?

STEP 2

Listen to the audio again and write any sentences with *may, might, could,* or *must* that show how certain the speaker feels.

ACTIVITY 5 speaking/listening

STEP 1

Look at the pictures below. What events are going to happen in each picture? What are you certain will happen? What is possibly going to happen? What are you not sure about?

STEP 2

Show the pictures to a friend. Ask him or her to tell you what he or she thinks might happen next. Take notes or record the answers he or she gives. Review your notes or listen to your recording and make notes. Do students have different ideas about the photos? Which ones are the most interesting? Tell your classmates.

ACTIVITY 6 speaking/listening

In the Opening Task, you looked at the contents of somebody's briefcase and made guesses about his or her identity. The purpose of this activity is to create your own "mystery person." Form groups and collect a number of items that somebody might carry in his or her pockets (tickets, bills, photographs, business cards, etc.). Choose six items, collect them in a bag, and bring them to class. Exchange bags with another group. With your group, examine the contents of the new bag and try to decide on the possible identity of the owner, using the same categories as in the Opening Task. When everyone is ready, share your conclusions with the rest of the class, showing how certain you are. Remember, your classmates might ask you to justify your conclusions, so be ready to justify each one.

ACTIVITY 7 writing

Write a profile of the "mystery person" your group presented to the class in Activity 6. Make sure you write an introductory sentence and that you provide evidence to support your conclusions. When you finish writing, read your profile to see how much of the language discussed in this unit you were able to use.

ACTIVITY 8 research on the web

On the Web: Look up one of these mysteries on the Internet using a search engine such as Google® or Yahoo® and make notes about what happened: 1) Stonehenge 2) the statues of Rapa Nui 3) the Mayan civilization. What is mysterious about them? Tell your classmates and ask them for suggestions about what might/may/could have happened.

ACTIVITY 9 reflection

Make a list of five things to do before taking an exam. Say what may/might/could happen if you don't follow this advice.

Example: *Don't stay up late the night before an exam, otherwise you might feel tired or sleepy during the exam.*

UNIT 6

PAST PROGRESSIVE AND SIMPLE PAST WITH TIME CLAUSES

When, While, and *As Soon As*

UNIT GOALS

- Choose between past progressive and simple past
- Form past progressive correctly
- Understand the meaning of *when, while,* and *as soon as*
- Form clauses with *when, while,* and *as soon as*

OPENING TASK

Miami Murder Mystery

Last night Lewis Meyer died at his home in Miami. Phil Fork, a police detective, was the first person to arrive at the house after Mr. Meyer died. This is what he found:

Mr. Meyer's wife, Margo, told Fork: "It was an accident. My husband took a shower at about 10:00 P.M. After his shower, he slipped on a piece of soap and fell down."

Do you believe her? What probably happened?

Look at the picture and work with a partner. Decide whether the following statements are **probably** true (T) or **probably** false (F). Be ready to share your answers with your classmates and to explain your choices.

1. Mr. Meyer died after Phil Fork arrived.	T	F
2. Mr. Meyer died when Phil Fork arrived.	T	F
3. Mr. Meyer died before Phil Fork arrived.	T	F
4. Mr. Meyer brushed his teeth before he died.	T	F
5. Mr. Meyer was brushing his teeth when he died.	T	F
6. Mr. Meyer was taking a shower when he died.	T	F
7. Mr. Meyer took a shower before he died.	T	F
8. Mr. Meyer died when he slipped on a piece of soap.	T	F
9. Somebody hit Mr. Meyer over the head while he was brushing his teeth.	T	F
10. The murder weapon is still in the bathroom.	T	F

You are the detective. In your opinion, how did Mr. Meyer die?

With your partner, use the picture and your answers above to try to solve the mystery. Make as many guesses as you like. For example: *We think somebody killed Mr. Meyer while he was brushing his teeth. This is how it happened. . . .* Be ready to share your ideas with the rest of the class. Write your ideas here:

WHAT REALLY HAPPENED:

(Solution to the Opening Task on page A-15)

FOCUS 1 Past Progressive and Simple Past

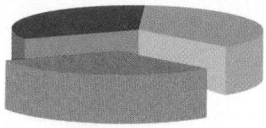

use

EXAMPLES	EXPLANATIONS
(a) Phil Fork **arrived** at 10:30. (b) Mrs. Meyer **drank** several cups of black coffee.	Use the simple past for an action that started and finished in the past. For a list of irregular past forms, see Appendix 5 on page A-13.
(c) Phil Fork **was eating** dinner at 10:00. (d) Mr. Meyer **was brushing** his teeth at 10:00	*Was eating* and *was brushing* are past progressive. Use the past progressive for an action that was in progress at a specific time in the past.
(e) Mr. Meyer **was brushing** his teeth when the murderer **entered** the room. (f) Phil Fork **was eating** dinner when he heard about the murder.	Use the past progressive with the simple past to show that one action began first and was still in progress when the second action happened. It is possible that the first action continued after the second action finished.
(g) Mrs. Meyer **was talking** on the phone while her husband **was taking** a shower. (h) Phil Fork **was reading** a newspaper while he **was eating** dinner.	Use the past progressive with the past progressive to show two actions in progress at the same time.

EXERCISE 1

Look back at what you wrote in the Opening Task on page 89. Did you use the past progressive and the simple past? If you did, underline all of your examples of the past progressive, circle all examples of the simple past, and check with your teacher to see if you used them correctly. If you didn't use these forms at all, write three sentences about Mr. Meyer's murder using the past progressive and the simple past. Check with your teacher to see if you used these forms correctly.

1. _____
2. _____
3. _____

FOCUS 2 Past Progressive

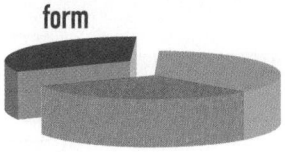

STATEMENT		NEGATIVE		QUESTION		
I She He It	was sleeping.	I She He It	was not sleeping. (wasn't)	Was	I she he it	sleeping?
We You They	were sleeping.	We You They	were not sleeping. (weren't)	Were	we you they	sleeping?

EXERCISE 2

Get together with a partner and complete this newspaper report of Mr. Meyer's murder. Use information from the Opening Task on page 88 and your own ideas about what happened to help you.

DAILY NEWS

BATHROOM MURDER

"I am innocent!" says Mrs. Meyer.

Last night police arrested Margo Meyer for the murder of her husband, Lewis. On her way to the police station, Mrs. Meyer told reporters: "I am innocent. I loved my husband very much. I didn't kill him."

According to Mrs. Meyer, on the night of his death, her husband _____

_____ when

_____.

However, Detective Phil Fork and his colleagues have a different theory about how Mr. Meyer died. According to them, _____

_____

_____ while _____

_____.

FOCUS 3 *When, While,* and *As Soon As*

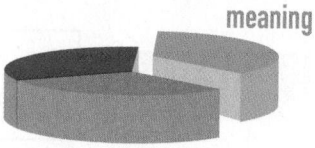

EXAMPLES	EXPLANATIONS
(a) **While** Mr. Meyer was getting ready for bed, Mrs. Meyer drank several cups of black coffee. OR (b) Mrs. Meyer drank several cups of black coffee **while** Mr. Meyer was getting ready for bed.	*When, while,* and *as soon as* give information about time. You can use them **either** at the beginning of a sentence **or** in the middle. *While* introduces an action in progress. It means "during that time." It is usually used with the past progressive.
(c) Mrs. Meyer called the police **when** she found the dead body. OR (d) **When** Mrs. Meyer found her husband's body, she called the police.	*When* introduces a completed action. It is usually used with the simple past. In (c) and (d), *when* introduces the action that happened first: **First** Mrs. Meyer found the body and **then** she called the police.
(e) Mrs. Meyer came to the door **as soon as** Phil Fork arrived. OR (f) **As soon as** Phil Fork arrived, Mrs. Meyer came to the door.	*As soon as* introduces a completed action and means "immediately after."

EXERCISE 3

Make meaningful statements about Mr. Meyer's murder by matching information from A with information from B. The first one has been done for you.

A	B
1. Mrs. Meyer called the police	she said that she was innocent.
2. While she was waiting for the police to arrive	Mrs. Meyer took him to the scene of the crime.
3. As soon as Phil Fork heard about the murder	as soon as her husband died.
4. When Fork asked to see the body	while the police were taking her to jail.
5. While Fork was searching the bathroom for clues	while he was brushing his teeth.
6. He saw that Mr. Meyer died	she placed a bar of soap on the bathroom floor.
7. When Fork accused Mrs. Meyer of murder.	he rushed to the Meyers' house.
8. A crowd of news reporters tried to interview Mrs. Meyer	he became suspicious of Mrs. Meyer's story.

EXERCISE 4

Look again at the sentences you created in Exercise 3. For each one, underline the part of the sentence that gives information about time. This is the part of the sentence that answers the question "When?"

Example: *Mrs. Meyer called the police as soon as her husband died.*

FOCUS 4 Time Clauses with *When, While, As Soon As, Before,* and *After*

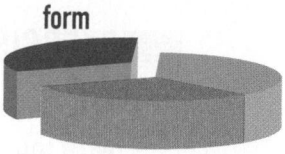

EXAMPLES		EXPLANATIONS
Dependent Time Clause	*Main Independent Clause*	A time clause is a **dependent** clause; this means that it is not complete by itself. It needs the rest of the sentence (**the main or independent** clause) to complete its meaning.
(a) When Amy returned home,	everyone ran out to greet her.	In order to understand *When Amy returned home,* we need more information.
(b) While my father was cooking dinner, our guests arrived.		A time clause can come at the beginning of a sentence (b) **or** at the end (c). If the time clause comes at the beginning of the sentence, use a comma between the time clause and the main clause.
(c) Our guests arrived while my father was cooking dinner.		**When** ~~~~~~~~, ~~~~~~~~
		If the main clause comes at the beginning of the sentence and the time clause comes last, do not use a comma between the two clauses (c).
		~~ **when** ~~~~~~~~

EXERCISE 5

Turn back to the sentences you created in Exercise 3. Write them below and add commas, as necessary.

1. _____
_____

2. _____
_____

3. _____
_____

4. _____
_____

5. _____
_____

6. _____

_____

7. _____

_____

8. _____

_____

EXERCISE 6

Check (✓) the sentence—(a) or (b)—closest in meaning to each statement.

1. While Mr. Meyer was brushing his teeth, someone entered the room.
   ___ a. Mr. Meyer finished brushing his teeth, before someone entered.
   ___ b. Mr. Meyer was alone when he started brushing his teeth.
2. When he got Mrs. Meyer's call, Phil Fork left his office and drove to her house.
   ___ a. Mrs. Meyer called before Phil Fork left his office.
   ___ b. Mrs. Meyer called after Phil Fork left his office.
3. As soon as he got into his car, he took out a cigarette and lit it.
   ___ a. He was smoking when he got into the car.
   ___ b. He started to smoke after he got into his car.
4. While Fork was driving to the Meyers' house, he was listening to his favorite opera on the radio.
   ___ a. He drove his car and listened to the radio at the same time.
   ___ b. He turned on the radio when he reached the Meyers' house.
5. When he got there, a number of police officers were searching the house for clues.
   ___ a. They started when he got there.
   ___ b. They started before he got there.
6. As soon as Fork started to question Mrs. Meyer, she burst into tears.
   ___ a. She was crying when he started to question her.
   ___ b. She started to cry when he began to question her.
7. Phil Fork carefully reviewed all his notes when he went home.
   ___ a. He went home first.
   ___ b. He reviewed his notes first.

EXERCISE 7

Work with a partner and write down five things you know about John Lennon.

Here is some more information about John Lennon's life. The wavy line (〰〰〰〰〰) indicates an action in progress. X indicates a completed action.

1. attend high school 〰〰〰〰〰 X his mother dies	2. attend high school 〰〰〰〰〰 X meet Paul McCartney
3. study at art school 〰〰〰〰〰 X form the Beatles	4. perform in clubs in Liverpool 〰〰〰〰〰 X sign his first recording contract
5. tour America 〰〰〰〰〰 X appear on the *Ed Sullivan Show*	6. live in London 〰〰〰〰〰 X fall in love with Yoko Ono
7. work for peace and write new songs 〰〰〰〰〰〰〰〰〰〰 X die	8. leave his apartment 〰〰〰〰〰 X one of his fans shoots him

Use this information to finish the short biography below. Fill in the blanks, using the simple past or the past progressive. The first one has been done for you as an example.

John Lennon was one of the most famous singer/songwriters of his time. He was born in Liverpool, England, in 1940, but his childhood was not very happy.

(1) His mother died while he was attending high school. Life was diffcult for John after his mother's death, but after a time things got better.

(2) _____ while _____. Soon Paul introduced him to George Harrison, and they began to play in a band together. After John left high school, he became an art student. (3) While _____, _____. After forming the Beatles, John married his first wife, Cynthia, and they had a son, Julian. (4) _____ when _____. John and the Beatles moved to London and became very famous. They traveled all over the world. (5) While _____, _____, a popular television show at the time.

(6) _____ while _____. A couple of years later, the Beatles split up. John and Yoko got married and moved to the United States, where their son Sean was born. John (7) _____ when _____. On December 8, 1980, (8) _____ while _____.

John Lennon died in 1980, but he still has lots of fans all over the world.

EXERCISE 8

Complete the sentences in the story below using the words in parentheses. Use the simple past or the past progressive. The first one has been done for you.

1. Wangari Maathai ___received___ (receive) the Nobel Peace Prize in 2004.
2. While Wangari _____ (grow up) in Kenya, the land around her home _____ (have) plenty of trees and water.
3. While she _____ (study) biology in college in the United States and at the University of Nairobi, she _____ (realize) the importance of plants and animals to the environment.
4. When she _____ (return) home, she _____ (find) that large companies _____ (destroy) the forests. Many of the trees and rivers were already gone.
5. When she _____ (ask) poor women from her village about their problems, they _____ (tell) her how they walked many miles every day to get firewood and water.
6. So she _____ (work) with these women to plant trees and _____ (create) the Green Belt Movement in1977. In thirty years, they planted 30 million trees.
7. Before she _____ (start) to work with the women, they _____ (not + feel) they had any power to change their lives.
8. Some people _____ (attack) her, and she was injured while she _____ (plant) trees in the Karura Public Forest in Nairobi, Kenya.
9. The Kenyan Government _____ (arrest) her many times.
10. When Wangari _____ (receive) the Nobel Peace Prize in 2004, she _____ (make) a speech. She said that wars start because of unequal distribution of resources: "A healthy environment is the path to peace."

Use Your English

ACTIVITY 1 speaking/listening/writing

Nan Silviera has just written her first book:

As you can see below, the author's life story on the back of the book is not complete. Work with a partner to finish writing it.

STEP 1 Student A: Turn to page 103. Student B: Turn to page A-16.

STEP 2 You both have information about Nan's life, but some of the information is missing. Do not show your pages to each other, but ask each other questions to get information about the parts marked "?".

STEP 3 Write down the information your partner gives you so that when you finish, you will have the complete story.

STEP 4 Use the information from your chart to write the story of Nan's life. You can use the biography on the back of her book to begin writing.

STEP 5 When you finish writing, check your work to see if you have used time clauses and the past progressive and simple past tenses appropriately.

ACTIVITY 2 speaking/listening/writing

In this activity, you will be gathering information about your classmates' lives by asking what they were doing at the times shown below. In the last box on the chart, add a time of your own choice (for example, on your last birthday, last New Year's Eve, etc.). Do not write information about yourself.

STEP 1 Think about the different students in your class. Can you guess what they were doing at these times? In the box marked *Guesses*, write what **you** think different people were doing at each time.

STEP 2 Go around the room and talk to as many people as possible to find out what they were really doing.

STEP 3 Write this information in the box marked *Facts*.

NOTE: Copy the chart into your notebook if you need more space to write. If you don't want to give information about a certain time, you can say, "I'm sorry but I'd rather not talk about that time." If you can't remember, you can invent something.

TIMES	GUESSES	FACTS
at 8:30 P.M last Sunday		
in May 1993		
five years ago		
ten years ago today		
????? (you choose a time)		

STEP 4 When you finish, review the information you collected. Choose the most interesting or surprising facts and make a short report (oral or written). Report on the facts, not on your original guesses. For example:

I asked my classmates about certain times in their lives. For example, at 8:30 P.M. yesterday, Sun Wu was working on her homework, and Tran was at home watching TV.

ACTIVITY 3 speaking/writing

STEP 1 Take a large sheet of paper and make a time line for your own life like the one used on page 103. Bring your time line to class and describe the story of your life to your classmates.

STEP 2 Exchange your time line with a partner. Use his or her time line to write the story of your partner's life. How many differences and similarities can you find between your partner's life history and yours?

ACTIVITY 4 speaking/listening/writing

On December 26, 2004, a huge tidal wave—called a tsunami—hit many countries of Southeast Asia including Indonesia, Thailand, Sri Lanka, and India. The giant wave—up to100 feet high in some places—was caused by an earthquake under the Indian Ocean off the coast of Sumatra. The tsunami killed about 275,000 people and was one of the worst natural disasters in modern history. The tsunami is sometimes called the Boxing Day Tsunami because it took place on December 26, which is a holiday called Boxing Day in many countries. Do you remember what you were doing when you heard about the Boxing Day Tsunami?

STEP 1 With a partner, interview one or two people about what they were doing when they heard the news of the Boxing Day or Asian Tsunami. If possible, record your interviews. Before the interview, get together with your partner to make a list of possible questions. You can use the questions below or make other questions of your own, if you prefer.

STEP 2 Share the results of your interviews with the class.

STEP 3 Listen to your recording and write down any sentences with the simple past or the past progressive. Underline any time clauses in these sentences.

- What were you doing when you heard the news of the Boxing Day Tsunami?
- Where were you living at that time?
- Who were you with?
- What did you do after you heard about it?
- How did you feel?
- Add your own questions.

ACTIVITY 5 listening

For this activity, you will hear three conversations with people being interviewed about what they were doing when they heard about the Boxing Day Asian Tsunami.

CD Tracks 9,10,11

STEP 1

Listen to the audio and take notes in the chart below.

CONVERSATION	PLACE	WHAT WAS THIS PERSON DOING?	WHAT DID THIS PERSON DO AFTER THAT?
Speaker 1	at home in Florida		
Speaker 2			
Speaker 3			

STEP 2

Listen to the audio again and write down any examples of the past progressive or simple past.

ACTIVITY 6 research on the web

On the Web: Think of a famous person you want to know more about. Go to the Internet and use a search engine such as Google® or Yahoo® to find information about his or her life. Type the name of the person and *biography*. Draw a brief time line of the main events in his or her life. Show the time line to your classmates and explain the sequence of events.

ACTIVITY 7 reflection

Think of three key events in your life. What happened? Why were they important? Make sentences using time clauses to describe these events. Try to use the different time clauses you learned in this unit.

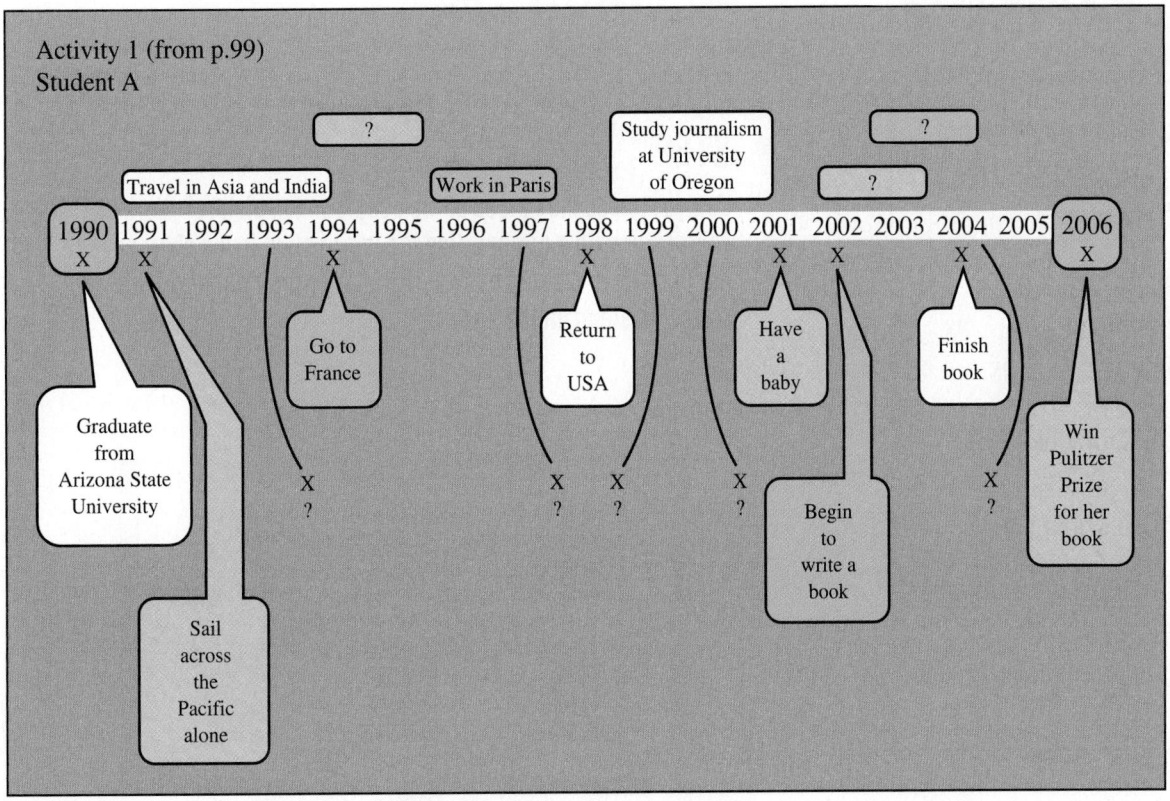
Activity 1 (from p.99)
Student A
?
Study journalism at University of Oregon
?
Travel in Asia and India
Work in Paris
?
1990 1991 1992 1993 1994 1995 1996 1997 1998 1999 2000 2001 2002 2003 2004 2005 2006
X X X X X X X X X
Go to France
Return to USA
Have a baby
Finish book
Graduate from Arizona State University
Win Pulitzer Prize for her book
X ? X ? X ? X ? X ?
Begin to write a book
Sail across the Pacific alone

UNIT 7

SIMILARITIES AND DIFFERENCES

Comparatives, Superlatives, *As . . . As, Not As . . . As*

UNIT GOALS

- Use comparatives and superlatives to express differences
- Understand the meaning of *as . . . as* and *not as . . . as*
- Form sentences with *as . . . as* and *not as . . . as*
- Use *as . . . as* and *not as . . . as* to make tactful comparisons

OPENING TASK

Friends

STEP 1

Can you guess the names of the people in the picture? Work by yourself or with a partner. Use the information in the chart and the list of clues to identify each person. Write their names in the correct position on the picture.

The Left

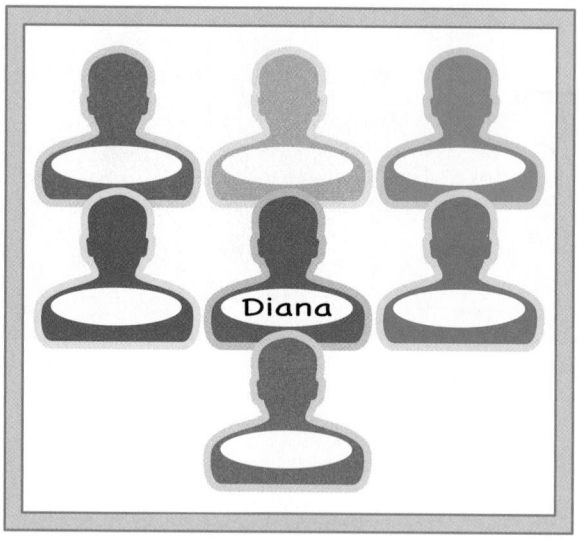

The Right

NAME	AGE	OCCUPATION	HAIR	HEIGHT
LINDA	75	doctor	short, white	5'9 1/2"
BOB	21	student	medium-length, brown	5'9 1/2"
SUSAN	25	student	long, blond	5'1"
FRANK	43	artist	short, gray	6'4"
CARLA	28	singer	medium-length, black	5'5"
GEORGE	44	writer	bald	5'10"
DIANA	58	engineer	medium-length, brown	5'10"

Clues

1. The oldest person is next to the youngest person.
2. The tallest woman is in front of someone thirty years younger than she is.
3. The shortest person is in front of someone with white hair.
4. The tallest man is next to the tallest woman.
5. The 28-year-old is in front of the youngest person.
6. The man with short wavy hair is not quite as tall as the person next to him on the right.
7. The man on the right of the youngest person is behind the tallest person.
8. The youngest person is as tall as the person next to him on the left.

When you finish, check your answers with the rest of the class to see if you all agree. You can find the solution to the Opening Task on page A-17.

STEP 2

Work in pairs. Describe one person in the picture by comparing him or her with the other people. Your partner will guess which person you are describing.

Example: *She's taller than Susan, but has shorter hair than Diana.* (*Answer:* Linda)

FOCUS 1 Expressing Difference: Comparatives and Superlatives

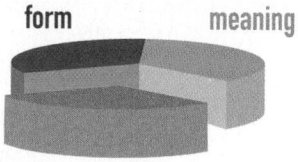

EXAMPLES

(a) Susan is **the shortest,** and Frank is **the tallest.**

EXPLANATIONS

The tallest and *the shortest* are superlatives.

Superlatives show extremes of difference among people or things. They show which has the greatest amount of a certain quality in a group of people or things.

(b) George is taller than Linda.

(c) Carla is shorter than George.

Taller than and *shorter than* are comparatives.

Comparatives show differences among people or things, but they do not show extremes of difference.

	Comparative	Superlative
young	**younger than**	**the** youngest
easy	easier **than**	the easiest
difficult	**more/less** difficult **than**	**the most/the least** difficult
carefully	**more/less** carefully **than**	**the most/the least** carefully
weigh	weigh **more/less than**	weigh **the most/the least**
money	**more/less** money **than**	**the most/the least** money

Comparatives and superlatives can be used with all parts of speech:

- adjectives with one syllable
- adjectives with one syllable + *-y*
- adjectives with two or more syllables
- adverbs
- verbs
- nouns

(d) George sings **better** (**worse**) than I do.

(e) Carla is the **best** (**worst**) singer in the family.

Some comparative and superlative forms are irregular. Examples (d) and (e) use irregular comparative and superlative forms of *good* and *bad.*

EXERCISE 1

First fill in the blanks with a word or word ending, and then use the information from the Opening Task to decide if the statements are true (T) or false (F).

1. The oldest woman is taller __than__ the oldest man. T (F)
2. George is tall _____ than the person beside him. T F
3. Diana is young ____ _____ the man beside her on the right. T F
4. George is tall ____ _____ Frank. T F
5. The singer is several years older _____ the person behind her. T F
6. The doctor is _____ old _____. T F
7. Bob is old ____ _____ the person in front of him. T F
8. The young _____ woman is in front of ____ old _____ woman. T F
9. Frank is _____ tall _____ man, but he isn't _____ old _____. T F
10. _____ old _____ man is short _____ _____ the young _____ woman. T F

Now write three statements about the people in the box found in the Opening Task. They can be True (T) or False (F). Show them to your partner. Your partner will decide if they are true or false.

Example: *The doctor is taller than Carla.* (False)

EXERCISE 2

Work with a partner. Read the information at right about working hours and vacation times. Ask your partner questions about each person, using the comparative and the superlative. Or, write down the questions and share them with a partner or the class.

NAME	WORKING HOURS	VACATION TIME
LINDA	8 A.M.–5 P.M.	4 weeks
BOB	9 A.M.–4 P.M.	12 weeks
SUSAN	9 A.M.–4 P.M.	12 weeks
FRANK	6 A.M.–1 P.M.	none
CARLA	9 P.M.–2 A.M.	6 weeks
GEORGE	7 A.M.–3 P.M.	3 weeks
DIANA	9 A.M.–5 P.M.	2 weeks

Examples: A: *Who starts work the earliest?*
B: *Frank does.*
A: *Who finishes work later, Susan or Linda?*
B: *Linda.*

FOCUS 2 Similarity and Difference: *As . . . As* and *Not As . . . As*

EXAMPLES	EXPLANATIONS
Linda is about 5'9". Bob is about 5'9". (a) Linda is **as tall as** Bob. OR Bob is **as tall as** Linda. 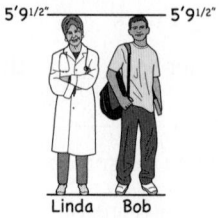 	To show similarity among people or things, you can use *as . . . as.*
(b) George is **exactly as tall as** Diana. OR Diana is **exactly as tall as** George.  	To show that people or things are the same, you can add *exactly.*
George is 5'10". Bob is 5'9 1/2". (c) Bob is { **almost** / **not quite** / **nearly** / **practically** / **just about** } **as tall as** George 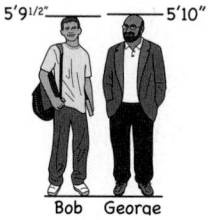 	To show that people or things are very similar, add: *almost, not quite, nearly, practically*, or *just about.*
George is 5'10". Bob is 5'9 1/2". (d) Bob is **not as tall as** George.	To show differences among people or things, you can use *not as . . . as.*
Susan is 5'1". Diana is 5'10". (e) Susan is { **nowhere near** / **not nearly** / **not anywhere near** } **as tall as** Diana.  	To show a great amount of difference, add: *nowhere near, not nearly*, or *not anywhere near.* *Nowhere near* and *not anywhere near* are only used in very informal conversation with friends.

EXERCISE 3

Get together with another student. Think of all the ways that you are similar and all the ways that you are different. You have five minutes to make as many sentences as you can, using *as . . . as* and *not as . . . as* to show these differences and similarities. Share your sentences with the rest of the class.

Example: *Fernando isn't quite as tall as I am.*

EXERCISE 4

Use the information in the Opening Task to write complete sentences about the following people. You can use a comparative, a superlative, *as . . . as,* or *not as . . . as* in each sentence. Show the amount of difference or similarity as necessary.

1. Linda/Bob/height
   Linda is as tall as Bob. _____
2. Susan/Frank/height
   _____
3. Linda/Diana/height
   _____
4. Linda/Carla/height
   _____
5. George/Susan/height and age
   _____
6. Bob/George/height
   _____
7. Frank/George/age
   _____
8. Diana/Linda/age
   _____
9. Frank/height
   _____
10. Linda/age
    _____
11. George/Diana/height
    _____

FOCUS 3 Using *As . . . As* and *Not As . . . As*

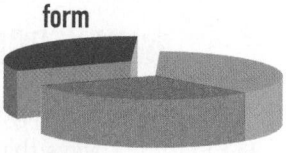

EXAMPLES	EXPLANATIONS
(a) Susan is **not as tall as** Carla. (b) Frank does not work **as quickly as** George. (c) Linda does not have **as much money as** Diana. (d) Diana does not have **as many friends as** Carla. (e) George **works as** much **as** Linda.	*As . . . as* and *not as . . . as* can be used with all parts of speech: • adjectives • adverbs • noncount nouns • count nouns • verbs
(f) Susan works as hard as **Carla works.** (g) Carla is not as tall as **Linda is.** (h) Susan works as hard as **Carla does.** (i) Susan works as hard as **Carla.** (j) Carla is not as tall as **her younger sister.** (k) Susan works as hard as **I/you/he/she/we/they.**	In sentences using *as . . . as* or *not as . . . as*, the second *as* can be followed by: • clauses • reduced clauses • noun phrases • subject pronouns
(l) Susan works as hard as he **works.** OR (m) Susan works as hard as he **does.**	In sentences where the verb is repeated after the second *as*, you can use a form of *do* instead.
(n) Susan works **as hard as he.** OR (o) Susan works **as hard as him.**	The same verb does not need to be repeated a second time. Using the subject pronoun (*he, she, I, we, you, they*) here is very formal. The object pronoun (*him, her, me, us, you, them*) is very common in conversation and informal writing.
(p) Susan's hair is not as short as **mine.** (q) Susan's hair is as long as **mine.** (r) Susan's hair is as long as me.	Remember to use a possessive pronoun where necessary. In examples (q) and (r), both sentences are correct, but there is a big difference in meaning!

EXERCISE 5

Correct the mistakes in the following sentences.

Example: *Miriam is more serious* ~~as~~ than *her sister, Hester.*

1. All her life, Hester has been lucky than her sister, Miriam.
2. Hester is not intelligent as Miriam, but she was always more successful than Miriam in school.
3. For example, Hester's grades were always better than Miriam.
4. Both sisters are pretty, but many people believe that Miriam is prettier that her sister.
5. However, Miriam does not have as many boyfriends than her sister does.
6. They both have excellent jobs, but Miriam thinks her job isn't as interesting as her sister.
7. They both travel as part of their work, but Hester goes to more exciting places than Miriam is.
8. In spite of these differences, Miriam thinks that she is happier that her sister is.
9. However, Hester thinks that good luck is important than good looks and intelligence.

What do **you** think is the most important: good luck, good looks, or intelligence? Why do you think so? Share your ideas with your classmates.

EXERCISE 6

Work in a group to create a problem like the one in the Opening Task. First use the picture and blank chart below to record your information and then write the clues. Each clue must contain at least one of the following: a comparative, a superlative, *as . . . as,* or *not as . . . as.* Finally, exchange your problem with that from another group and see if you can solve each other's problems.

NAME	AGE	HEIGHT	OCCUPATION	WORKING HOURS

Clues

_____

_____

_____

_____

_____

FOCUS 4 Making Tactful Comparisons with *As . . . As* and *Not As . . . As*

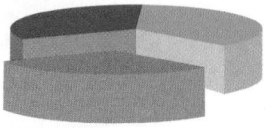

Sometimes it is important to be tactful (more polite and less direct) when you are making comparisons. The adjective you choose can show how tactful your comparison is.

EXAMPLES	EXPLANATIONS
Some adjectives commonly used in making comparisons: Express "MORE": / Express "LESS": *tall* / *short* *old* / *young* *large* / *small* *fast* / *slow*	When you use *as . . . as*, it is more common or usual to use an adjective that expresses "more." When you use an adjective that expresses "less," you draw special attention to it because it is an unusual use.
(a) Linda is **as tall as** Bob.	In (a), the use of *tall* is usual. It does not make us think about **how** tall or **how** short Bob and Linda are, but only that they are the same height.
(b) Linda is **as short as** Bob.	In (b), the use of *short* is unusual. It makes us think that both Bob and Linda are very short.
(c) Patricia is **as old as** Virginia.	In (c), the use of *old* is usual. It shows only that they are the same age.
(d) Patricia is **as young as** Virginia.	In (d), the use of *young* is unusual. It therefore puts special emphasis on *young*.
(e) Bob is **not as tall as** Frank. (f) Frank is **not as short as Bob.** Bob Frank	Both (e) and (f) show that Frank is taller than Bob. However, the use of *short* in (f) is unusual, so it draws special attention to the fact that Bob is short. It is more tactful and more polite to choose (e).
(g) Otis is **not quite as smart as** Rocky. (h) His latest book is **not quite as good as** his earlier ones.	When you want to be really polite and tactful, you can use *not quite as . . . as.*

EXERCISE 7

You are the manager of a large company. A smaller company wants to do business with you but there are several problems to discuss. They will have to improve their overall performance before you are willing to do business with them.

Use the adjectives in parentheses with *not as . . . as*. Add *not quite* if you want to be even more tactful. The first one has been done for you.

1. Your company is smaller than ours. (large)
   Your company is not as large as ours.
2. Your factories are more old-fashioned than ours. (modern)
   _____
3. Your workers are lazier than ours. (energetic)
   _____
4. Your products are less popular than ours. (well known)
   _____
5. Your advertising is less successful than ours. (effective)
   _____
6. Your designs are more conservative than ours. (up-to-date)
   _____
7. Your production is slower than ours. (fast)
   _____
8. The quality of your product line is lower than ours. (high)
   _____
9. Your factories are dirtier than ours. (clean)
   _____
10. Your factories are more dangerous than ours. (safe)
    _____

EXERCISE 8

Omar is president of the International Students' Association at an American college. He wants to write an article for the college newspaper about international students' reactions to life in America. He made a survey of the international students. Help him to write the answers in a more tactful and polite way.

1. Children in America watch more TV.
   Children in my country don't watch as much TV as they do in America.
2. People have dinner very early in America.
   _____
3. People eat more fast food in America.
   _____
4. Food is cheaper in America.
   _____
5. Americans work longer hours than people in my country.
   _____
6. People change jobs more easily in America.
   _____
7. Cities are cleaner in America.
   _____
8. People drive longer distances in America than in my country.
   _____

Do you agree or disagree with these comments? Do you have any comments of your own that Omar could include in his article? Add them here:

_____

_____

_____

_____

Use Your English

ACTIVITY 1 speaking/writing

STEP 1 Work in groups. Imagine that someone from your country (or a country that you know well) is going to stay with a family in America. Discuss and make notes about the differences in culture and customs they may find surprising. Include information about the best places in town for international students to meet new people and to practice English.

STEP 2 Divide your group into small groups of two or three people. One small group will write a brief guide for the American host family. The other pair will write a guide for the visiting student. Be tactful where necessary!

ACTIVITY 2 writing

You are staying with an American family for the summer. Write a letter to your own family describing some of the differences you have experienced between life in America and life in your country. Before you start, make a list of interesting, surprising, or reassuring topics.

ACTIVITY 3 speaking/listening

There are many common idioms in English that use the construction *as . . . as*. Some common idioms are:

- as strong as an ox
- as stubborn as a rule
- as quiet as a mouse

Interview several speakers of English and ask them to tell you as many idioms as they can remember. Write the idioms in your notebook and also write an example of when they might use each idiom. Choose one of these new idioms to explain to your classmates.

ACTIVITY 4 speaking/listening

The purpose of this activity is to think of as many differences as possible between two objects. Your teacher will tell you what you are to compare. Form teams. You have five minutes with your team to make a list of as many differences as possible. After five minutes, the teams take turns sharing their differences. The team with the most differences scores a point. Your teacher will then give you the next two objects to compare. The team with the most points is the winner.

STEP 1 To score a point, your comparison must be meaningful **and** accurate.

STEP 2 You cannot repeat a comparison that another team has already given. However, you **can** express the same idea, using different words. For example:

Team A says: *A Harley Davidson motorcycle is more expensive than some cars.*

Team B can say: *Some cars aren't as expensive as a Harley Davidson.*

Team C can say: *Some cars are cheaper than a Harley Davidson . . .* and so on.

If possible, try to record your team as you play this game. Afterwards listen to the recording and see how many comparative, superlative, and (*not*) *as . . . as* forms you used.

ACTIVITY 5 speaking/listening

STEP 1 Choose one set of objects that you compared in Activity 4. Ask three different people outside of class to compare these two objects and record their replies. Listen to the recording. Did they make more comparisons than you did? Or did you make more comparisons than them? Compare your findings with classmates.

STEP 2 Listen to your recording again and write down any sentences with examples of comparative, superlative, and (*not*) *as . . . as* forms.

ACTIVITY 6 listening/speaking

CD Track 12

STEP 1

Before you listen to the audio for this activity, get together with a partner. Make a list of all the differences you can think of between working for a small company and working for a large company. Write them on the left side of a chart in your notebook.

What are the differences between working for a small company and a large company?

DIFFERENCES: _____ (partner) and I	DIFFERENCES: TERRY AND ROBIN
A small company is friendlier than a large company.	

STEP 2

Listen to the audio. You will hear two people, Terry and Robin, compare working for a small company and working for a large company. Add the differences they describe to the right side of the chart. How many differences did you and your partner find? How many did Terry and Robin find?

STEP 3

Now listen to the audio again, and write down any sentences with comparative, superlative, or *(not) as . . . as* forms in them.

ACTIVITY 7 speaking

STEP 1

Think of two jobs that you had in the past. Tell your partner about them. Say which one you liked better and why. Report to the class about your partner's jobs.

STEP 2

Make a list of adjectives or adverbs you used in your report. Group the words according to those that use *-er* or *-est* , those that use "more" or "most," and other words that show similarity or difference. Can you find a pattern?

ACTIVITY 8 speaking/listening

We sometimes honor people with special awards for achievements in different fields. For example, the film industry presents Oscars every year for "the best picture," "the best director," and so on. This year, your school will give several special awards for different achievements. You and your classmates are on the committee that will decide who should get these awards.

STEP 1 In small groups, make a list of awards you would like to give. For example, you can give awards for "the best dressed student," "the most talkative student," "the most creative dancer," "the student who is the most likely to become president of his or her country," and so on. Decide on who should receive these awards. You can also give awards to other people on campus or to places that you like in the community, for example, "the teacher who gives the most homework," "the best hamburger," "the quietest place to study," "the best place to meet other students."

STEP 2 Hold a class awards "ceremony" to announce the winners and present the awards.

ACTIVITY 9 research on the web

***InfoTrac® College Edition*:** Go to *InfoTrac* to read facts about two countries: for example, Russia and the United States. Type: "Compare facts: Russia and the United States" Write five sentences comparing these two countries and tell the class. What explanations can you think of for the similarities and differences you found?

ACTIVITY 10 reflection

What similarities or differences are there between English and your first language (or another language you know well)? Which one is easier or more difficult and why? Make a list of differences and similarities and present your list to the class.

UNIT 8

MEASURE WORDS AND QUANTIFIERS

UNIT GOALS

- Understand special measure words used with foods
- Use measure words with count and noncount nouns
- Know how to use common quantifiers

OPENING TASK

Getting Ready for a Potluck Dinner

STEP 1

Jim has been invited to a potluck dinner—a meal where each guest brings a dish. The hostess asked him to bring cookies and a salad for six people. Look at the picture of Jim's kitchen. Can you name the different foods? How much does he have of each food?

STEP 2

Jim wants to make everything himself. He already has these ingredients in his kitchen.

INGREDIENTS	
mustard	chocolate chips
sugar	tomatoes
salt	flour
lettuce	olive oil
hard-boiled eggs	butter
cheese	eggs
vinegar	garlic

Help Jim decide which ingredients he can use in each dish. Write each ingredient in the box below.

SALAD	SALAD DRESSING	CHOCOLATE CHIP COOKIES

STEP 3

How much of each ingredient do you think Jim should use? Write an amount beside each ingredient. Remember, there will be six people at the party.

STEP 4

Are there any other ingredients you would include? Add them to the boxes above, with suggested amounts.

FOCUS 1 Measure Words with Food

CONTAINERS

Some measure words are **containers** that we can find in a store.

a bottle of (soy sauce, ketchup)

a jar of (peanut butter, mustard)

a box of (cereal, crackers)

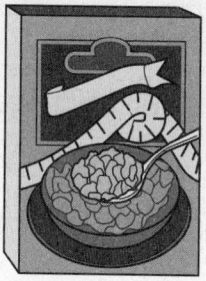

a bag of (potato chips, flour)

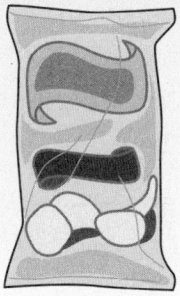

a carton of (milk, eggs)

a can of (tuna fish, soup)

EXERCISE 1

Turn back to the Opening Task on page 121. Look at the ingredients and the amounts. Did you use the right measure words? Make any necessary corrections.

EXERCISE 2

Turn back to the Opening Task and look carefully at the ingredients. Some of these are count nouns (tomatoes) and some are noncount nouns (flour). Write C beside each count noun and NC beside each noncount noun.*

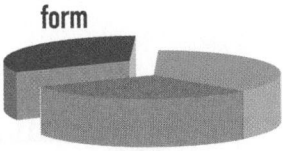

FOCUS 2 Measure Words with Count and Noncount Nouns

Measure words express specific quantities. They also allow us to make noncount nouns countable.

three bottles of water

two scoops of ice cream

six pounds of coffee

three cartons of milk

*For more information on count and noncount nouns, see *Grammar Dimensions* Book 1, Unit 4.

Most measure expressions follow this pattern.*

A/An/One Two Three	+	Measure Word (Singular/Plural)	+	*of*	+	Noun (Noncount/Plural)
a		cup		of		milk
a		pound		of		apples
two		cups		of		milk
two		pounds		of		apples

* Exception: specific numbers (including *dozen*):
a dozen eggs NOT a dozen of eggs
ten strawberries NOT ten of strawberries

EXERCISE 3

These are the recipes that Jim finally used. Complete the missing parts. (The picture may help you.)

Jim's Super Salad

1 large (a) _____ of red lettuce
1 medium-sized (b) _____ of romaine lettuce
1 large cucumber, cut into (c) _____
6 tomatoes, cut into quarters
$^1/_2$ (d) _____ of Swiss cheese, cut into small strips

1 (e) _____ cooked chicken, shredded into small pieces
2 hard-boiled eggs, shelled and cut into quarters

1. Line a large salad bowl with red lettuce leaves.
2. Tear the romaine lettuce leaves into medium-sized pieces.
3. Place in the bowl in layers: slices of cucumber and tomato, cheese, lettuce, and chicken.
4. Add olives and eggs. Cover and refrigerate for one hour. Toss with Jim's Super Salad Dressing just before serving.

Jim's Super Salad Dressing

1 (a) _____ Dijon mustard
4 (b) _____ red wine vinegar
1 (c) _____ sugar
$^1/_2$ (d) _____ salt
$^1/_2$ (e) _____ pepper
$^1/_2$ (f) _____ olive oil

1. Put the mustard into a bowl. Whisk in vinegar, sugar, salt, and pepper.
2. Slowly add the oil while continuing to whisk the mixture.

Jim's Granny's Old Time Chocolate Chip Cookies

$^1/_2$ (a) _____ butter
1 (b) _____ brown sugar
$^3/_4$ (c) _____ granulated sugar

2 eggs
2 (d) _____ flour

1 (e) _____ baking soda
1 (f) _____ vanilla extract
1 (g) _____ salt

1 $^1/_2$ (h) _____ chocolate chips

1. Preheat the oven to 350°F. Grease a cookie sheet.
2. Cream the butter and both the sugars together until light and fluffy. Add the eggs and vanilla and mix well.
3. Sift the flour, baking soda, and salt. Mix thoroughly.
4. Add the chocolate chips.
5. Form into cookies. Place on a cookie sheet and put on the middle rack of the oven for 8–10 minutes.
6. Cool for 5 minutes.
7. Enjoy! (This recipe makes about 40 cookies.)

Turn back to the Opening Task on page 121 and look at the ingredients (and the amounts) you suggested for these dishes. How many differences can you find between your suggestions and Jim's recipes? Whose recipe do you think will taste better?

EXERCISE 4

Last week Matthew ate a delicious spaghetti sauce at his friend Nancy's house. He enjoyed it so much that Nancy lent him the recipe so that he could make a copy of it. However, Nancy has obviously used this recipe many times and it is quite difficult to read. Can you help Matthew figure out the recipe? Fill in the missing words below.

Spaghetti Sauce

(from Nancy's kitchen)

First, cut 3 _____ of bacon into small pieces and cook over a very low heat. Stir in ½ a _____ of ground meat along with 4 _____ of garlic and 2 _____ of onion, very finely chopped. Add 1 _____ of salt, a _____ of cayenne pepper, and 2 _____ of dried herbs. Mix in two 8-ounce _____ of tomato sauce. Cook on low heat for about 30 minutes. Serve over fresh pasta.

If you were making this recipe yourself, would you change or add anything? Share any changes or additions with your classmates. Try to be as precise as possible.

FOCUS 3 Common Quantifiers

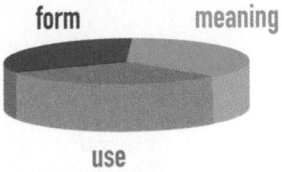

AMOUNT	EXAMPLES	EXPLANATIONS
all	(a) **All** of the dishes at the potluck were delicious. (b) He spends **all** of his money on wine.	Some quantifiers (words that talk about quantity/number or amount) can be used with **both count and noncount** nouns. Use *all* to mean *everything* or *everyone.*
most	(c) **Most** of the people in North America take vacations in the summer. (d) **Most** people in my town work in tourism.	Most means *almost everyone* or *almost everything.* Use *most* of when there is an article before the noun. Use *most* when there is no article.
many/much	(e) We heard that ***many*** people were coming. (f) We don't have ***much*** time. (g) A: Were ***many*** people hurt? (h) B: No, not ***many.***	*Many* is used only with count nouns to talk about a large number. Use *much* with noncount nouns to talk about a large amount. *Many* and *much* are usually used in questions or negative statements.
a lot of *lots of* *a great deal of*	(i) We make ***a lot of*** trips back and forth over the mountains. (j) I heard that there was ***lots of*** new snow. (k) ***A great deal of*** current information is available on the Internet.	Use *a lot of* or *lots of* with very large numbers or amounts, and with either count or noncount nouns. *Lots of* is used in informal situations. Use *a great deal of* in formal situations, and only with noncount nouns. It means the same as *a lot of* or *lots.*
some	(l) We needed ***some*** milk for the recipe. (m) We were glad that we had put ***some*** new snow tires on our car.	*Some* is a smaller amount or quantity than a *lot of/lots of.* *Some* is used with both count and noncount nouns.

Continued on next page

Continued from previous page

AMOUNT	EXAMPLES	EXPLANATIONS
several	(n) We couldn't travel on ***several*** days last winter because the mountain passes were closed.	*Several* is used only with count nouns. *Several* means more than a small number.
a few / a little	(o) In a ***few*** days, we'll be ready to go. (p) There was ***a little*** snow on the mountains. (q) Let's buy ***a little*** food and ***a few*** cans of soda.	A *few* means more than two, but not many more. A few and *a little* have similar meanings. *A little* is used only with noncount nouns and *a few* is used only with count nouns.
few/little	(r) We have ***few*** friends and ***little*** money. (s) ***Few*** people know that she has ***little*** time left.	*Few* and *little* refer to the same amounts or numbers as *a few* and *a little*; however, they have a negative meaning. They mean *almost none*. *Few* is used only with count nouns, *little* only with noncount nouns.
a couple (of)	(t) I'd like to get ***a couple of*** blankets to keep in the car. (u) Let's ask ***a couple (of)*** people to come with us.	*A couple of* means two, but it is sometimes used informally to mean two or more. *A couple of* is used only with count nouns. In informal English, *of* is sometimes omitted.
none/no	(v) ***None of*** the people went to the meeting. (w) We heard that there was ***no*** new snow.	*None* means *not any*, and is used with count nouns. *No* has the same meaning, and is used with noncount nouns.

EXERCISE 5

Choose the correct quantifier for each sentence.

1. There are _____ big supermarkets in my town.
   a. a lot b. a little c. much d. several
2. We usually get _____ of rain in the summer.
   a. a little b. some c. most d. a lot
3. There are _____ fast-food restaurants near my house.
   a. a couple of b. most c. a little d. a great deal of
4. _____ people have the Internet at home.
   a. None b. Little c. Few d. A lot of
5. _____ education at my university concerns the use of new technology.
   a. All of b. None of c. Many of d. A great deal of

EXERCISE 6

Find a partner and take turns asking each other questions about your native countries or countries you know about. Use the topics in (A) to ask general questions. In your answers to the questions, give specific examples to explain what you mean. You must use a quantifier (from Focus 3) in your answer. Column (B) gives you ideas for quantifiers you can use in your answers, but you may use others.

Example: Q: *Is clothing expensive in (Vietnam)?*

A: *No, not really. A lot of people go to the big cities to buy clothes. There are lots of factories in the cities, so you can usually find clothes that are pretty cheap.*

(A) Topic	(B) Quantifier
1. clothing	some lots of/a lot of
2. tourist attractions	a few a couple of
3. holidays	most some
4. climate	no/none a great deal of
5. fast-food restaurants	some several
6. technology	a few many
7. English speakers	most a lot of
8. entertainment	all much

EXERCISE 7

Some of the sentences in the following letter have errors with nouns and with quantifiers. Find the errors and correct them. When you have finished, check your answers with another student.

Dear Nell,

I think I'm going to like my new job. So far it's interesting, and I hope that it stays that way! There are several of people who work in the same office with me. At the moment I share a desk with Jessica, who just started a couple week ago, but our office manager just ordered new furnitures so that soon we will each have a desk of our own. There are lot of people in the building who share desks and computers, so I feel pretty lucky to have my own to work on.

Every morning Martha, the staff assistant, brings us each a cup of coffee. She already knows that I like sugars in my coffee but no milks. Martha also brings the mails to us, and she likes to give us many advice about how to be efficient. Two times a day I get at least fifty letter which I have to respond to, so I do listen to Martha's advices. A few her ideas have really been useful!

Some days I can do most of my business on the computer. Other days I need a little more informations from my customers, so I need to talk to them on the telephone. Every day there are some problem that I cannot handle. If there are only couple of problems, my coworker helps, but on the days when there are lot of problems, we call in Anna, the office supervisor. Already there have been several time when even Anna couldn't handle the problems, and so she has had to call in her supervisor.

So you can see that I'm busy, and at this point, I'm not bored.

Talk to you soon—

Love,

Elliott

Use Your English

ACTIVITY 1 writing/speaking

This "recipe" was written by an English teacher:

"Recipe" for the Perfect Student

Ingredients:

1 cup of motivation	1 cup of imagination
1 cup of determination	1 $^1/_2$ cups of willingness to make a guess
$^1/_2$ cup of patience	1 cup of independence
$^1/_2$ cup of tolerance	1 $^1/_2$ cups of cooperation with others
1 cup of laughter	1 pinch of fun

Combine ingredients and stir gently to bring out the best flavor.

What do you think the teacher meant by this?

Get together with a partner and create a "recipe" of your own. Here are some ideas, but you probably have plenty of your own:

- Recipe for a long-lasting marriage
- Recipe for the perfect partner
- Recipe for the perfect teacher
- Recipe for the perfect house
- Recipe for the perfect mother/father

Share your recipes with the rest of the class.

ACTIVITY 2 writing

Write a paragraph describing your perfect birthday party (real or imaginary). Before writing, make notes on the people, food, music, and activities. When you have written your paragraph, exchange it with another student. Underline the quantifiers. Were they used correctly?

Example: *My ideal birthday party would have a lot of food, many friends . . .*

ACTIVITY 3 speaking

Your class is scheduled for a weekend trip to a nearby national park or state forest. Transportation is provided, and a few small overnight cabins are available. But you will need to decide what food to bring, and also what other things you will need. Here are some ideas: sleeping bags, cooking pots, eating utensils (plates, cups, silverware), firewood, sports equipment, depending on the season (fishing poles? swimsuits? skis?).

Work in groups and come up with a list. Be specific about the quantities. Compare lists to make sure you haven't forgotten anything!

ACTIVITY 4 speaking/listening/writing

STEP 1

Organize an international potluck. Everyone in the class should prepare and bring a dish, preferably from his or her country. After the meal, have each person describe his or her recipe. If possible, record the descriptions.

STEP 2

Listen to the recording and write down the recipes. Collect all the recipes for an international cookbook. Make copies and distribute them to the class.

ACTIVITY 5 listening

CD Track 13

STEP 1

Listen to the audio of a person describing a recipe for a traditional North American dish.

1. What dish is the speaker describing?
2. When is this dish usually eaten?
3. What are the important ingredients in the dish?

STEP 2

Listen to the audio again, and this time write down the ingredients and amounts.

Work with a partner to make sure that you understand what each ingredient is, and then take turns reading each ingredient and the amount aloud. If you decide to make this dish, it is important that your recipe is accurate!

For each ingredient with a measure word, write the kind of measure word:

- If it is a **container,** mark it C.
- If it is a **shape/typical state,** mark it S.
- If it is a **portion,** mark it P.
- If it is a **measurement,** mark it M.

1. Do you recognize the measurements?
2. Do you know what teaspoon/tablespoon/cup is?

ACTIVITY 6 research on the web

On the Web: Go on the Internet using a search engine such as Google® or Yahoo® and find a recipe for one of these dishes: potato salad/cheesecake/apple pie/carrot soup. Make a list of the ingredients. Then compare your list with a partner. What differences in the ingredients did you find?

ACTIVITY 7 reflection

Make a list of food and drink you had today. Organize your list with the correct measure word for each item. Compare your list with a partner.

Example: *a teaspoon of sugar, a slice of bread*

UNIT 9

DEGREE COMPLEMENTS

Too, *Enough*, and *Very*

UNIT GOALS

- Understand the meaning of *enough*, *not enough*, and *too*
- Form correct sentences with *enough*, *not enough*, and *too*
- Know how to use *too much*, *too many*, *too little*, and *too few*
- Understand the difference between *too* and *very*

OPENING TASK

Looking for Somewhere to Live

What's your ideal home?

STEP 1

Get together with a partner and try to guess what these housing abbreviations mean. Read the classified housing ads below to help you work out the answers.

apt *kit* BR DR *lg* *furn* *kit* *mo*

For Rent

1 1200 SQ FT BASEMENT 2 BR APT $700 Newly Painted. Walk to center. Furn/unfurn. No pets. Call owner before 9 P.M. (718) 555-1320	2 EAST VILLAGE Renovated lg studio apt w/new wood flrs. High ceilings: sunny: lg windows: lg walk-in closet: mod kit $650/mo 555-0479
3 GREENWICH VILLAGE Charming 1BR; new kit & bath. Very quiet building $875/mo. 555-4345	4 GREENWICH ST. 3 BR Bright: Big closets: full bath: lge kit. Nice gdn. Call Tim 555-8246 $1250/mo.

STEP 2

Read the classified ads about different types of housing rentals. Then match the ads with the descriptions of different home hunters. Explain which homes are NOT suitable for these people.

a. Maria is looking for an unfurnished house or apartment with lots of light and plenty of closet space. She cannot pay more than $900 a month.
Best home: _____

b. Sandra and Suzanne are looking for a two-bedroom apartment with at least 1000 square feet. They can pay $800 a month.
Best home: _____

c. Tony and Carla have two children and a dog. They need a garden and a big kitchen. They can pay around $1200 a month.
Best home: _____

d. Peter is looking for a sunny furnished studio apartment in good condition. He can pay $700 a month.
Best home: _____

STEP 3

Work with a partner and complete the sentences. Make similar sentences about the other people.

Maria likes apartment _____ because _____. She does not like apartment _____ because _____. She does not like apartment _____ because _____. She does not like apartment _____ because _____.

STEP 4

Look back at all the ads. Which place would you choose? Why? Which places would you definitely NOT choose? Why?

(Solution to the Opening Task on page A-16)

meaning

FOCUS 1 Enough, Not Enough, Too

EXAMPLES	EXPLANATIONS
(a) There are **enough** closets. (b) This apartment is big **enough** for both of us.	*Enough* shows something is sufficient. You have as much as you need and you do not need any more. *Enough* usually shows that you are satisfied with the situation.
(c) There are **not enough** windows in this apartment. (I want more windows!) OR: There aren't **enough** windows in this apartment. (d) The bedroom is **not** big **enough.** (I want a bigger bedroom!) OR: The bedroom isn't **enough.**	*Not enough* shows that something is insufficient. In your opinion, there should be more. *Not enough* usually shows that you are not satisfied with the situation.
(e) The rent is **too** high. (It is more than I want to pay.) (f) The kitchen is **too** small. (I want a bigger one.) (g) That coffee is **too** hot. (I can't drink it.) (h) He speaks **too** fast. (I can't understand him.) (i) She's **too** young to drink. (She has to be 21 to drink alcohol in this state.)	*Too* shows that something is **more** than you want or need OR that it is **less** than you want or need. It depends on the meaning of the word that follows. *Too* usually shows that you are not satisfied with the situation.

EXERCISE 1

Look back at Step 2 of the Opening Task on page 137. Did you use *too, not enough,* or *enough*? If not, rewrite your reasons and see if you can use *too, enough,* or *not enough* in them.

Choose one of the families listed on page 137. In your opinion, what would each family say about these apartments? Where possible, use *too, enough,* and *not enough.*

1. Tiny but charming studio apartment. Large skylights. Limited storage space. $700.

_____

_____

2. Gorgeous penthouse apartment. Fabulous views of Central Park. 3 bedrooms, 2 bathrooms. Dining room and roof gardern. $1800.

_____

_____

3. Bright two-bedroom apartment. Big closets. Next to fire station. $825.

_____

_____

EXERCISE 2

In this exercise, people are talking about problems that they are having, and their friends are responding by saying what they think caused these problems. For example:

Read the list of problems and the list of causes below. What do you think caused the problems? Work with a partner and match the problems and their causes.

PROBLEMS		CAUSES
1. My feet really hurt.	d	a. You don't go to the dentist often enough.
2. I'm broke!	_____	b. Maybe you shouted too much at the ball game.
3. I failed my math test.	_____	c. You didn't add enough salt.
4. I've gained a lot of weight recently.	_____	d. Perhaps your shoes aren't big enough.
5. I never feel hungry at mealtimes.	_____	e. You spend too much money.
6. I can't sleep at night.	_____	f. Your stereo is too loud.
7. I have a sore throat.	_____	g. You don't get enough exercise.
8. This soup is tasteless.	_____	h. You eat too many snacks.
9. My neighbors are always angry with me.	_____	i. You drink too much coffee.
10. My teeth hurt.	_____	j. You didn't study enough.

FOCUS 2 *Enough, Not Enough, Too*

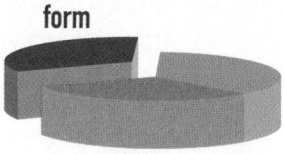

EXAMPLES	EXPLANATIONS
(a) This house is **big enough.** That apartment is **not big enough.**	Place *enough* or *not enough*: • after adjectives
(b) Po speaks **clearly** enough. Tan does not speak **clearly enough.**	• after adverbs
(c) She **ate enough.** He **did not eat enough.**	• after verbs
(d) We have **enough money.** They **do not** have **enough money.**	• before nouns
(e) She is **(not) old enough to vote.**	Notice how *enough* can be used with: • an adjective + an infinitive
(f) They studied **hard enough to pass** the test, but they didn't study **hard enough to get** a good score.	• an adverb + an infinitive
(g) We **(don't) earn enough to pay** the rent.	• a verb + an infinitive
(h) I (don't) have **enough chocolate to make** a cake.	• a noun + infinitive
(i) She is **too young.**	Place *too* before adjectives and adverbs.
(j) They work **too slowly.**	
(k) This tea is **too hot to drink.**	*Too* + adjective or adverb is often followed by an infinitive.
(l) We worked **too late to go to** the party.	
(m) That book is **too difficult for me to understand.**	*Too* + adjective or adverb is often followed by *for* + noun/pronoun + infinitive.
(n) He walked **too fast for the children to keep up.**	

EXERCISE 3

Nazmi has some problems in his English classes. Rewrite the sentences using *too*, *enough*, or *not enough*. Compare your answers with a partner.

1. The teacher speaks too quietly.
   She doesn't speak loudly enough.
2. Her writing is too small.
   Her writing is _____.
3. My seat is too far away from the board.
   My seat isn't _____.
4. The test time is too short and we never finish.
   There is _____.
5. I am too busy to finish all my homework.
   I don't _____.
6. Our grammar book isn't easy enough.
   Our grammar book is _____.
7. Our lessons aren't long enough.
   Our lessons are _____.
8. I have a lot of questions but I don't ask them.
   I don't _____.
9. I want to take the exam but I need to study more.
   I do _____.
10. I don't check my answers carefully enough.
    I check my answers _____.

Think of some other problems you have or know about. Describe the problem using *too*, or *not enough*. Take turns with a partner saying the same things in a different way.

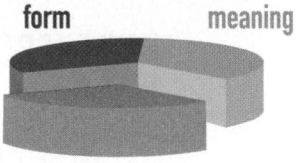

FOCUS 3 *Too Much* and *Too Many; Too Little* and *Too Few*

EXAMPLES	EXPLANATIONS
(a) Walt has **too much money.**	Use *too much* with noncount nouns.
(b) There are **too many students** in this class.	Use *too many* with count nouns. *Too much* and *too many* show that there is more than you want or need. They show that you are not satisfied with the situation.
(c) There's **too little time** to finish this.	Use *too little* with noncount nouns.
(d) The class was canceled because **too few students** enrolled.	Use *too few* **with count nouns.** *Too little* and *too few* show that there is less than you want or need. They show that you are not satisfied with the situation.

EXERCISE 4

Read the following description of a wedding reception where everything went wrong. Underline all the words or phrases that show there was not enough of something. Where possible, replace these with *too little* or *too few* and change the verbs as necessary.

My sister's wedding was a disaster. First of all, she decided to get married very suddenly, so there was too little time to wasn't enough time to plan it properly. Nevertheless, about fifty of her friends came to the reception in her studio. Unfortunately, there wasn't enough room for everyone, so it was rather uncomfortable. She only had a few chairs, and our ninety-six-year-old grandmother had to sit on the floor. My father had ordered lots of champagne, but there weren't enough glasses, so some people didn't get very much to drink. In addition, we had several problems with the caterers. There wasn't enough cake for everyone, but there was too much soup! We also had problems with the entertainment. My sister loves Latin music, so she hired a salsa band; however, it was hard to move in such a small space, and my sister got upset when not enough people wanted to dance. I got into trouble too. I was the official photographer, but I didn't bring enough film with me, so now my sister is mad because she only has about ten wedding photographs—and all of them are pictures of people trying to find a place to sit down!

EXERCISE 5

You and your friends decided to give a big party. You made lots of plans, but unfortunately everything went wrong and the party was a total disaster. Get together with one or two other students and make a list of all the things that can go wrong at parties. Use this list to make a description of **your** disastrous party, using *too*, *too much*, *too many*, *too little*, *too few*, or *not enough*. Share your description with the rest of the class and decide who had the "worst" possible party.

meaning

FOCUS 4 *Too* versus *Very*

EXAMPLES	EXPLANATIONS
(a) *This writing is small.*	*Very* adds emphasis, but *too* shows that something is more than is necessary or desirable.
(b) *This writing is very small.*	In (b) the writing is small, but I can read it.
(c) *This writing is too small.*	In (c) the writing is smaller and I cannot read it.
	In these situations, *too* shows that you are unable to do something, but *very* does not.

EXERCISE 6

Complete the following with *too, too + to,* or *very,* as appropriate.

A: Hi Pam! I haven't seen you for ages!

B: I'm sorry. I've been (1) *too* busy *to* call. I've been house-hunting.

A: Did you find anything yet?

B: Yes, I found a place downtown. It's (2) _____ expensive, but I think I'll have enough money.

A: What was wrong with your old apartment?

B: I need a place where I can work on my art designs, and my old apartment was (3) _____ dark _____ work in. This apartment is (4) _____ large and sunny.

A: It sounds great. The problem with my apartment is that it's (5) _____ noisy. But it's also (6) _____ cheap, so I guess I'll stay there till I have some more money. Do you need any help moving?

B: Oh yes, please. Could you bring your car? My car is (7) _____ small _____ carry all my stuff. Afterwards we can go out for lunch together.

A: Yes, I'd like that (8) _____ much.

EXERCISE 7

Complete the following with *very, too, too + to, enough, not enough,* or *too much/many/little/few,* as appropriate.

Dear Tom and Wendy,

I'm writing to answer your questions about life in New York. In fact, this is quite hard to do because my opinions keep changing!

My apartment is nice, but the rent is (1) ___very___ high. Luckily, I earn a good salary and I can afford it. The main problem is that the apartment just is (2) _____ big _____ I had to sell about half my furniture because I didn't have (3) _____ room for everything. I can't invite people for dinner because the kitchen is (4) _____ small _____ eat in. Luckily, the apartment has lots of windows, so all my plants are getting (5) _____ light. I live (6) _____ close to a subway station; it only takes me a couple of minutes to walk there. However, I never take the subway to work because it's (7) _____ crowded. You wouldn't believe it! There are just (8) _____ people crammed in like sardines, and you can't breathe because there is (9) _____ air. I haven't had the courage to ride my bike yet because there's just (10) _____ traffic. Mostly I walk everywhere, so the good news is that I am getting (11) _____ exercise!

Despite all this, there are lots of wonderful things about living here. There are (12) _____ museums and art galleries to keep me happy for years! However, at the moment, I have (13) _____ time to enjoy them because my job is driving me crazy. It's impossible to get all the work done because there are (14) _____ projects and (15) _____ good people to work on them. As a result, I am (16) _____ busy to make new friends or meet people. I don't sleep (17) _____ and so I am always tired. Worst of all, I don't even have (18) _____ time to stay in touch with dear old friends like you! Nevertheless, I'm certain things will get better soon. Why don't you come and visit? That would really cheer me up!

Love,

Mary

Use Your English

ACTIVITY 1 speaking

Work with a partner or in teams to play this version of tic-tac-toe.

STEP 1 Decide who will be "X" and who will be "O" and toss a coin to see who will start the game.

STEP 2 For each round of the game, select a different topic from the list below.

STEP 3 Choose the square you want to start with. With your team, agree on a meaningful sentence expressing the idea written in the square and relating to the topic of the round. For example: TOPIC: This classroom. *"This classroom is very small," "There aren't enough chairs in this classroom," "There are too few windows in this classroom,"* and so on. If your sentence is correct, mark the square with "X" or "O".

STEP 4 The first team to get three across, down, or diagonally is the winner.

TOPICS

1. This campus
2. Television
3. North America
4. This town or city

very	too + to	too
too few	not enough	too much
enough	too many	too little

ACTIVITY 2 writing

Write a letter to your local city councilor or mayor about a problem in your city or neighborhood. Describe the problem, and say why it is important. Be sure to use *too, enough,* and *very.* Suggest a possible solution.

ACTIVITY 3 speaking/writing

STEP 1

Look at the chart below. If you were responsible for making the laws in your community, at what ages would you permit the following activities? Write the ages in the column marked *Ideal Age.*

STEP 2

Go around the room and collect information from your classmates about the ages at which these activities are permitted in the parts of the world (countries, states, provinces) that they know about. You can include information about this country (or state or province) as well. Write this in the last column.

ACTIVITY	IDEAL AGE	REAL AGE/WHERE
drive a car		
drink alcohol		
vote		
join the military		
get married		
own a gun		
leave school		

STEP 3

When you have collected the information, prepare a report (oral or written) on the differences and similarities you found among different parts of the world. Include your own opinions about the ideal ages for these activities and give reasons to support them. Remember to announce the purpose of your report in your introduction and to end with a concluding statement. You can use these headings to organize your information: Introduction: Purpose of this report, Most interesting similarities among parts of the world, Most interesting differences among parts of the world, Your opinions on ideal ages, with reasons to support them, and Brief concluding statement.

STEP 4

If you make a written report, remember to read it through carefully after you finish writing. Check to see if you were able to use any of the language in this unit. If you make an oral report, record your presentation and listen to it later. Write down any sentences that you used containing *too, very*, not enough, or *enough.*

ACTIVITY 4 speaking

The purpose of this activity is to share opinions on different social issues. Work with a partner and look at the issues listed below. For each one, think about what is sufficient (enough), what is insufficient (not enough), and what is excessive (too much) in this country and in other countries you and your partner know about. For example, you might think that public transportation in this country is too expensive and that there is not enough of it, but that public transportation in Egypt is very inexpensive but too slow. Record your opinions in your notebook. Be ready to share your ideas with the rest of the class.

- Public Transportation
- Health Care
- Law and Order
- Education
- Care of the Elderly
- Housing
- Employment
- Access for Disabled People to Public Buildings and Transportation

ACTIVITY 5 writing

Choose **one** of the social issues you discussed in Activity 4. Review the information you collected on different countries. In your opinion, which country has the best solution? Which country, in your opinion, is the least successful in dealing with this issue? Write a short report, describing the best and worst solutions. Give reasons to support your opinions. Remember to introduce your topic; we have suggested one possibility below, but you can probably think of a better way. When you finish writing, read your report carefully and check to see if you were able to include any of the language discussed in this unit.

In the modern world, many countries are trying to find solutions to the same social issues, and it is interesting to see that different countries and cultures deal with these issues in different ways. In my opinion, some countries have better solutions than others. To illustrate this point, I will talk about _____ (social issue) and show how _____ (country) and _____ (country) both deal with it.

ACTIVITY 6 speaking/listening

STEP 1 Use the information from Activity 4. As a class, choose four topics that interest you. Then, by yourself or with another student, interview a friend or another student about these topics. Record your interview. Listen to your recording and make a brief summary of the person's opinions. Share your findings with others. What similarities and differences did your class find in these interviews?

STEP 2 Listen to your recording again and write down any sentences containing examples of language discussed in this unit.

ACTIVITY 7 listening

CD Track 14

STEP 1 List three serious problems facing the environment today.

STEP 2 Listen to the audio of two people discussing environmental problems. Which opinions do you agree or disagree with and why?

STEP 3 Listen to the audio again. Write down as many phrases containing *too*, *enough*, and *very* as you can.

ACTIVITY 8 research on the web

InfoTrac® College Edition: What are the causes of world hunger? Why do some countries have too much food, and others not enough? Go to *InfoTrac* and search using the keywords 'causes of hunger'. What are the different ways this topic can be understood and explained? Make notes and present your ideas to the class.

ACTIVITY 9 reflection

What do you like and dislike about your classroom or library? What do you have too much/many of? What do you have too little/too few of? Tell your partner.

UNIT 10

GIVING ADVICE AND EXPRESSING OPINIONS

Should, Ought To, Need To, Must, Had Better, Could, and *Might*

UNIT GOALS

- Use *must, had better, need to, should, ought to, could, might,* and imperatives to give advice appropriately
- Use *should, ought to,* and *should not* to express opinions

OPENING TASK

How to . . .

In North America, many "self-improvement" or "self-help" books are published every year. These books give people advice on how to improve their lives.

STEP 1

With a partner, look at the titles of the books below. What kinds of advice do you expect to find in each one? Make up short dialogs about each book, similar to the example below.

Example:

Student A: *I need to learn about a healthy diet.*

Student B: *You should read* Live Longer, Eat Better.

STEP 2

Now read the sample passages from these books and match each one to the book you think it probably comes from.

A
As an important first step, you really ought to eliminate red meat. This may be hard at first, but you will be amazed to find that there are many healthy—and delicious—alternatives.

B
This is never as easy as it sounds, so you should be prepared to put time and effort into it. For example, doing volunteer work is one way to meet people who share your interests, and you may get to know them better as you work on projects together.

C
It's easier than you think. To really make a difference, you should start slowly and establish a routine. Think about one thing that you can easily do (carpool? recycle paper, cans, and glass?) As soon as this becomes a habit, you should start to think about what to do next.

D
You should never settle into a regular, predictable routine. Surprise each other with fun activities, like picnics after work or moonlight barbecues on the beach.

E
You ought to make every effort to motivate yourself to stay on your diet! Buy a dress that is just a little bit too small for you and hang it in your closet. You should look at it every day and dream of the time when it will really fit you.

F
You shouldn't draw attention to yourself. Choose conservative but attractive styles. Navy blue is a good color choice. Remember that you ought to look competent and professional at all times.

STEP 3

With your partner, choose one of these self-help books. What advice would you give on the topic? Come up with at least three pieces of advice. Write these in your notebook.

FOCUS 1 Giving Advice with *Should, Ought To, Shouldn't*

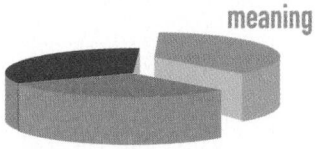

EXAMPLES	EXPLANATIONS
(a) A: I'm so tired. B: You **should/ought to** get more sleep. (b) A: I can't understand my teacher. B: You **ought to/should** talk to her about it.	*Should/should not* and *ought to* are often used to give advice (to tell someone what you think is a good or bad idea for him or her to do). Use *should* or *ought to* to show that you think something is a good idea. *Ought to* is often pronounced as *oughta* in spoken English.
(c) A: I have a terrible cough. B: You **should not (shouldn't)** smoke so much.	Use *should not* (*shouldn't*) to show that you think something is a bad idea. *Ought to* is not usually used in negatives or in questions in American English.
(d) Nami works too hard. She **should/ought to** take a vacation. (e) NOT: She shoulds/oughts to take a vacation.	*Should* and *ought to* are modal auxiliaries. They do not take third person *s*. For more information about the form of modals, see Unit 5.

EXERCISE 1

Look at the advice that you and your partner wrote in the Opening Task on page 151. Did you use *should, ought to, should not?* Check to see if you used them correctly. If you didn't use them at all, rewrite your advice to include them.

Share your advice with the rest of the class. Do not tell your classmates which book you were thinking about when you wrote the advice and see if they can guess correctly.

FOCUS 2 Using *Need To* and Imperatives to Give Advice

EXAMPLES	EXPLANATIONS
(a) A: My tooth hurts. B: You **need to** see a dentist. (b) A: My tooth hurts. B: You **should/ought to** see a dentist.	*Need to* + base verb can also be used to give advice. It is stronger than *should* or *ought to*. *Need to* is not a modal verb.
(c) A: My tooth hurts. B: **Go** to a dentist. (d) A: I can't sleep. B: **Don't drink** so much coffee! (e) A: I can't sleep. B: You **shouldn't** drink so much coffee.	You can also use an imperative to give advice. An imperative is much stronger and much more direct than *need to*. If you do not know the person you are addressing very well, it is usually better to use *should/shouldn't* or *ought to*.

EXERCISE 2

Thompson Heinle ELT,
A Thompson Learning Company

We are proud to announce an exciting new book, *by* language learners *for* language learners:

HOW TO BE A BETTER LANGUAGE LEARNER

Language learners from all over the world give you advice about ways to learn a second, third, or fourth language. This book will change the way you learn languages . . .

THOMSON HEINLE

Australia · Canada · Mexico · Singapore · Spain · United Kingdom · United States

You have been asked to contribute to this exciting new "self-help" book. First, think about your own experience as a language learner. Then, in your notebook write down at least three important things that you think someone who wants to learn **your** language should or should not do. Get together with a partner and compare your lists. How many similarities and differences can you find in your advice? Share your advice with the rest of the class.

FOCUS 3 *Should* and *Ought To* versus *Must*

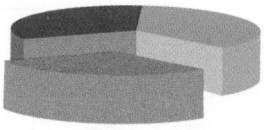

EXAMPLES	EXPLANATIONS
(a) **Alma:** I can't sleep at night. **Bea:** You **should** drink a glass of milk before you go to bed.	*Should* and *ought to* shows that something is a good idea. In (a), Bea is giving advice, but Alma is not obliged to follow that advice; she is free to do what she pleases.
(b) **Dora:** Do I need to get a special visa to visit Taiwan? **Wen:** Yes, you **must** go to the Taiwanese consulate here and get one before you leave. You **must not** try to enter the country without one.	*Must* is stronger. In (b), it is obligatory for Dora to follow Wen's advice. She is not free to do what she pleases. For more information about this use of *must,* see Unit 11.

EXERCISE 3

Oscar has just bought a used car. Complete the following, using *should, shouldn't, must,* or *must not* as appropriate. Different people may have different opinions about some of these, so be ready to justify your choices.

1. He ___should___ get insurance as soon as possible.
2. He _____ take it to a reliable mechanic and have it checked.
3. He _____ get it registered.
4. He _____ drive it without insurance.
5. He _____ drink and drive.
6. He _____ wear a seat belt.
7. He _____ lock the doors when he parks the car.
8. He _____ keep a spare key in a safe place.
9. He _____ let other people drive his car.
10. He _____ drive too fast.

FOCUS 4 *Should* and *Ought To* versus *Had Better*

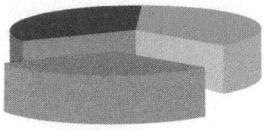

EXAMPLES	EXPLANATIONS
(a) You **should** go to all your classes every day. (b) You **had better** go to all your classes every day.	You can also use *had better* to give advice. *Had better* is much stronger than *should* and *ought to*, but not as strong as *must*. In (a), it is a good idea for you to do this. In (b), if you don't go, something bad will happen.
(c) You **should** see a doctor about that. (It's a good idea.) (d) You'd **better** see a doctor about that. (It's urgent.) (e) You **must** see a doctor about that. (It's obligatory.)	*Had better* often shows that you think something is urgent. *Had better* is often contracted to *'d better*.
(f) *Teacher to student:* If you want to pass this class, you **had better** finish all your assignments. (g) *Student to teacher:* If you come to my country, you **should** visit Kyoto. (h) NOT: You had better visit Kyoto.	*Had better* is often used in situations where the speaker has more power or authority (for example, boss to employee or teacher to student). In these situations, *had better* sounds like an order or a command. If you want to be sure that you sound polite, use *should* or *ought to*.
(i) You **had better** finish this tomorrow. (j) I **had better** leave now. (k) He **had better** pay me for this.	*Had better* refers to the present and the future. It does not refer to the past (even though it is formed with *had*).
(l) She'd **better not** tell anyone about this. (m) You'd **better not** be late.	Notice how the negative is formed.

EXERCISE 4

Angie is planning a trip to India and asks Sushila for some advice. Choose the most appropriate words from the box to complete the conversation. Use each word or phrase only once.

~~should~~	should not	ought to	must	'd better not	must not	'd better

Angie: I am planning a trip to India. Can you give me some advice?

Sushila: It's very hot there in the summer. You (1) ___should___ go there in January or February when the weather is cooler.

Angie: Do I need a visa?

Sushila: Yes, if you have a U.S. passport, you (2) _____ get a tourist visa. And you (3) _____ get some vaccinations before you go. It's easy to get sick when you're not used to the food and water. You (4) _____ take some insect repellant and some stomach medicine, too.

Angie: What about money?

Sushila: It's a good idea to change some money before you go and take your credit card, but you (5) _____ keep your credit card and passport together. If you lose both, you'll be in trouble!

Angie: What kind of clothes do I need?

Sushila: Take some light clothes for the day. But it can be cool at night, so you (6) _____ forget to take a sweater and jacket, too.

Angie: Are there any special customs I should know about?

Sushila: Yes, you (7) _____ wear shoes when you enter someone's home.

EXERCISE 5

Circle your choice in each of the following sentences.

1. You (should not/must not) smoke when you are in a movie theater in the United States.
2. While you are in Los Angeles, you (had better/should) try to visit Disneyland.
3. In the state of Michigan, people under the age of 21 (should not/must not) try to purchase alcohol.

4. You ('d better not/must not) talk on your cell phone while you are driving in New York City; it's against the law!
5. You ('d better not/must not) take your car into downtown New York, because you may not find a parking space.
6. Everybody who comes into the United States (must/should) show a valid passport or picture ID.
7. If you are interested in Egyptian art, you (should/had better) visit the Metropolitan Museum in New York. They have a fantastic collection.
8. It's difficult to find a hotel room in Boston. We (must/should) make a reservation before we go there.
9. You (had better/should) visit Washington DC in the spring because the cherry trees are very beautiful at that time of year.
10. You (must/should) have an appointment before you can visit the White House.

FOCUS 5 *Should* versus *Could* and *Might*

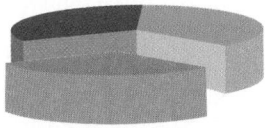

EXAMPLES	EXPLANATIONS
(a) A: I heard there's a new movie playing in town. B: Yeah, you **should** see that movie. It's great. (b) A: I don't know what to do on Friday night. B: You **could** see a movie.	You can also use *could* to give advice. *Could* is not as strong as *should* because it only expresses choices or possibilities. *Could* does not show that the speaker thinks that something is a good idea to do or that it is the right thing to do.
(c) If you want to improve your Spanish, you **could** take classes, you **might** listen to Spanish-speaking stations on the radio, you **could** find a conversation partner, or you **might** take a vacation in Mexico.	We often use *could* or *might* to express many different possibilities, without saying which one we think is best.

EXERCISE 6

Your friends always come to you when they have problems because you usually have lots of great ideas about what to do.

STEP 1 **For each problem, write down as many possible solutions as you can think of, using *could* and *might*.**

STEP 2 **Get together with two or three other students and compare your ideas. Decide who has the best solution to each problem and write it down, using *should*.**

Example: Your neighbors play loud rock music all night.

Possibilities: You could talk with them. You could play very loud opera in the morning when they are still asleep. You might move. You might buy earplugs. You could call the police.

In our opinion, the best solution: You should buy earplugs.

1. Your friend's husband snores. Possibilities: _____

   _____

   In our opinion, the best solution: _____

   _____

2. Your friend's father is planning to come and visit for a few days. Unfortunately, he is a heavy smoker and your friend's roommates are nonsmokers who do not permit smoking in the house. Possibilities: _____

   _____

   In our opinion, the best solution: _____

   _____

3. A classmate has just spilled coffee on her favorite white shirt. She doesn't know what to do. Possibilities: _____

   In our opinion, the best solution: _____

   _____

4. Your friend can't sleep at night. She feels exhausted every morning and doesn't have enough energy to do anything all day. Possibilities: _____

   _____

   In our opinion, the best solution: _____

   _____

5. One of your classmates wants to learn more about American culture and customs and would really like to make friends with some Americans. He doesn't know how to start. You have lots of ideas. Possibilities: _____

   _____

   In our opinion, the best solution: _____

   _____

6. Your partner never has enough money. At the end of the month, he is always broke. He comes to you for some ideas about what to do. Possibilities: _____

_____

In our opinion, the best solution: _____

_____

7. Two of your friends are taking a university class. The professor speaks very fast and they find it hard to follow the lectures. They are afraid that they are going to flunk the class. Possibilities: _____

_____

In our opinion, the best solution: _____

_____

8. Your friend's fiancée has two dogs. She has had these dogs since she was a child and is very attached to them. Unfortunately, your friend is allergic to dogs. He loves his fiancée very much, but the dogs are making him sick. He doesn't want to upset her. Possibilities: _____

_____

In our opinion, the best solution: _____

_____

EXERCISE 7

The following story is a well-known logic problem. Get together with some of your classmates and decide on the best solution.

A woman went shopping. First she bought a large piece of cheese. Next she walked to a pet store where she bought a white mouse for her nephew's birthday. Just as she was leaving the store, she saw an adorable black and white cat. She couldn't leave the store without it, so she bought the cat as well.

Unfortunately, her car is parked a long way from the pet store, and it's only possible for her to carry one thing at a time. What could she do in order to get everything to her car? How many solutions can you find?

She could _____

_____

_____

There are no parking areas near the pet store, so she cannot move her car, and there is nobody around to help her. Unfortunately, cats eat mice and mice eat cheese. This means that if she leaves the cat with the mouse, the cat will eat the mouse, and if she leaves the mouse with the cheese, the mouse will eat the cheese. What should she do? What is the best solution to her problem?

She could _____

_____

_____

You can find the solution to this problem on page A-16.

There are many different versions of this problem. Do you know one? Share it with the rest of the class.

FOCUS 6 *Should* and *Ought To* versus *Might, Could, Need To, Had Better,* and *Must*

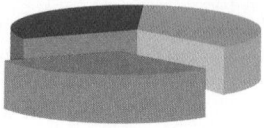

EXAMPLES	EXPLANATIONS
WEAK ↑ might could should/ought to need to had better ↓ must STRONG	All these verbs can be used to give advice. However, they express different degrees of strength.

EXERCISE 8

Read the following situation and follow the instructions given:

Jennifer is an American student. As she is planning to major in international business, she decided that it would be important for her to know how to speak Japanese. She managed to get some money from her father and left for Japan for six months.

She has now been in Tokyo for three months, taking classes in Japanese language and conversation. When she first arrived, she missed home a lot, so she quickly made friends with other Americans she met. Instead of living with a Japanese host family, she decided to move in with two other American women, and now she spends all her time with her new friends. She takes Japanese classes every day, but she seldom spends any time with the students who do not speak any English. As a result, she rarely speaks Japanese and has not made much progress in the language. She hasn't learned much about Japanese culture either.

Jennifer is having a great time in Tokyo with her American friends, but now she's in a terrible panic. Her father has just called to tell her that he will be coming to Tokyo on business, and he wants her to help him while he is there. He wants her to help interpret for him, as well as advise him on Japanese culture and customs. She is feeling very anxious about meeting her father. . . .

First, make a list of all the possible solutions to Jennifer's problem that you can think of in two minutes. Get together with another student and role-play a conversation with Jennifer. Then switch roles.

Example: You must try to meet some Japanese people.

FOCUS 7 Expressing Opinions with *Should*, *Ought To*, and *Should Not*

EXAMPLES	EXPLANATIONS
(a) Iryna believes that more people **should** drive electric cars. (b) In Mune's opinion, more students **ought to** continue their education after high school. (c) Most of my friends think that we **shouldn't** eat meat.	You can also use *should, ought to*, and *should not* to express your opinions about what you think is right or wrong.

EXERCISE 9

In your opinion, which of the following occupations should receive the highest salaries? Number the occupations in order of the highest to the lowest salaries (Number 1 is the highest salary).

_____ TV news announcer	_____ CEO of a large company
_____ firefighter	_____ bus driver
_____ professional football player	_____ politician
_____ social worker	_____ elementary school teacher
_____ attorney	_____ plastic surgeon
_____ plumber	_____ police officer
_____ emergency room doctor	_____ nurse
_____ model	

When you finish, compare your answers with a partner's. Be ready to share and justify your opinions with the rest of the class.

Use Your English

ACTIVITY 1 speaking/listening

STEP 1

Sometimes, for fun, people give each other advice on the best way to accomplish a negative goal—for example, the best way to lose your job or how to annoy your neighbors. Get together with another student and choose one of the following humorous topics. How many different ideas can you come up with?

- How to get a traffic ticket
- How to get rid of your boyfriend or girlfriend
- How to avoid learning English
- How to get an F in this class
- How to annoy your roommate

STEP 2

With your partner, make a poster presentation on the topic you chose. Display your poster and use it to explain your ideas to the rest of the class.

STEP 3

Record yourself as you make your poster presentation. Listen to your recording and write down all the sentences where you used *should, shouldn't, ought to, need to, must, had better, might,* or *could.* Did you use them appropriately?

ACTIVITY 2 speaking

Many American newspapers have advice columns. People write to these columns for help with their problems. Three famous ones are "Dear Abby," "Ann Landers," and "Miss Manners." Clip any advice columns you can find in various newspapers and bring them to class. Cut off the answers to the letters and circulate the letters without their replies. (But do not throw away the replies.) In groups, try to come up with helpful advice. Share your responses with the rest of the class. Compare your advice with the advice the professionals gave.

ACTIVITY 3 writing

In groups, write a letter to "Dear Abby," asking for advice on a particular problem. Exchange your problem letter with another group and write solutions to their problem. Share both problem and solution with the rest of the class.

ACTIVITY 4 writing

Write a short report, giving advice to someone who is planning to visit your hometown, your country, or the community where you grew up. Advise him or her on places to visit, clothes to wear, things to bring, things to do, and how to act.

Remember to start your report with an introductory statement.

Example: My hometown/country, (name), is very interesting, and if you follow my advice, I am sure that you will have an enjoyable and rewarding visit. . . .

When you finish writing, check and see if you have used *should, shouldn't, must, ought to, might, need to, could,* and *had better.* It is not necessary to use one in every sentence, as this would sound very unnatural!

ACTIVITY 5 speaking

Is honesty always the best policy? Should we **always** tell the truth? Think about the following situations. Share your opinions on each one with your classmates. How many people share your point of view? How many have different ideas?

1. You saw your best friend's girlfriend out on a date with someone else. Should you tell your friend what you saw? Why? Why not?
2. A classmate cheated on the last test. Should you tell your teacher? Why? Why not?
3. Your friend has a new haircut. She is really happy with her new "look," but you don't like it at all. In fact, you think it makes her look quite ugly. She asks for your opinion. Should you tell her what you really think? Why? Why not?
4. You catch your 8-year-old son telling a lie. Should you tell him that it is wrong to lie? Why? Why not?

ACTIVITY 6 speaking/writing

STEP 1

Read the following and circle *should* or *should not* to express the point of view that is closest to your own opinion on the topic.

1. School uniforms should/should not be obligatory.
2. Animals should/should not be used in laboratory experiments.
3. Doctors should/should not reveal the identity of an AIDS patient to the patient's employer or school.
4. Mothers should/should not work outside the home while their children are young.
5. A woman should/should not take her husband's family name when she marries.
6. Smoking should/should not be permitted in public places.

STEP 2

Choose the topic that interests you the most and then go around the room until you find one or two other students who share your opinion on that topic. Form a group with these students and brainstorm all the reasons and examples you can think of to support your point of view and then write them down. Choose the strongest ones, with the best examples, and use them to make a short report (oral or written) presenting your opinion. Share your report with the rest of the class and be ready to justify your position as necessary.

STEP 3

If you make a written report, read your report carefully and underline every example you can find of the modal auxiliaries from this unit.

If you choose an oral report, record your report. Listen to your recording and write down every sentence where you use one of the modal auxiliaries from this unit.

ACTIVITY 7 listening

CD Track 15

In this activity, you will hear an interview on the topic of smoking. Listen to the person's opinion. Does she think smoking should be banned in public places? What other ideas does she express? Check (✓) the statements you think the speaker agrees with.

_____ Smoking should be banned in public places.

_____ People should not be able to buy cigarettes in drugstores and supermarkets.

_____ Parents should not smoke at home in front of children.

_____ Teachers need to teach students about the dangers of smoking.

Listen to the audio again. Write down any sentences that contain examples of the verb forms in this unit.

ACTIVITY 8 speaking/listening

Many people have strong opinions about smoking. Ask five different people questions like these: "What's your opinion about smoking in public places?" "Do you think it's a good or bad idea to ban smoking in public places?"

Record their answers. Listen to your recording and be ready to share the information that you collect with the other people in your class. What do most of the people you interviewed think about this topic?

Listen to your recordings again. What are some of the words and the ways people used to express their opinions? Write down any sentences that contain examples of the verbs from this unit.

ACTIVITY 9 research on the web

InfoTrac® College Edition: Go to *InfoTrac* and search articles for advice on how to stop smoking. Type keywords "how to stop smoking." Take notes of the main points. What do you think should be done to stop people from smoking? Discuss this issue with your class.

ACTIVITY 10 reflection

What problems do you have studying English? Write down three problems. Tell your partner and ask for some advice.

UNIT 11

MODALS OF NECESSITY AND PROHIBITION

Have To/Have Got To, Do Not Have To, Must/Must Not, Cannot

UNIT GOALS

- Use *must*, *have to*, and *have got to* to show something is necessary
- Use *must not* and *cannot* to show something is prohibited
- Choose between *have to* and *have got to*
- Use *do not have to* to show something is not necessary
- Use *have to* for *must* in the past

OPENING TASK

Customs and Immigration

STEP 1

Every country has rules about what you can bring with you when you enter the country. What is one rule you must follow to enter the United States? What is one rule you must follow to enter the country you are from?

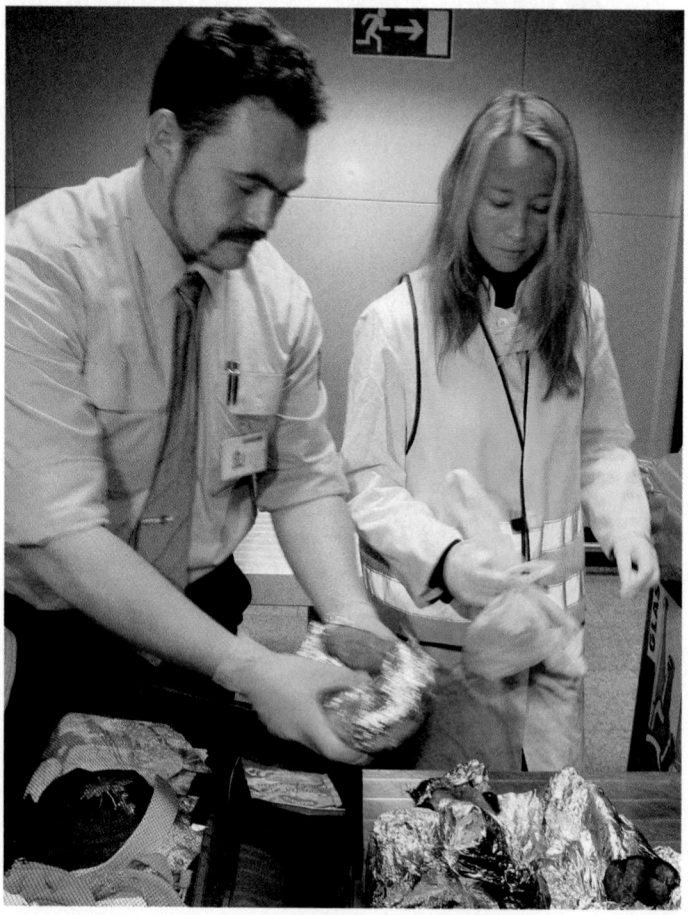

STEP 2

A friend of yours in Taiwan is planning a short vacation to California. He doesn't have much room to pack a lot of things because he's planning to travel with just a backpack. Here are some of the things he is thinking of taking with him:

a passport	a map of the United States	an umbrella
a surfboard	fireworks	a business suit
fresh fruit	a laptop computer	hiking boots
an international driver's license	a credit card	a cell phone
traveler's checks	a tourist visa	Chinese pop music CDs
books about China	California guide books	
a return airline ticket	photographs of his hometown	

STEP 3

Use the box below to help your friend organize the things he wants to take to the United States. Work with a partner and put them in the category where you think they belong.

1. It's necessary and obligatory: You can't enter the United States without this: You must take this with you.	3. It's a good idea to bring this: You should take this with you.
2. It's prohibited by law: You must not take this into the United States.	4. It's O.K. to bring this, but it isn't really necessary: You don't have to take this.

STEP 4

With your partner, write sentences about one or two items in each category, explaining why you think they belong there.

FOCUS 1 Modals of Necessity, Prohibition, and Permission

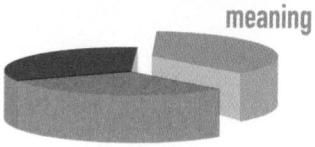

EXAMPLES	EXPLANATIONS
(a) You **must** have a passport. OR (b) You **have to** have a passport. OR (c) You **have got to** have a passport.	Use *must, have to,* or *have got to* to show something is necessary and obligatory (something that is strongly required, often by law).
(d) You **must not (mustn't)** bring fresh fruit into the United States. OR (e) You **cannot (can't)** bring fresh fruit into the United States.	Use *must not (mustn't)* or *cannot (can't)* to show something is prohibited and absolutely not permitted (often by law).
(f) When I traveled to Iceland last year, **I couldn't** take any meat products.	In the past, use *couldn't.*
(g) If you go to live in Japan next year, you **won't be able to** take any pets with you.	In the future, use *will not (won't)* be able to.
(h) You **can** bring a surfboard.	Use *can* to show that something is permitted.
(i) About ten years ago, you **could** smoke on an airplane.	In the past, use *could.*
(j) In the future, you **will be able to** go to bed on an airplane.	In the future, use *will be able to.*
(k) You **should** bring a credit card.	Use *should* to show something is a good idea. For more information about this use of *should* see Unit 10.
(l) You **don't have to** bring a surfboard.	Use *do not (don't) have to* to show something is permitted, but not necessary. You can do this if you want to, but you are not required to.

EXERCISE 1

Look back at the sentences you wrote in Step 4 of the Opening Task. Did you use *must, have to, have got to, should, can, can't, mustn't,* and *don't have to?* If you did, check to see that you used them correctly. If you didn't use them, rewrite the sentences.

Example: *He must have a valid passport—it is required by law.*

In the rest of this unit, you will have the opportunity to practice all of these in more detail.

FOCUS 2 Modals and Phrasal Modals: *Must*, *Have To*, and *Have Got To*

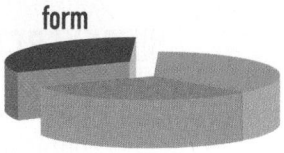

EXAMPLES	EXPLANATIONS
(a) International students **must** get visas before they enter the United States. (b) My Taiwanese friend **must** get a tourist visa before he goes to the United States on vacation.	*Must* is a modal and does not change to agree with the subject.
(c) International students **have to** get visas before they enter the United States. (d) My Taiwanese friend **has to** get a tourist visa before he goes on vacation in the United States.	*Have to* is a phrasal modal. It changes to agree with the subject. *Have to* and *has to* are usually pronounced "hafta" and "hasta" in fast speech and informal conversation.
(e) International students **have got to** get visas before they enter the United States. (f) My Taiwanese friend **has got to** get a tourist visa before he goes to the United States on vacation.	*Have got to* is a phrasal modal. It changes to agree with the subject. *Have got to* and *has got to* are usually pronounced " 've gotta" and " 's gotta" in fast speech and informal conversation.
(g) **Do** we **have to** go? Does she **have to** go too?	Notice how questions with *must, have to,* and *have got to* are formed. Use *do/does* with *have to.*
(h) **Have** we **got to** go? **Has** she **got to** go too?	Use *has/have* with *have got to.* Do not use *do/does.*
(i) **Must** we go? **Must** she go too?	Do not use *do/does* with *must.* However, *must* is rarely used in questions in American English.

EXERCISE 2

Many road signs are used internationally, but some used in the United States are confusing for tourists from other countries. What do you think the following road signs mean? Complete the sentences, using *have to* and *have got to* in your answers.

1. 

   In the United States, drivers _____ when they see this sign.

2. 

   Also, when they see this one, they _____

   _____

3. 

   This sign tells you that you _____

   _____

4. 

   A driver who sees this sign _____

   _____

5. 

   Be careful when you see this one. It means that you _____

   _____

6. 

   Q: What happens when there are two or three cars waiting at this sign?

   A: The car that arrives last _____

   _____

How many of these road signs on page 170 are also found in your country? Are there are any road signs from your country that are not found in North America? Draw the signs and write sentences showing what you have to do when you see them.

EXERCISE 3

Work with a partner and decide which of the following are necessary and obligatory to do if you want to get a driver's license in the United States.

speak English very well
take driving lessons
practice before the test
take an eye test
take a written test
have a medical examination
have a passport or birth certificate as ID
pass a driving test
have a high school diploma
own a car
study the information booklet from the DMV (Department of Motor Vehicles, the department that issues driver's licenses)
have an international driver's license

EXERCISE 4

Role-play this situation with your partner. Your friend will ask you questions about how to get a driver's license. Answer the questions and explain what is necessary to get a driver's license in the United States; then explain what is necessary to get a driver's license in the country you are from. Then switch roles.

Example: A: *Do I have to take a written test?*
B: *Yes, you have to take a written test and a driving test.*

FOCUS 3 *Have To* versus *Have Got To*

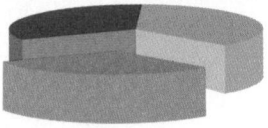

use

EXAMPLES	EXPLANATIONS
(a) Joe **has to** go on a diet. (b) Joe **has got to** follow a very strict diet because he has a serious heart condition. (If he doesn't follow the diet, he will die.) (c) You **have to** pay your phone bill once a month. (d) You **have got to** pay your phone bill immediately. (If you don't, the phone company will disconnect the phone.)	Both *have to* and *have got to* show that something is necessary and obligatory. However, many people use *have got to* when they want to emphasize that something is **very** important and **very** necessary.
(e) Hey Steve, you'**ve got to (gotta)** see this movie. It's really great.	In very informal conversation among friends, some people use *have got to* to show they think something is a really good thing to do. In (e), Steve's friend is not saying that Steve is obliged to see the movie; she is just strongly advising Steve to see it.

EXERCISE 5

Make a statement for each situation. Work with a partner and decide which you would use for each one: *have to* or *have got to*.

1. Your sister's 4-year-old son takes a nap every day and goes to bed at 8:00 every night. But today he didn't take a nap, and it's now 10:00 P.M.

   She says to her son, "You _____ go to sleep now."

2. The last time your friend went to the dentist was four years ago. He doesn't think he has any problems with his teeth, but he feels he should probably go to the dentist for a checkup.

   He says, "I _____ make an appointment to see the dentist sometime soon."

3. You haven't been reading the assignments for your history class, and you did very badly on the first two quizzes. You are afraid that you'll fail the course.

   You tell your classmate, "I _____ study every day if I don't want to fail my history class."

4. Your roommate is making dinner. She has just put a loaf of bread in the oven. Suddenly she realizes that she doesn't have an important item that she needs for dessert.

   She says, "I _____ go to the store. If I'm not back in ten minutes, can you take the bread out of the oven? It _____ come out at 7:00 or it'll be ruined."

5. You are at a friend's house. You are feeling a little tired and want to go to sleep early.

   You say, "I _____ leave now. I'll see you after class tomorrow."

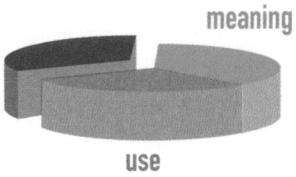

FOCUS 4 Using *Cannot* (*Can't*) and *Must Not* (*Mustn't*) to Show Something Is Prohibited or Not Permitted

EXAMPLES	EXPLANATIONS
(a) You **cannot (can't)** bring fresh fruit into the United States. OR (b) You **must not (mustn't)** bring fresh fruit into the United States. (c) You **cannot (can't)** smoke in here. OR (d) You **must not (mustn't)** smoke in here.	Use *cannot* and *must not* to show that something is completely prohibited or not permitted (often by law). *Cannot* is more common than *must not* in American English. *Cannot* and *must not* are usually contracted to *can't* and *mustn't* in fast speech.
(e) Herbert, you **must not (mustn't)** eat any more of those cookies!	*Must not/mustn't* is also often used as a strong command in situations where you want someone to obey. In (e), eating cookies is not prohibited by law, but the speaker **really** wants Herbert to stop eating them.

EXERCISE 6

Look at the cartoon. Write statements in your notebook that use *cannot* and *must not* to describe each prohibited activity.

EXERCISE 7

Where would you see each of the signs below? Match the signs with the places. Say what you *can, must, cannot,* or *must not* do there. (Some signs may be found in more than one place.)

airport

supermarket

museum

restaurant

movie theater

school

1.

_____

2.

_____

3.

_____

4.

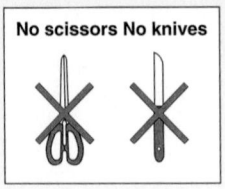

_____

5.

_____

6.

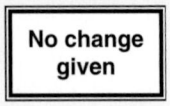

_____

FOCUS 5 *Must* and *Have To* versus *Must Not, Cannot,* and *Do Not Have To*

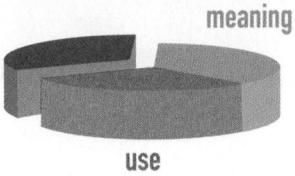

EXAMPLES	EXPLANATIONS
(a) To enter the United States you **must** have a valid passport. OR (b) To enter the United States you **have to** have a valid passport.	Showing something is necessary and obligatory: Use either *must* or *have to.* In this situation, they have the same meaning.
(c) You **cannot** bring fireworks into the United States. OR (d) You **must not** bring fireworks into the United States. (e) NOT: You don't have to bring fireworks into the United States.	Showing something is prohibited: Use *cannot* or *must not.* Do not use *do not have to.* In negative sentences, they do not have the same meaning. In this situation, *must not* means it is prohibited.
(f) You **don't have to** bring a surfboard to California because you can rent one there. (g) NOT: You must not bring a surfboard to California because you can rent one there. (h) There aren't any classes on Saturdays, so we **don't have to** come to school.	Showing something is not necessary: Use *do not have to.* Do not use *cannot* or *must not.* In this situation, *do not have to* means you can do something if you want to, but you are not obliged to do it if you don't want to.

EXERCISE 8

Look back at the places and signs in Exercise 7. Can you use *don't have to* to describe any of these signs?

EXERCISE 9

With your partner, make a list of rules for your classroom, using *must, must not, cannot,* and *don't have to.* Take a vote to see which ones your classmates want to put on your classroom walls. Draw signs to go with your rules.

Example: *You cannot smoke in this room.*

EXERCISE 10

The magazine article below is about traffic laws in different European countries.

STEP 1 **Before you read the article, look at the following statements. Do you think they are probably true or probably false? Circle T (for *true*), or F (for *false*). After you finish reading, look at the statements again and change your answers if necessary.**

1. In Germany, you mustn't use bad language or make rude and insulting gestures if you get angry with other drivers. T F
2. You must be careful when you honk your horn in Greece. T F
3. You have to honk your horn when you pass another car in Gibraltar. T F
4. You cannot flash your lights at other drivers in Luxembourg. T F
5. In Scandinavian countries, you cannot drive with your headlights on during the day. T F
6. You have to drive more slowly at night in Austria. T F
7. In Romania, you don't have to keep your car clean. T F

How not to collide with local road laws

If you are planning on driving in Europe, you should know that driving laws and customs vary greatly from country to country.

Be careful not to allow frustration with other drivers to develop into swearing or offensive gestures in Germany: They are illegal. Displays of anger are not welcome in Greece, either.

It is unlawful to honk your horn too loudly (although this may surprise many visitors to Athens!). In Gibraltar, using your horn at all is completely prohibited. In Luxembourg, the law says that drivers have to flash their lights each time they pass another car.

In Scandinavian countries, you have to drive with your headlights dimmed during the day, but in Poland, this is obligatory only in winter.

Make sure you fill your tank before you get on the Autobahn in Germany: It is illegal to run out of gas. Speed limits vary too, not just from country to country, but within countries as well. Beware of speed limits that change from one moment to the next. For example, in Austria, speed limits are lower at night and in France, the speed limit on the freeways drops from 130 kmh* to 110 kmh when it rains. (And if the French police catch you speeding, you have to pay a massive on-the-spot fine!)

But perhaps the strangest law of all is from Romania, where you must not drive your car if it is dirty.

Adapted with permission from *The European* (Magazine Section), 6/9/95
*kmh = kilometers per hour

STEP 2 **Make statements using *must, have to, cannot, mustn't,* or *do not have to* about the following topics from the article.**

1. Driving in Poland during the winter: _____

   _____

2. Driving on the Autobahn in Germany: _____

   _____

3. Driving on the freeways in France: _____

   _____

STEP 3 **Are there any traffic laws that are sometimes confusing to visitors to the country you come from? Describe them to the rest of your class, using *must, have to, cannot, must not,* and *do not have to* where you can.**

FOCUS 6 Talking about the Present, Past, and Future with *Have To* and *Must*

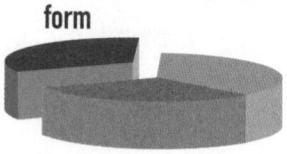

PRESENT	PAST	FUTURE
must	—	must
have to	had to	have to/will have to
do not have to	did not have to	do not have to/will not have to

EXAMPLES	EXPLANATIONS
(a) Students **have to** start school at 8:00 A.M. (b) Students **must** start school at 8:00 A.M. (c) Students **don't have to** go to school on Saturdays.	Use *must (not), have to,* and *do not have to* to show that something is (or is not) necessary in the present.
(d) We **had to** stay late after school yesterday. (e) We **didn't have to** take the test last week.	Notice that there is no past tense form of *must* when it shows necessity. Use *had to* to show that something was necessary in the past.
(f) Ron **must** go to a meeting tomorrow. OR (g) Ron **has to** go to a meeting tomorrow. OR (h) Ron **will have to** go to a meeting tomorrow.	You can use *must, have to,* or *will have to* to talk about events that will be necessary in the near future.
(i) He **doesn't have to** go to school next week. (j) He **will not (won't) have to** go to school next week.	You can also use negative forms *do not have to* or *will not have to* to talk about the near future.

EXERCISE 11

Maggie and her friend Jan are talking about jobs. Maggie is describing a job she had last summer. Complete their conversation with *have to,* and *do not have to* in the present, past, or future.

Maggie: The worst job I ever had was last summer, when I worked as a waitress in that tourist restaurant down by the aquarium.

Jan: Oh really? What was so terrible about it?

Maggie: For a start, I (1) _____ get up at 5:00 A.M. and, as I didn't have a car then, I (2) _____ walk.

Jan: Why didn't you take the bus?

Maggie: It doesn't start running until 7:00, and I (3) _____ be at the restaurant by 6:30 to set the tables for breakfast.

Jan: That's tough. Did they make you wear a silly uniform or anything?

Maggie: No, thank goodness. We (4) _____ wear any special uniforms, except for hats. We all (5) _____ wear really stupid sailor caps. Mine was too small and it kept falling off.

Jan: So you're probably not planning on working there again next summer.

Maggie: Absolutely not. I'm earning twice as much at my present job, so with a bit of luck, I'll be able to save some money and I (6) _____ work at all next summer.

Jan: That sounds good. What's your present job like?

Maggie: It's much better. I start work at 11:00 A.M.

Jan: So you (7) _____ get up early. What about weekends?

Maggie: I (8) _____ work on weekends, but if I want to make some extra money, I can go in on Saturdays. It's ideal.

Jan: Maybe I should try to get a job there. Our landlord raised the rent last month and I just can't afford to stay there on my present salary.

EXERCISE 12

Read the letter and choose the correct answer for each blank from the list below.

Dear Kimberley,

It's almost the end of the school year and we are in the middle of final exams. We (1) _____ take a lot of different tests and write essays. Luckily, my grades in English language are quite good, so I (2) _____ take any extra tests. Last year I (3) _____ go to summer school for two months because my grades were so bad, but I hope I (4) _____ go this year. My parents say I (5) _____ come to stay with you this summer unless I pass all my classes.

It's getting late now and I (6) _____ finish writing this letter. I have a history exam tomorrow morning and I (7) _____ go over all my notes tonight. In middle school, we (8) _____ take our notes into the exam, but here we (9) _____. I want to get a good average, so I (10) _____ fail this exam. I'm looking forward to seeing you again this summer. You (11) _____ write and tell me when I can come to visit you. There's a new Johnny Depp movie coming out in July and we (12) _____ go and see it together!

Love from,

Charlene

1. ○ (a) have got to ○ (b) must not ○ (c) have to
2. ○ (a) must not ○ (b) couldn't ○ (c) don't have to
3. ○ (a) had to ○ (b) should ○ (c) must
4. ○ (a) can't ○ (b) won't have to ○ (c) must not
5. ○ (a) must not ○ (b) can't ○ (c) don't have to
6. ○ (a) can ○ (b) have to ○ (c) had to
7. ○ (a) have got to ○ (b) had to ○ (c) could
8. ○ (a) can ○ (b) should ○ (c) could
9. ○ (a) couldn't ○ (b) don't have to ○ (c) can't
10. ○ (a) must not ○ (b) don't have to ○ (c) couldn't
11. ○ (a) had to ○ (b) don't have to ○ (c) must
12. ○ (a) can't ○ (b) had to ○ (c) have got to

Use Your English

ACTIVITY 1 speaking

In Exercises 2, 6, and 7 you saw some examples of signs. The local tourist board has asked you and your classmates to create some signs for tourists visiting the area. Get together with two or three other students and draw at least three signs. For example: *You must not feed the ducks. You must have exact change for the bus. You must not drink this water*. Draw each sign on a different piece of paper. Do not write anything next to the sign—your classmates must guess what it is. Look at their signs and write down what you think they mean.

ACTIVITY 2 speaking

In this activity, you will be comparing your childhood memories with those of your classmates. Think back to when you were a child. Write down five things you had to do then that you do not have to do now. Example for Childhood: I had to go to bed early. Then write down five things you did not have to do then that you have to do now. Example for Now: I can stay up late.

Next, compare your list with those of two or three other classmates and be ready to report on your findings to the rest of the class.

YOU		YOUR CLASSMATES	
Childhood	Now	Childhood	Now
1	1	1	1
2	2	2	2
3	3	3	3
4	4	4	4
5	5	5	5

ACTIVITY 3 writing

A friend of yours is interested in studying at a North American university. Write him or her a letter explaining what he or she will have to do in order to enter a university.

ACTIVITY 4 speaking/listening

CD Tracks 16,17,18

STEP 1

Do you know what a person has to do in order to get any of the following?

- a green card (for permanent residence in the United States)
- a Social Security number
- a marriage license
- a credit card
- United States citizenship

With a partner, make a list of what you think a person must or has to do in order to get each of these.

STEP 2

Listen to the audio. You will hear somebody discussing three of the above topics. Which topics are the speakers talking about? What do they think you have to do to get these things? Make notes in the chart below or in your notebook.

TOPIC	WHAT YOU HAVE TO DO
1	
2	
3	

STEP 3

Now look at the list you and your partner made on the same topic. How many differences and how many similarities can you find?

STEP 4

Listen to the audio again. Write down any sentences containing examples of modals and phrasal modals expressing necessity and prohibition. Refer to Focus 1 and Focus 2 for review of these modals.

ACTIVITY 5 speaking/listening

STEP 1 Choose a topic from Activity 4 that you don't know anything about.

STEP 2 Interview three different people and ask them what they know about the topic. For example, you can ask: *What does somebody have to do if they want to get a green card?*

Record your interviews. Listen to your recording and take notes. Did all the people you interviewed tell you the same information? Or did they tell you different things? Share your findings with the rest of your class.

STEP 3 Listen to your recording again and write down any sentences containing *must, have to, must not, cannot, do not have to, have got to,* or *should.*

ACTIVITY 6 research on the web

On the Web: Use an Internet search engine such as Google® or Yahoo® to get more information about one of the topics in Activity 4. Take notes on what you read. Summarize your findings and tell the class. Be sure to make a note of which Web sites you used.

ACTIVITY 7 reflection

Make a list of helpful guidelines for a new student who is going to start studying English. Divide your list into things that are necessary things that are not necessary. Compare lists with a partner. What things did you need to do in the past that you do not need to do now?

UNIT 12

EXPRESSING LIKES AND DISLIKES

UNIT GOALS

- Express similarity with *too/either* and *so/neither*
- Express similarity with *so* clauses
- Use short phrases to show agreement and weak agreement
- Express likes and dislikes with gerunds and infinitives

OPENING TASK

What Kind of Food Do You Like?

STEP 1

Work in a group. Name the different foods in the pictures. Which ones do you like most? Which ones do you dislike?

STEP 2

Work with a partner. One of you is A, the other is B. Talk about food that you like and don't like, and complete the chart on the next page together.

STEP 3

In the top left-hand box, write three kinds of food that A and B both like. In the top right-hand box, write three kinds of foods that A does not like, but B does. In the bottom left-hand box, write three kinds of food B doesn't like, but A does. In the last box, write three kinds of food that both A and B do not like.

STUDENT B	STUDENT A	
	LIKES	DOESN'T LIKE
LIKES	(A likes, and B does, too.)	(A doesn't like, but B does.)
DOESN'T LIKE	(B doesn't like, but A does.)	(B doesn't like, and A doesn't either.)

STEP 4

Share some of these findings with the class. Make a list of statements with *like* and *dislike* (or *doesn't/don't like*).

Example: *I like spicy food and Tina does too.*

FOCUS 1 Expressing Similarity with *Too* and *Either*

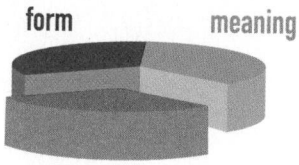

EXAMPLES	EXPLANATIONS
(a) I like fruit, **and** Roberta **does too.** (b) NOT: I like fruit, and Roberta likes fruit.	To avoid repetition in affirmative sentences (sentences without *not*), use *and* (X) *do/does too.*
(c) Roberta doesn't eat meat, and I **don't either.** (d) NOT: I don't eat meat, and Roberta doesn't eat meat.	To avoid repetition in negative sentences (sentences with *not*), use *and* (X) *do/doesn't either.*

EXERCISE 1

Check the statements you made in Step 4 of the Opening Task on page 185. Did you use *too* and *either* correctly? If not, rewrite these statements using *too* and *either.*

FOCUS 2 Expressing Similarity with *So* and *Neither*

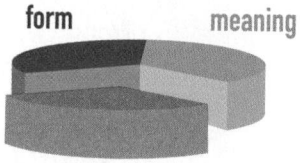

EXAMPLES	EXPLANATIONS
(a) I like fruit, **and so does** Roberta. (b) Roberta doesn't eat meat, **and neither do I.**	Another way to avoid repetition is with *and so do/does* (X) in affirmative sentences, and with *and neither do/does* (X) in negative sentences. Invert subject and verb after *so* and *neither.*

EXERCISE 2

Now work with a different partner and share the information on your charts in the Opening Task. Use this information to complete the following report. Make sure that your statements are not only grammatical but also true.

My classmates and I have strong opinions about the kinds of food we like and dislike. For example, _____ and so _____.

_____ and neither _____.

_____ too.

_____ either.

We also found other similarities in our taste in food. _____ either. _____

neither _____.

_____ so _____. _____ too.

FOCUS 3 Expressing Similarity with *So*

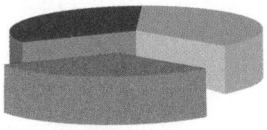

use

EXAMPLES	EXPLANATIONS
(a) I speak French, and so **does** my mother. (b) My mother exercises every day, and so **do** I.	Use *do* when you do not want to repeat the verb. Make sure that there is subject/verb agreement: I *do he/she does they/you do*
(c) I **can** speak French, and so **can** she. (d) I **have** studied it, and so **has** she. (e) I **am** happy, and so **is** she.	Use an auxiliary verb (*can, have, should*) if the first verb uses one. Use a form of *be* if the first verb is a form of *be.*

EXERCISE 3

Read Lucille's story about her friend Barbara. Match the first half of the sentences in column A with the second half in column B. Draw an arrow to show the connection. The first one has been done for you.

1. Barbara is 18 years old
2. Barbara went to Clarke High School
3. I didn't study very hard
4. She likes to travel
5. I can't drive
6. Barbara's job isn't interesting
7. She'll quit her job soon
8. Barbara's parents want to go to California
9. They don't have much money
10. Barbara has never been to California
11. Barbara has studied Spanish
12. We're excited about going to California

a. and neither do we.
b. and so have I.
c. and so will I.
d. and so am I.
e. and neither have I.
f. and so do my parents.
g. and I did too.
h. and Barbara didn't either.
i. and Barbara can't either.
j. and I do too.
k. and they are too.
l. and neither is mine.

FOCUS 4 Showing Agreement with Short Phrases

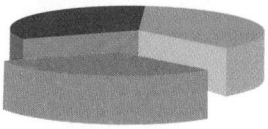

EXAMPLES	EXPLANATIONS
(a) **Tina:** I love going to movies. **Rob:** So do I.	Short phrases such as *so do I, neither do I, I can't either,* and *I do too* are used to show agreement with somebody else's opinions and ideas. They are very common in informal conversation.
(b) **Tina:** I never go to violent movies. **Rob:** **Neither do I.**	
(c) **Tina:** I can't stand watching violence. **Rob:** **I can't either.**	
(d) **Tina:** I prefer comedies. **Rob:** Really? **I do too.**	

EXERCISE 4

Read the comic strip. Can you find the missing parts of the conversation in the list below? Write the letters in the appropriate cartoon bubble.

A I don't either!

B I do too!

C Neither can I!

D So did I!

E Neither will I!

F So is mine!

G I will too!

H So am I!

I I can't either!

FOCUS 5 Short Phrases or Hedges and Emphatic *Do*

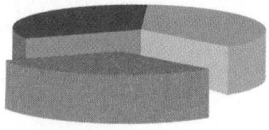

EXAMPLES	EXPLANATIONS
(a) **Sue:** I love ballet. What about you? **Tien:** Kind of. (b) **Sue:** Do you like opera? **Tien:** Sort of.	If you do not agree strongly with the speaker's opinions, you can use hedges (*sort of, kind of*) in informal conversation. In fast speech, *sort of* sounds like "sorta" and *kind of* sounds like "kinda."
(c) **Tien:** You really **are** a good swimmer. (d) **Sue:** Thanks! I **do** love swimming. (e) **Tien:** You know, I **really do** enjoy our conversations, Sue.	You can add emphasis to a sentence by stressing the auxiliary or the *be* verb. In sentences where there is no auxiliary or *be* verb, you can add *do* and stress it for emphasis. You can add extra emphasis by adding *really* or *certainly* before the auxiliary verb.

EXERCISE 5

Claire and Chris have just met at a party and are finding out how much they have in common. Look at the chart showing their likes and dislikes.

✓ ✓ ✓ = really a lot ✓ ✓ = a lot ✓ = a little

Use the information from the chart to complete the conversation. Use agreement phrases with *so* or *neither*, hedges, or emphatic structures with *really* or *certainly* where appropriate. The first one has been done for you.

	LIKES		DISLIKES
Chris	swimming ✓✓✓ cats ✓✓ cooking ✓✓	hiking ✓✓ music ✓ Chinese food ✓✓	TV ✓✓ getting up in the morning ✓✓✓ country music ✓✓
Claire	cats ✓ eating in restaurants ✓✓ Chinese food ✓✓✓	cooking ✓ music ✓✓ swimming ✓✓ hiking ✓	country music ✓✓✓ getting out of bed ✓✓ staying home ✓✓ watching TV ✓✓

Chris: Well, let me see . . . what are some of my favorite things? The ocean . . . I (1) ___really do___ love swimming in the ocean.

Claire: (2) _____. Maybe we should go for a swim sometime.

Chris: Yes, that'd be great! Do you like hiking too?

Claire: (3) _____. In general, I prefer to be active. I mean I don't like sitting at home and watching TV.

Chris: (4) _____. But I (5) _____ like getting up in the morning.

Claire: Well, (6) _____. Most people don't like getting out of bed in the morning! What about music? Do you like music?

Chris: (7) _____. I don't know too much about it, actually.

Claire: Really? I love all kinds of music, except for country. I hate country!

Chris: (8) _____. We (9) _____ do agree on that one! What else? I love cooking, don't you?

Claire: (10) _____. I really prefer eating out in restaurants, especially in Chinatown. I (11) _____ love Chinese food.

Chris: (12) _____. I've heard that the new Chinese restaurant on Grant Avenue is supposed to be really good.

Claire: (13) _____. Why don't we give it a try?

Chris: That sounds good. By the way, I have six cats. Do you like cats?

Claire: Well, (14) _____.

Chris: That's O.K.—as long as you don't *hate* them. . . .

EXERCISE 6

One way to meet people is through personal ads in newspapers or magazines. These personal ads appeared in a local newspaper. Read them quickly and then read the statements that follow. Circle T (true) if you think the statement is true and F (false) if you think it is false.

(A) COULD THIS BE YOU?
You are attractive, slim, and athletic. You like dancing, eating candlelit dinners, and walking on the beach by moonlight. Like me, you also enjoy camping and hiking. You love dogs and you don't smoke. If you are the woman of my dreams, send a photo to Box 3092.

(B) BEAUTY & BRAINS
Warm, humorous, well-educated SF loves walking on the beach, dancing, cycling, and hiking. Seeks intelligent life partner with computer interests. P.S.—I'm allergic to cats, dogs, and smoking. Box 875.

(C) I'VE GOT YOU ON MY WAVELENGTH
Athletic, professional, DF, animal lover seeks active man who knows how to treat a lady. Box 4021.

(D) A FEW OF MY FAVORITE THINGS:
Cooking for my friends, cycling, walking on the beach with my dog, wise and witty women. I can't stand: snobs, cheap wine, jogging, people who smoke, women who wear makeup. DM looking for a special woman. Box 49.

1. A likes walking on the beach, and so do D and B. T F
2. B does not like smokers, and neither do A and C. T F
3. Cooking for friends is one of B's favorite pastimes. T F
4. D does not like women who wear a lot of makeup. T F
5. D likes dancing, and A does too. T F
6. A wants to find someone who likes hiking, and so does D. T F
7. Jogging and cycling are two of B's favorite sports. T F

Do you think any of these people would make a good couple? If so, why? If not, why not?

FOCUS 6 Likes and Dislikes with Gerunds and Infinitives

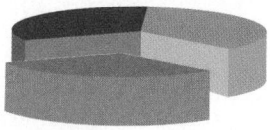

EXAMPLES	EXPLANATIONS
(a) **Cooking** is my favorite hobby. (b) I love **cooking.** Do you? (c) My favorite hobby is **cooking.**	*Gerunds* (nouns formed from verb + *-ing*) can be used as: the subject of a sentence the object of a sentence the complement of a sentence (something needed to complete the sentence)
(d) I like **to cook.** (e) I don't like **to swim.** (f) I hate **to go** to the dentist. (g) AWKWARD: **To cook** is my favorite hobby.	*Infinitives* (*to* + verb) are also used in talking about likes and dislikes. In this context, infinitives are usually used as objects of sentences or as complements, but they sound awkward as subjects.
(h) I don't like **swimming.** (i) I hate **going** to the dentist	When talking about likes and dislikes, you can usually use infinitives or gerunds. The verbs *hate, like,* and *love* can be followed by either a gerund or an infinitive.

EXERCISE 7

Look back at numbered list in Exercise 6.

1. Underline all the gerunds.
2. Check (✓) all the gerunds that are subjects and circle the gerunds that are objects or complements.
3. Replace the gerunds with infinitives where possible.
4. Rewrite sentences 2 and 4, using a gerund or an infinitive.

Sentence 2:

_____

_____

Sentence 4:

_____

_____

Use Your English

ACTIVITY 1 speaking

The purpose of this activity is to share information with one other person and then to report what you find to the rest of the class. While sharing information with your partner, try to find out **how many things you have in common.** Some ideas for starting your conversation are given below. When you have nothing more to say on this topic, decide on another one and find out what you have in common on that topic. Use the chart for your notes.

TOPIC	NOTES
family	Examples: any brothers and sisters?/grandparents alive?/father older than mother?

ACTIVITY 2 speaking

Form teams. Your job as a team is to find as many similarities as possible among the pairs of things listed below. The team that finds the most similarities is the winner.

1. an apple and an orange
2. tennis and golf
3. hiking and jogging
4. learning a foreign language and learning to ride a bike

ACTIVITY 3 speaking

Form pairs or groups of three.

STEP 1 Think of fifteen to twenty statements using *so/too/either/neither.* Make sure they are meaningful. Write each statement on two cards, like this:

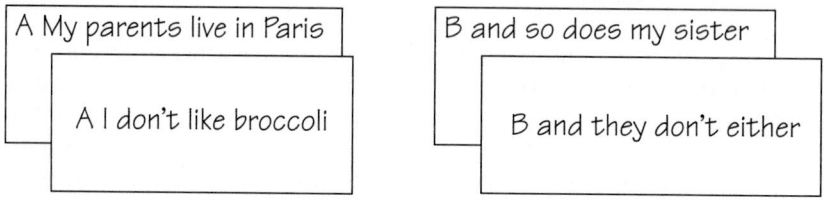

Therefore, if you have twenty statements, you will have forty cards.

STEP 2 Get together with another pair or threesome. Place all the A cards in one pile and all the B cards in another pile. Shuffle each deck of cards carefully.

STEP 3 Put the A pile facedown on the table. Then distribute the B cards among the players. Do not look at the cards; place them facedown on the table in front of you.

STEP 4 The first player turns the first card from the A pile on the table and puts the first card from his or her B pile beside it. The player must not look at his or her card before putting it down on the table. The object of the game is to create meaningful sentences. If the two cards on the table do not make a meaningful match, the next player puts his or her B card down. The game continues in this way until a meaningful match is created. The first player to spot a match shouts "Match" to stop the game. If the match is acceptable, he or she collects all the B cards on the table. The next A card is then turned over and the game continues.

STEP 5 The player with the most cards at the end is the winner. This game should be played as quickly as possible.

ACTIVITY 4 writing

Who are you most similar to in your family? Write a description of your similarities and differences. If you wish, think of someone in your extended family—for example, a cousin, aunt, or grandparent.

ACTIVITY 5 speaking/listening

STEP 1 Make a list of five popular musicians that you like or dislike. Or you can choose movies, movie stars, types of music, sports, writers, or books. Walk around the classroom and ask other students their opinions about your list. Find out how many students agree or disagree with you. Record your conversations or interviews.

STEP 2 Make a report on your findings. Listen to the recording to make sure your report is accurate. Did your classmates use short phrases such as *I do too, so do I*, *I don't either, neither do I*, *sort of*, and *kind of*? If not, what did they use instead to agree and disagree with each other?

ACTIVITY 6 listening

CD Track 19

STEP 1 Listen to the audio of people talking about what they like and dislike. What general topic are they talking about? What specific topics do they mention?

STEP 2 Number the statements below in the order that you hear them. Mark the first statement as number 1 and so forth.

_____ *I do too.*	_____ *I don't either.*	_____ *Sort of.*
_____ *So do I.*	_____ *Neither do I.*	_____ *Kind of.*

STEP 3 Which statements do you agree and disagree with?

ACTIVITY 7 research on the web

***InfoTrac® College Edition* Option:** Go to *InfoTrac* to look up a review of your favorite movie or music. Do you agree with the reviewer? Tell the class.

ACTIVITY 8 reflection

Work with a partner. Complete a chart like the one in the Opening Task on page 185 with things you both like and don't like about learning English. Then tell your class.

UNIT 13

PRESENT PERFECT WITH *SINCE* AND *FOR*

UNIT GOALS

- Use present perfect to show a connection between past and present situations
- Form correct sentences with present perfect
- Know how to use *for* and *since* correctly
- Know which verbs not to use with present perfect

OPENING TASK

Personal Information

STEP 1

Look at the picture. Where are they? What are they talking about?

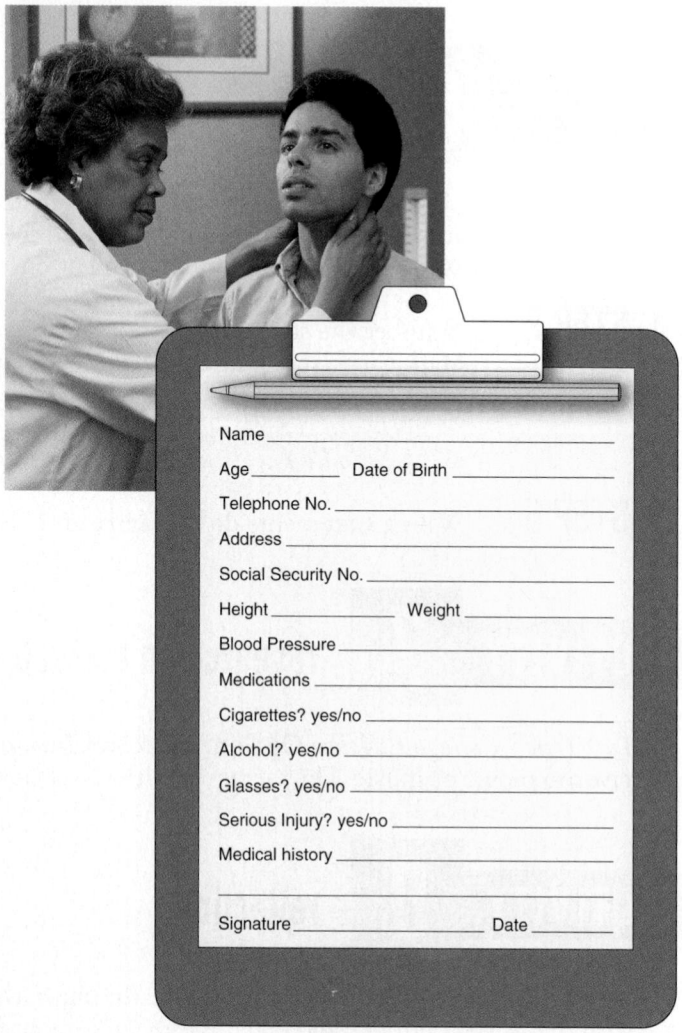

STEP 2

Work in pairs. Student A, look at this page. Student B, look at page A-17.

Student A: Complete the information on the medical history form by asking your partner questions about Michael Menendez. Your partner will answer your questions by looking at pages A-16 and A-17. Use complete questions.

Example: **Student A:** *Does he smoke?*
Student B: *Yes, he does.*
Student A: *How long has he smoked?*

MEDICAL HISTORY					
Name	Michael Menendez				
Date of birth *08/24/75*	Cigarettes? Yes/No	Alcohol? Yes/No	Glasses? Yes/No	Serious Injuries? *Broken ankle*	Health Problems? _____
Height *5ft 11in* Weight _____	How long? _____ *Started* _____ *Stopped* _____	How much? *A glass of wine with dinner every night*	How long? *Since* _____	When? *In 1992*	How long? *For* _____

STEP 3

Use the information above to make sentences about Michael Menendez. Write complete sentences.

PAST:

1.
2.

PRESENT:

1.
2.

PAST AND PRESENT:

1.
2.

FOCUS 1 Present Perfect: Connecting Past and Present

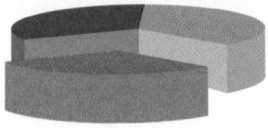

EXAMPLES	EXPLANATIONS
PAST (a) **I moved** to New York in 2002. (simple past)	Use the simple past for completed action in the past.
PRESENT (b) **I live** in New York now. (simple present)	Use the simple present for facts about present situations.
PAST AND PRESENT (c) **I have lived** in New York since 2002. (present perfect) (d) It is now 2006. **I have lived** in New York for four years. (present perfect)	Use the present perfect (*have* + past participle) to connect the past and present. One use of the present perfect is to tell us about something that began in the past and continues to the present. (For other uses of the present perfect, see Unit 14.)

EXERCISE 1

Use the information about Michael Menendez from the Opening Task on page 197 and page A-17 to complete the doctor's report below. Circle the simple present, simple past, or present perfect.

Medical Report on Michael Menendez

Michael Menendez spoke with me yesterday about serious headaches. He (1) has/had/has had these headaches for two months. His previous medical history is good. He (2) doesn't have/didn't have/hasn't had any serious illnesses. In 1992, he (3) is/was/has been in the hospital for three weeks, when he (4) breaks/broke/has broken his ankle in a skiing accident. He (5) doesn't smoke/didn't smoke/hasn't smoked: (6) he stops/stopped/has stopped six years ago, and he (7) doesn't smoke/didn't smoke/hasn't smoked since that time. He (8) wears /wore/has worn glasses when he reads and he (9) wears/wore/has worn them since 2003. He works/worked/has worked with computers since 1998. I examined Mr. Menendez and did several tests. I asked him to return next week.

Signed: Dr. Roberts

FOCUS 2 Forming the Present Perfect

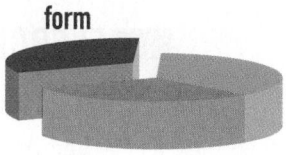

To form the present perfect use *have/has* + past participle.*

STATEMENT		NEGATIVE		QUESTION		
I You We They	have gone. ('ve)	I You We They	have not gone. (haven't)	Have	I You We They	gone?
She He It	has gone. ('s)	She He It	has not gone. (hasn't)	Has	She He It	gone?

* See Appendix 5 on page A-13 for the past participles of some common irregular verbs.

EXERCISE 2

Write the questions that the doctor probably asked Mr. Menendez in order to get these responses.

Example: 1. Do you drink? _____

Yes, a little. I drink a glass of wine with dinner every night.

2. _____

Yes, I do. I wear them when I read.

3. _____

I started wearing them in 1987.

4. _____

I've worn them since 1987.

5. _____

No, I don't smoke now.

6. _____

I stopped ten years ago.

7. _____

No, I haven't smoked since that time.

8. _____

Yes, I have had these headaches for two months.

EXERCISE 3

Work with a partner. Ask and answer questions about each other's medical history. Feel free to make up information on the following topics, or use the information about Michael Menendez on pages 197 and A-17 to answer questions.

Example: A: Have you had any serious illnesses?

B: Yes, I once had pneumonia when I was ten years old.

serious illnesses

smoking

eyesight

present health problem(s)

time in hospital

drinking

allergies

when problem(s) started

EXERCISE 4

Go back to Exercises 1 and 2. Look for the words *for* and *since*. In the boxes below, write down the word or words that directly follow *for* or *since*. The first example is *two months* with *for*, from Exercise 1.

SINCE	FOR
	two months

What does this tell you about the use of *since* and *for*? What kinds of words or phrases follow *since* and *for*?

meaning

FOCUS 3 *For* and *Since*

EXAMPLES	EXPLANATIONS
(a) **for** two weeks (b) **for** ten years (c) **for** five minutes	*For* is used to show length of time (how long the period of time was).
(d) **since** 1985 (e) **since** my birthday (f) **since** I turned 40 (g) **since** Monday (h) **since** April	*Since* is used to show when a period of time began.

EXERCISE 5

What difference in meaning (if any) is there in each pair of statements? Discuss with a partner.

1. a. Anthony and Eva lived here for ten years.
   b. Anthony and Eva have lived here for ten years.
2. Anthony and Eva met in 1998.
   a. They have known each other for over ten years.
   b. They have known each other since 1998.
3. a. They have worked for the same company for a long time.
   b. They worked for the same company for a long time.
4. It is May. Eva started studying Italian three months ago.
   a. Eva has studied Italian for three months.
   b. Eva has studied Italian since February.
5. It is July.
   a. Anthony hasn't drunk any coffee for six months.
   b. Anthony stopped drinking coffee in January.

FOCUS 4 *For* and *Since*

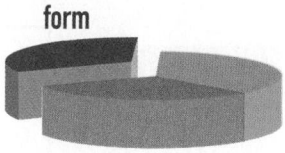

EXAMPLES	EXPLANATIONS
(a) She's worked here **(for)** several years. (b) (For) how long have you lived here? (c) **Since** when have you lived here? (d) NOT: When have you lived here? (e) I've lived here **since** January. (f) NOT: I've lived here January.	The word *for* can be omitted in statements. *For* can also be omitted in questions. *Since* cannot be omitted. *"How long . . ."* is more common than *"Since when . . ."* in questions.

EXERCISE 6

Look at the hotel register below. How many people are staying in the hotel right now? Who has stayed there the longest? Use the information from the register to make statements with the words given below.

Example: *Mr. and Mrs. Gordon stayed in the hotel for six nights.*

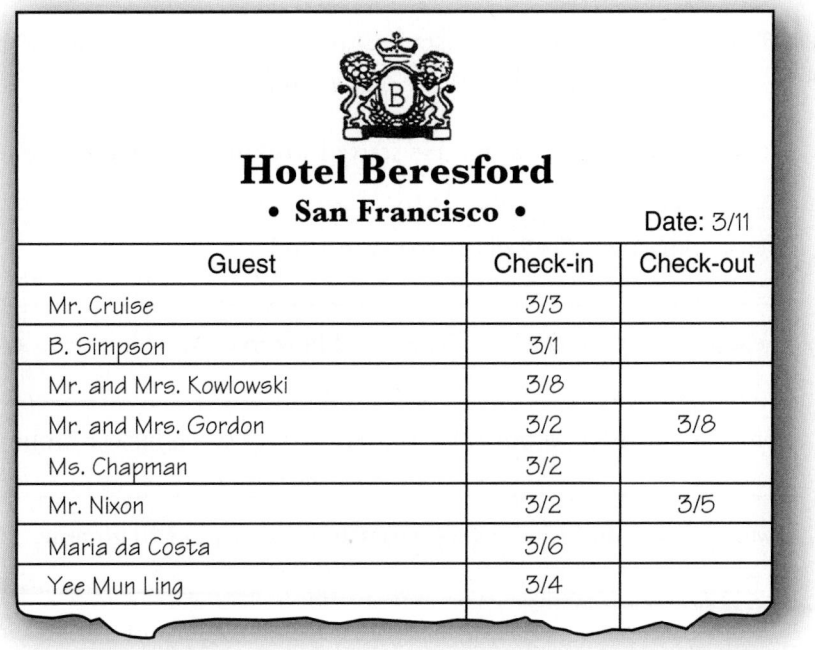

Hotel Beresford

• San Francisco •

Date: 3/11

Guest	Check-in	Check-out
Mr. Cruise	3/3	
B. Simpson	3/1	
Mr. and Mrs. Kowlowski	3/8	
Mr. and Mrs. Gordon	3/2	3/8
Ms. Chapman	3/2	
Mr. Nixon	3/2	3/5
Maria da Costa	3/6	
Yee Mun Ling	3/4	

1. Mr. and Mrs. Gordon/for
2. Maria da Costa/since
3. Yee Mun Ling/since
4. B. Simpson/for
5. Mr. and Mrs. Kowlowski/for
6. Ms. Chapman/since
7. Mr. Cruise/for
8. Mr. Nixon/for

FOCUS 5 Verbs Not Used with Present Perfect and *For*

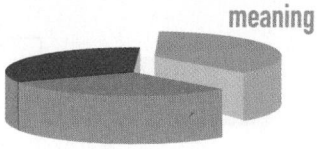

EXAMPLES	EXPLANATIONS
(a) Shin **arrived** in the United States three years ago. (b) NOT: Shin has arrived in the United States for three years.	Some verbs talk about an action that happens all at once, an action that doesn't continue for a period of time.
(c) Shin **has lived** in the United States for three years.	In (c) we understand that it is the living in the United States that continues, not the arriving.
begin *arrive* *meet* *end* *leave* *stop*	For the same reason, these verbs are not usually used with present perfect and *for*.

EXERCISE 7

Rewrite these sentences. Be sure to use the present perfect and *since* or *for*.

Example: Karen wears glasses. She started to wear glasses when she was a child.
Karen has worn glasses since she was a child.

1. He works for the TV station. He started working there eight years ago.

   _____

2. They are married. They got married in 1962.

   _____

3. She knows how to fix a car. She learned how to do it a long time ago.

   _____

4. Tom rides his bike to work. He started to do it when his car broke down.

   _____

5. I wanted to go to China several years ago. I still want to go now.

   _____

6. My brother started painting when he was in college, and he still paints now.

   _____

7. I was afraid of bats when I was a child, and I am afraid of them now.

   _____

8. My mother is in France. She went there last week.

   _____

9. My sister runs two miles every morning before breakfast. She started to do this when she was fifteen years old.

_____

10. They go to Cape Cod every summer. They started to do this twelve years ago.

_____

EXERCISE 8

Fill in the blanks with *since* or *for* OR the appropriate form of the verb in parentheses.

Leroy and Paula are having a party. Two of their guests, Lee and Bob, have just met.

Lee: (1) _____ Have you known Leroy and Paula (2) _____ a long time?

Bob: I (3) _____ (know) Paula (4) _____ my senior year in college. I first (5) _____ (meet) Leroy at their wedding two years ago. What about you?

Lee: I'm a colleague of Leroy's. We (6) _____ (work) together (7) _____ several years.

Bob: Oh, Leroy (8) _____ (show) me some of your work last week. It's great.

Lee: Thanks. What do you do?

Bob: I (9) _____ (teach) French (10) _____ ten years, but I (11) _____ (quit) a couple of years ago. Now I'm an actor.

Lee: An actor! I thought you looked familiar.

Bob: Well, not really. I (12) _____ (not work) as an actor (13) _____ last October. In fact, last night I (14) _____ (start) to work as a waiter at the Zenon.

Lee: Really? I (15) _____ (eat) there last night. *That's* why you look familiar!

EXERCISE 9

Look for mistakes in the following passage. Correct any mistakes that you find. One mistake has been corrected for you.

1. My sister is very good at languages. She studies
2. Italian at the language institute. She started studying
3. Italian in 1993, so she ~~studies~~ has studied Italian several years. When
4. she was a child, she wanted to learn Russian and she still
5. wants to learn it. She has wanted to learn Russian
6. since a long time, but Russian courses are not offered
7. at the language schools near her home. Two years ago
8. she has found out that the local community college offers
9. courses in Chinese, so she started learning Chinese.
10. Unfortunately, she doesn't have a car, so she takes the bus
11. to school since two years.

Use Your English

ACTIVITY 1 speaking

Work in pairs or groups of three. Complete the following with information about your partner(s). Make a list of appropriate questions and then ask your partner(s) the questions. Here are some sample questions:

How long have you studied English? *How long have you lived in this town?*

1. _____ for _____ hours.
2. _____ since _____.
3. _____ for _____.
4. _____ for _____ years.
5. _____ since _____.

ACTIVITY 2 speaking

Work individually. Respond to this survey. Each response is a number.

———The number of people you have talked to today

———The number of weeks, months, or years you have known your oldest friend

———The number of weeks, months, or years you have studied in this school

———The number of hours or minutes since you last ate something

———The number of minutes you have been in this classroom

Work in pairs. Say one number to your partner (in random order). Your partner has to guess what each number means.

Example:
A: *Five*
B: *Is that the number of weeks you have studied in this school?*

ACTIVITY 3 speaking/listening

STEP 1 Work with a partner. Read the statements in the chart on page 208 and try to match each statement to someone in your class. Write the name in the column marked Guesses.

STEP 2 Next, ask your classmates questions using *How long have you . . . ?* in order to find out who has done each thing the longest and shortest amounts of time. Fill in the answers in the column marked Facts.

Continued on the next page

ACTIVITY 3 continued

GUESSES	WHO.	FACTS
_____	has studied English the longest time?	_____
_____	has been married the longest time?	_____
_____	has owned his or her watch the longest time?	_____
_____	has known how to drive the longest time?	_____
_____	has known how to drive the shortest time?	_____
_____	has had the shoes he or she is wearing today the longest time?	_____
_____	has worn glasses the longest time?	_____
_____	has worn glasses the shortest time?	_____
_____	has had the same hair style the longest time?	_____

ACTIVITY 4 speaking/listening/writing

In this activity, you will find out how different countries are governed.

STEP 1 Get together with a group of classmates from different countries, if possible. First use the three charts on page 209 to note and list information about your own country or another country you are familiar with. We have done some for you, as examples.

STEP 2 When you have all filled in the charts, begin sharing your information. Then use the charts to take more notes on what your classmates tell you. In the first two charts, check (✓) the appropriate box or write in the box marked other. In the third chart, write notes.

STEP 3 Be ready to share this information with the rest of the class.

COUNTRY	TYPE OF LEADERSHIP				
	President	Monarch*	Prime minister	Military	Other
Great Britain		✓	✓		

* King, queen, emperor, etc.

COUNTRY	HOW CURRENT LEADER CAME INTO POWER				
	Election	Succession*	Coup**	Other	
Great Britain	✓ (Prime Minister)	✓ (Queen)			

* *Succession:* the act of a position or title passing from one person to another, usually a relative
** *Coup*: a sudden or violent seizure of power by a group that has not been elected

COUNTRY	WHAT CURRENT LEADER HAS DONE		
	Length of time the current leader has been in power	Best thing he or she has done while in power	Worst thing he or she has done while in power***

*** Talk about the leader of your country or another country for which you've listed information in the blank

ACTIVITY 5 listening

CD Track 20

STEP 1

You are going to hear a job interview with a man applying for a job as an office manager. Listen to the job interview carefully. Do you think the man will get the job? Why or why not? Discuss with a partner.

STEP 2

Match the first part of each sentence in column A with the second part in column B.

A	B
1. I've worked	a. being part of a team.
2. I've been	b. able to solve every problem.
3. I've enjoyed	c. there for about three years.
4. I have found out	d. in charge of training the new staff.
5. I've learned	e. more or less everything there is to know about the job.
6. I haven't always been	f. how to work with people.

STEP 3

Listen to the audio again. This time, listen to all the interviewer's questions. Write them in the chart.

INTERVIEWER'S QUESTIONS
1.
2.
3.
4.
5.
6.

STEP 4

Role-play the interview with a partner. Change any of the questions or answers if you want.

ACTIVITY 6 speaking/listening

STEP 1 Find a classmate, a friend, or an acquaintance who is studying the same field as you, or who has or wants a job like yours. Conduct a practice job interview. You can work together to come up with questions, which should include when things happened and for how long: work experience, job history, and education. Feel free to make up information!

STEP 2 Decide who will be the "employer" (the interviewer) and who will be the "employee" (the interviewee). Take turns if there is time. Record the interviews.

STEP 3 Listen to the recording. Write down all the sentences with the present perfect. In each case, was it used correctly? Were *since* and *for* used? Were there cases where the present perfect should have been used but wasn't?

ACTIVITY 7 research on the web/writing

STEP 1 Choose a country that you are interested in. Go on the Internet and use a search engine such as Google® or Yahoo® to find out about the political system in that country. What kind of government does it have? When and how did the current leader come into power? What has the current leader done while he or she has been in power?

STEP 2 Write a brief summary of the information you found. Exchange reports with a classmate and check to make sure that the present perfect was used correctly.

ACTIVITY 8 reflection

Write three things you have done that have helped you to learn English. Make a class list and display the results as a class poster.

UNIT 14

PRESENT PERFECT AND SIMPLE PAST

Ever, Never, Already, and *Yet*

UNIT GOALS

- Use present perfect and simple past appropriately
- Understand the meaning of *ever* and *never* in questions and statements
- Use present perfect questions appropriately
- Understand the meaning of *already* and *yet*

OPENING TASK

Around-the-world trip

STEP 1

Look at these pictures. Do you know any of these places?

STEP 2

Tosh and Yumiko are on a trip around the world. The cities are marked on the map on the next page. Starting in Tokyo, they are going to visit eight cities in four weeks. Look at Tosh and Yumiko's travel souvenirs. With a partner, draw Tosh and Yumiko's route on the map. Which places have they already visited? Which places haven't they visited yet?

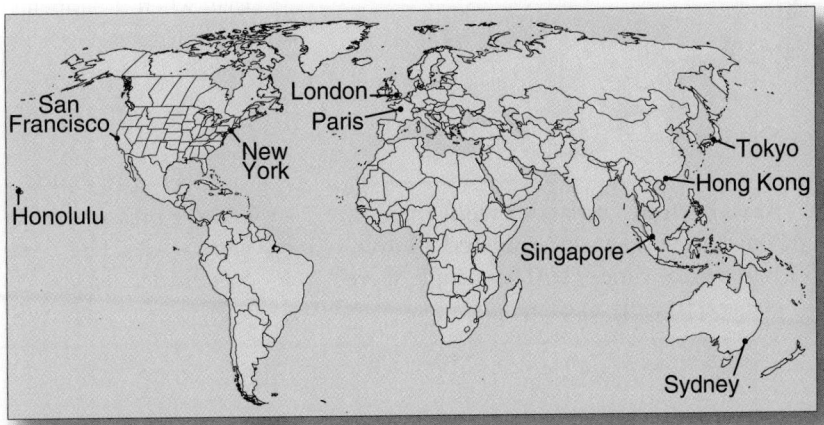

STEP 3

Write down one city you have visited (in the world or in your state), one city you haven't visited, and one city you would like to visit. Walk around the classroom and find three people who have the same place names for each category. Discuss why you chose to write down those places.

FOCUS 1 Present Perfect versus Simple Past

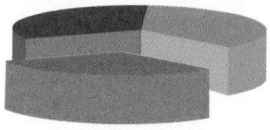

EXAMPLES	EXPLANATIONS
(a) Last year, she **graduated** from high school. 	Use the simple past to talk about something that happened at a **specific time** in the past.
(b) He **lived** in this house from 1880 to 1888. 	Use the simple past to show when something happened.
(c) He **has been** to Mexico. (d) They **have run** a marathon. 	Use the present perfect when you talk about something that happened in the past without mentioning the specific time it happened. The experience is more important than when it happened.
(e) I **have been** to Thailand. I **went** there about ten years ago and **traveled** all over. I **had** a great time. The Thai people **were** open and friendly to tourists.	Use the present perfect to introduce the general idea. Use the simple past to give specific details.

EXERCISE 1

There is a "classic" film festival in town featuring a number of famous American movies at several different movie theaters. Robert loves classic movies, and so he is planning to invite some friends to a movie on Saturday night. Naturally, he wants to suggest a movie that nobody has seen. Use the information below to help him choose.

FILM FESTIVAL SCHEDULE		
BALBOA 38th & Balboa 555~8184	*CORONET* Geary & Arguelio 555~4400	*METRO* Union-Webtser 555~1835
HIGH NOON 4:55 8:30 10:55	ON THE WATERFRONT 1:20 3:30 5:37 7:30	CASABLANCA 1:00 3:15 5:30 10:00
ROMAN HOLIDAY 6:50 10:25	*GALAXY* Van Ness & Sutter 555~8700	*REGENCY* Van Ness & Sutter 555~6773
PSYCHO 12:30 4:45 8:40 11:15	THE GODFATHER 6:10 8:30 10:55	THE GRADUATE 4:40 7:40 10:30

Ann has seen the movie at the Coronet.
Patty and Mark went to the Metro last night.
Karen went to the Balboa on Tuesday to see the movie that started at 8:30.
Tom went to the Galaxy last weekend.
Carolyn and Terry have seen the movie at the Regency.
A couple of days ago Robert went to the Balboa and saw the movie that started at 8:40.

1. Which movie should they see?
2. Have you seen any of these movies?
3. Find out how many of your classmates have seen these movies.

EXERCISE 2

Use the information from Exercise 1 to make questions that fit with the following answers. The first one has been done for you.

1. Did Carolyn and Terry go to the movies yesterday?

   Yes, they did. They went to see *The Graduate* yesterday.

2. _____

   Yes, Tom has seen *The Godfather.*

3. _____

No, Patty and Mark haven't seen *High Noon.*

4. _____

No, she didn't see it last weekend. She saw it on Tuesday.

5. _____

No, they didn't see *Psycho.* They saw *Casablanca.*

6. _____

Yes, he has. He saw it a couple of days ago.

7. _____

No, they haven't seen *Roman Holiday*, but they have seen *The Graduate.*

8. _____

No, he didn't. He saw it last weekend.

EXERCISE 3

Alice is on vacation in New York City. Complete her postcard written to her family choosing verbs from the list below (some of the verbs can be used more than once). Use either the simple past or present perfect form of the verb.

try	see	walk	eat
have	go	spend	take

Hi Folks!
Having a great time! I **(1)** _____ at least 50 miles, but I **(2)** _____ lots of interesting things. Yesterday I **(3)** _____ the Staten Island Ferry, and on Thursday I **(4)** _____ to the top of the Empire State Building. I **(5)** _____ several shows. Two nights ago I **(6)** _____ to see "Chicago" I **(7)** _____ great tickets. Wonderful food!!! I **(8)** _____ some delicious meals. Yesterday I **(9)** _____ sushi for the first time.
See you next week.
Love, Alice
P.S. I **(10)** _____ lots of money!

The Murphys
1403 Eastwood
Ann Arbor, MI
48103

meaning

FOCUS 2 *Ever* and *Never* in Questions and Statements

EXAMPLES	EXPLANATIONS
(a) A: **Have** you **ever eaten** Mexican food?	Use *ever* in questions with the present perfect to mean "at any time before now."
(b) Yes, **I have eaten** it. (c) NOT: Yes, I have **ever** eaten it. (d) **I haven't ever eaten** it.	*Ever* is not usually used in affirmative statements (those that mean or use *yes*). *Ever* is used in negative statements.
(e) **I have never eaten** it.	Use *never* with the present perfect to mean "at no time before now."
(f) No, **never.**	You can also use *No, never* as a short answer.

EXERCISE 4

Read the conversation. Underline and correct any mistakes.

Mick: Have you ever visit Europe? (visited)

Dave: Yes. I've been there several times, in fact. Three years ago I've gone to France.

Mick: Really? Where did you go?

Dave: I went to Paris, of course. And then I rode my mountain bike in the Pyrenees. Last year I've ridden my bike in Germany and Switzerland. Have ever you been there?

Mick: I've never been to Germany, but I've ever been to Switzerland.

Dave: When was that?

Mick: I've taken an international business course there about eight years ago.

FOCUS 3 Present Perfect in Questions

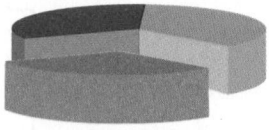

EXAMPLES	EXPLANATIONS
(a) A: **Have** you **ever eaten** frogs' legs? B: No, I haven't.	Use the present perfect with *ever* when you want to know **if** something has happened.
(b) A: **Have** you **ever been** to Sub-Saharan Africa? B: Yes, I have.	When you ask these questions, you usually expect the answer to be *Yes, I have* or *No, I haven't.*
(c) A: When **did** you **go** there? B: I went there last year.	Use the simple past in questions when you want to know **when** something happened.

EXERCISE 5

Complete the conversations, using the present perfect or the simple past of the verb in parentheses. The first one has been done for you.

1. **A:** Excuse me, sir, we're doing a survey. Can I ask you a few questions?
   B: Sure, go ahead.
   A: (1) Have you ever used (you/use/ever) WonderWhite detergent?
   B: No, (2) _____ (I/try/never)it.
   A: Why not?
   B: (3) _____ (I/do/never) laundry in my life. My wife always does it.
   A: What about you, sir? (4) _____ (you/wash/ever) your clothes with WonderWhite?
   C: Yes, (5) _____ (I/try) it.
   A: When (6) _____ (you/try) it for the first time?
   C: (7) _____ (I/use) it for the first time about six months ago.

2. **A:** (1) _____ (you/read/ever) any books by Latin American writers?
   B: Yes, I (2) _____. I (3) _____ (read) a great novel by a Colombian writer a few years ago.
   A: Which one?
   B: I (4) _____ (forget) his name. He (5) _____ (win) the Nobel Prize several years ago.
   A: Oh, you mean Gabriel García Márquez.

3. **A:** My brother is coming to stay with us for a few days next week. Do you have any ideas about how we can entertain him?
   B: (1) _____ (he/be/ever) here before?
   A: Yes. He (2) _____ (come) once about three years ago.
   B: (3) _____ (he/go) to Chinatown then?
   A: No, (4) _____ (he/be/never) to Chinatown, but (5) _____ (he/travel) a lot in China and in the Far East.
   B: Maybe you'd better not take him to Chinatown then! (6) _____ (you/take) him to the Greek restaurant when he was here three years ago?
   A: No, and (7) _____ (he/visit/never) Greece.
   B: Great! Why don't you take him there?

4. **A:** _____ (you/go out) last night?
   B: Yes. (2) _____ (we/go) to that new Italian restaurant.
   A: What's it like? (3) _____ (I/be/never) there.
   B: It's O.K., but (4) _____ (I/eat) better Italian food in other restaurants.
   A: (5) _____ (you/try/ever) the one on Main Street?
   B: Yes. (6) _____ (we/have) great meal there last weekend.

meaning

FOCUS 4 *Already* and *Yet*

EXAMPLES	EXPLANATIONS
(a) I've **already** eaten. (b) I haven't eaten **yet.**	Use *already* to show that an event was completed earlier. Use *yet* when an event has **not** been completed before the time of speaking.
(c) Have you eaten **yet**? (d) Have you eaten **already**? OR (e) Have you **already** eaten?	*Yet* in questions is more neutral than *already.* The use of *already* in questions shows that the speaker expects that an event has happened before the time of speaking.

EXERCISE 6

Get information from your classmates about the following topics and add topics of your own. Use *already, yet, ever*, and *never* in your questions when appropriate.

1. study other languages (besides English)
2. receive an F in a class
3. receive an A in a class
4. give a speech
5. be a teacher/teach students
6. feel nervous about speaking another language
7. feel excited about studying/learning
8. earn a Bachelor's degree
9. forget about a test that was scheduled
10. finish studying this chapter
11. master the present perfect tense

EXERCISE 7

Sue and her roommate Betsy are discussing their evening plans. Fill in the missing parts of their conversation. Use *already*, *yet*, *ever*, and *never* when appropriate.

Sue: (1) _____?

Betsy: No, not yet. But I'm hungry. I didn't eat lunch.

Sue: Well, should we go out to eat? I'd love to try that new Mexican restaurant down the street. (2) _____?

Betsy: No, (3) _____. I was going to go with Deb and Rebecca last week, but at the last minute they changed their minds. (4) _____ out to eat with them? They have a hard time making decisions!

Sue: No, (5) _____. One time we made plans to, but at the last minute they canceled.

Betsy: I'd rather be invited to their house for _____ dinner, anyway. Deb's a great cook. She went to a chef's school in Paris. (6) _____?

Sue: (7) _____. She makes the best chicken curry. Yum! Which reminds me. . . . You're not the only one that's hungry! Do you need to stop at the ATM on the way to the restaurant?

Betsy: No, (8) _____.

Sue: Well, good, let's go then.

Use Your English

ACTIVITY 1 listening/speaking/writing

STEP 1

In this activity, you will be finding out about some of the things that your classmates have done. Look at the list in the box below. Move around the class and ask questions to see if you can find anyone who has ever done any of these things.

First you need to find who has had the experience (name); then you need to get specific details about the experience (when) (where) (how/why). Take notes below; it is not necessary to write full sentences at this point. In the box marked ***, you can add an experience of your own if you want to.

Be ready to share your findings with the rest of the class.

HAVE YOU EVER .....?				
Experience	Name	When	Where	How/Why
met a famous person				
climbed a mountain				
seen a shark				
felt really frightened				
flown in a hot-air balloon				
***				

STEP 2

Now use the information you collected to write a report on your findings. Here is one way you can start your report:

I have interviewed some of my classmates about things they have done before now, and I have learned some interesting things about their past experiences. For example,...

ACTIVITY 2 speaking/listening

Move around the class and ask questions to find out if the following statements are true or false. If the statement is true, write T beside it; if it is false, write F.

1. Somebody in this room has appeared on TV. _____
2. Everybody here has eaten tacos. _____
3. At least three people have never ridden a motorcycle. _____
4. Somebody has swum in more than two oceans. _____
5. Several people have seen a ghost. _____
6. At least three people have been to Disneyland. _____
7. Nobody has been to Paris. _____
8. Somebody has run a marathon. _____
9. Half the class has never played soccer. _____
10. Somebody has never driven a car. _____

ACTIVITY 3 speaking/listening

The purpose of this activity is to confuse your classmates. You will tell the class about three things you have done in your life. Two of these things are true, but one is false. Your classmates will try to guess which one is false. For example:

I have ridden a bicycle from San Francisco to Los Angeles.
I have traveled by boat down the Nile.
I have broken my leg twice.

Which statement is false?

In order to decide which one is false, your classmates can ask you questions about the specific details of each experience. For example: "When did you ride your bike to Los Angeles?" "How long did it take?" "Which leg did you break?" and so on. After they have listened to your answers, the class will vote on which experience is false.

Take turns talking about your true and false experiences until everyone has taken part.

ACTIVITY 4 writing or speaking/listening

STEP 1 Write down one of the true stories you told in Activity 3, this time providing lots of details. Read the story aloud and record it.

OR If you want practice in telling the story without writing it down first, take a few minutes to think about the details you want to include. Then tell the story to a classmate and record it.

STEP 2 Listen to your own or each other's recordings for verb tense usage. Was the present perfect used? If it wasn't, were there cases where it should have been used? Was the simple past used correctly? Did you use already, yet, ever, and never appropriately?

ACTIVITY 5 speaking/listening

You have probably had many different experiences since you came to this country, this city, or this school. In this activity you will be finding out the best and worst experiences your classmates have had since they came here. First, go around the room and get as much information as you can from at least three different people. Use the chart to take notes on the information your classmates give you.

NAME	LENGTH OF STAY	BEST EXPERIENCE	WORST EXPERIENCE

ACTIVITY 6 writing

You have been asked to write a short article for your college newspaper on the experiences of international students. Review the information you collected in Activity 5. Choose the two most interesting or surprising "best" experiences and the two most interesting or surprising "worst" experiences. Organize your article so that you talk first about the bad experiences and then about the good experiences. Start your article with a brief introduction to the topic and to the students you interviewed.

ACTIVITY 7 listening

CD Track 21

Listen to the audio of two people talking about their travels.

STEP 1

Take notes in the chart below, using information from their conversation.

	SPEAKER 1/THE MAN	SPEAKER 2/THE WOMAN
WHERE? area of the world countries (list them)		
WHEN? what year(s)? length of stay		
HOW? transportation hotels/guesthouses		
WHY? reasons for traveling types of experiences		

STEP 2

Discuss these questions with a partner: How would you describe each speaker's traveling style? In other words, what type of travel do they enjoy? What types of places do they stay in? Do they enjoy being tourists or residents? How does your own style of traveling compare or contrast with those described?

STEP 3

Now listen to the audio again for the way the speakers used verb tenses. List the phrases from the conversation where the speakers used the present perfect verb form in their questions or answers. Compare your list with your classmates' lists. Did the speakers use yet, ever, or never with the present perfect?

ACTIVITY 8 writing

Write a letter to a family member or a friend and tell him or her about the best and the worst experiences you have had since you left home. Review your letter for the use of the present perfect. If you feel comfortable sharing your letter with someone, you can review each other's letters. Was the present perfect used? If it wasn't, were there cases where it **should** have been used? Was the simple past used correctly? Did you use *already, yet, ever*, and *never* appropriately?

ACTIVITY 9 research on the web

Ask your partner if he or she has ever used the Internet for any of the following, or done any of the following on the Internet. Then choose one of the topics. Go on the Internet and use a search engine such as Google® or Yahoo® and find a Web site to recommend to your classmates.

An online dictionary
An online grammar reference
Examination practice
Grammar practice
A job search
A college program search

ACTIVITY 10 reflection

Which of these activities have you done this week in English? Check your answers. Then circle the activities you want to do but haven't done yet. Share your answers with a partner.

Have you written ...?	☐ a check	☐ a letter	☐ an email	☐ an essay
Have you read ...?	☐ a grammar book	☐ a newspaper	☐ a novel	☐ a magazine
Have you spoken to...?	☐ a friend	☐ a co-worker	☐ a teacher	☐ a counselor
Have you listened to...?	☐ a radio program	☐ a song	☐ a story	☐ the news

UNIT 15

PRESENT PERFECT PROGRESSIVE

UNIT GOALS

- Correctly use present progressive with *just*
- Form present progressive correctly
- Use present progressive to describe unfinished actions and new habits
- Correctly choose between present perfect and present perfect progressive

OPENING TASK

Recent Activities

STEP 1

Look at the picture. How does she feel? Why do you think she feels like this?

STEP 2

Work with a partner. Match the pictures with the words and phrases below.

1.

Alan

2.

Linda

3.

Melina

4.

Julia and Fred

5.

Sue

6.

Tom and Brian

_____ muddy boots
_____ baking bread
_____ fixing a car
_____ exhausted

_____ running a marathon
_____ chopping onions
_____ wet hair
_____ gardening

_____ crying
_____ swimming
_____ covered in oil
_____ covered in flour

STEP 3

Work in pairs. Student A chooses a picture and asks student B a question about it. Student B responds.

Example: A: *Why are Alan's hands covered in flour?*
B: *He's been baking bread.*

FOCUS 1 Present Perfect Progressive and *Just*: Recent Activities

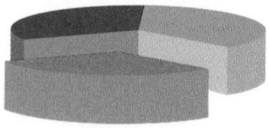

EXAMPLES	EXPLANATIONS
(a) A: Why are your hands greasy? B: I **have been fixing** my car.	Use the present perfect progressive to talk about an activity that was happening (in progress) very recently in the past. In (a) the activity is so recent that you can still feel or see the effect or result.
(b) A: How come you're so thirsty? B: I've just been running.	To emphasize that the activity is recent, use *just*.

EXERCISE 1

Look at the Opening Task on page 227. Write sentences that give explanations for each situation. Check that you have formed the present perfect progressive correctly.

1. Alan's hands are covered in flour because he has been baking bread.
2. _____
3. _____
4. _____
5. _____
6. _____

FOCUS 2 Present Perfect Progressive

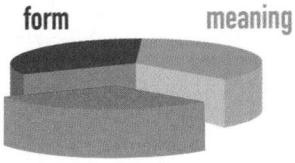

Use *has/have* + *been* + verb + *-ing* to form the present perfect progressive.

STATEMENT	NEGATIVE	QUESTION
I / You / We / They have been sleeping. ('ve)	I / You / We / They have not been sleeping. (haven't)	Have I / you / we / they been sleeping?
She / He / It has been sleeping. ('s)	She / He / It has not been sleeping. (hasn't)	Has she / he / it been sleeping?

EXERCISE 2

You are riding the subway in a big city late at night. There are several other people in the same car. You observe them carefully and try to figure out what they have been doing recently. Use the verb in parentheses to make sentences about what each person has, or hasn't, been doing.

1. A young man with a black eye and ripped clothing. (fight)
   He's been fighting with somebody.
2. Two young men wearing sweats and carrying tennis racquets. (play)
   _____
3. Two young women with many bags and packages from well-known department stores. (shop)
   _____
4. A couple wearing shorts and walking shoes and backpacks. They seem very tired. (hike)
   _____
5. A man with dark shadows under his eyes who looks very tired. (sleep)
   _____
6. A woman with ketchup on her T-shirt. (eat)
   _____
7. A man with a two-day beard. (shave)
   _____

FOCUS 3 Perfect Progressive: Unfinished Actions

EXAMPLE	EXPLANATION
(a) He **has been waiting** for twenty minutes. (He's still waiting.)	Use the present perfect progressive to describe situations or actions that started in the past and are still going on.

EXERCISE 3

For each conversation, complete the following sentences. The first one has been done for you.

1. **Lee:** What are you doing?
   Mary Lou: I'm waiting to make a phone call. This woman has been talking (talk) on the phone for the last twenty minutes.
2. **Dan:** Haven't you finished writing that book yet?
   Heidi: No, we're still working on it.
   Dan: You _____ (write) it for almost three years!
3. **Steve:** What's up? You look miserable.
   Tom: I am. I want to go for a bike ride, but it _____ (rain) since eight o'clock this morning.
4. **George:** Excuse me, but is this your dog?
   Barbara: Yes. Is there a problem?
   George: I can't get to sleep because that dog _____ (bark) for hours! Please keep it under control, or I'll call the police.
5. **Martin:** Are these your glasses?
   Gin: Yes! Thank you so much. I _____ (look) for them everywhere!
6. **Sarita:** How are things going in New York?
   Anastasia: We don't live there anymore.
   Sarita: Really?
   Anastasia: Yes. We _____ in Philadelphia since January. (live)

7. **Diane:** Why are Kemal and Cynthia so depressed?
Marianne: They _____ grammar for ages, but they still don't understand how to use the present perfect progressive. (study)

8. **Pam:** Aren't you ready yet?
Andrew: No. I've lost my keys and I _____ to find them for the last half hour. (try)

FOCUS 4 Present Perfect Progressive for New Habits

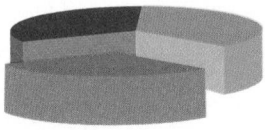

EXAMPLES	EXPLANATIONS
(a) They've **been eating** out a lot recently.	Use the present perfect progressive to talk about a regular habit or activity that is still happening.
(b) He's been exercising a lot **lately.** (c) I've been walking to work **recently.**	Add a time phrase or word to show that the activity started recently.

EXERCISE 4

Stan is talking with his old friend Janet. They have not seen each other for several months, and Janet is surprised by some of the changes in Stan's appearance. Complete their conversation, using the verbs from the list below.

happen	sail	cook	do
feel	take	go	study
eat	ride	date	ski
talk	think	see	spend

Janet: Pat, you look great! You've lost a lot of weight, too.

Stan: Well, I (1) 've been riding my bike to school recently, and I (2) _____ an aerobics class.

Janet: Is that all? No special diets or anything?

Stan: Not really. I (3) _____ (not) to any fast-food restaurants. I (4) _____ at home instead — a lot of fresh vegetables and salads and other healthy stuff like that. It really makes a difference. I (5) _____ much better, with lots more energy.

Janet: Well, you seem to be very busy these days. You're never home when I call. What else (6) _____ you _____?

Stan: I (7) _____ somebody special. She's got a boat, so we (8) _____ a lot, and she also has a cabin in the mountains, so we (9) _____ time there, too. And also, we (10) _____ about taking some longer trips together. So it's all pretty exciting. But what about you? What (11) _____?

Janet: Nothing. I (12) _____ for my final exams, but when they're over, I'm going to start having fun!

FOCUS 5 Present Perfect versus Present Perfect Progressive

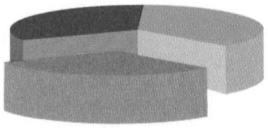

use

EXAMPLES	EXPLANATIONS
(a) Jim **has worked** here for ten years. (b) Jim **has been working** here for ten years. (c) Jim **has started** a new job. (d) NOT: Jim **has been starting** a new job.	With verbs that show actions or states over time (example: *work, live, study*), there is often little difference between the present perfect and present perfect progressive. However, if the verbs refer to one time only, then the present perfect should be used, not the present perfect progressive.

EXAMPLES	EXPLANATIONS
(e) They **have painted** their house. (f) They **have been painting** their house.	In other cases the present perfect progressive: • shows that the action is incomplete (unfinished). In (e), the painting is complete. In (f), it is not complete (see Focus 3). OR
(g) Jean **has visited** her grandmother. (h) Jean **has been visiting** her grandmother.	• emphasizes that the action was in progress recently. (g) tells us that the visit occurred earlier. (h) tells us that the visit occurred recently and perhaps is still in progress (see Focus 1). OR
(i) Geraldo **has exercised.** (j) Geraldo **has been exercising** lately.	• talks about a new habit. (i) tells us that Geraldo exercised at some time earlier. (j) suggests that he has started a new habit (see Focus 4).

EXERCISE 5

Read each situation and circle the statement that best describes the situation.

1. Sally ate frogs' legs in September 1998, and again in December 1999.
   a. Sally has eaten frogs' legs.
   b. Sally has been eating frogs' legs.
2. Bill started reading that book last week and he's not finished yet. He will probably finish it tonight.
   a. Bill has read that book.
   b. Bill has been reading that book.
3. I rode a motorcycle once when I was 16 and once last year.
   a. I've been riding a motorcycle.
   b. I've ridden a motorcycle.
4. We first studied English grammar in school, ten years ago. This year we have grammar class for one hour every day, five days a week.
   a. We've been studying English grammar.
   b. We've studied English grammar.
5. My brother just can't quit smoking, even though he knows it's a bad habit. He started smoking when he was seventeen, and now he's almost thirty.
   a. My brother has been smoking for a long time.
   b. My brother has smoked for a long time.

EXERCISE 6

What would Doug and Sandy say in each situation below? The words in parentheses will help you, but you will need to add some other words.

1. It's 4:00, and Doug's partner Sandy has been napping since 1:00. Doug is waiting for her to wake up. When she finally does, he says: (I/wait/three hours)
2. Sandy has promised to change the oil in Doug's car. While she is sleeping, Doug decides to try to do it himself, but he can't. When Sandy wakes up, he says: (I/try/forty-five minutes)
3. Sandy's mother calls to tell her that Sandy's sister has had another baby. Her mother asks, "When are you and Doug going to have kids?" Sandy tells her: (we/discuss/ten years)
4. After her nap, Sandy is hungry and she wants Doug to go out with her to eat pizza. Doug doesn't want to go because he bought fresh fish for dinner and wants to try out a new recipe. He tells Sandy, "I don't want to go out because (I/plan/dinner/all day)"

EXERCISE 7

Complete the dialogues below, using present perfect progressive, present perfect, or simple past. Be prepared to explain your choice.

Dialogue 1

Keven: What's the matter? You look frustrated.

Tsitsi: I am. I (1) _____ (try) to study all day, but the telephone never stops ringing. People (2) _____ (call) all day about the car.

Keven: That's great. I (3) _____ (hope) to sell that car for six months now. Maybe today's the day!

Dialogue 2

Maria: I'm sorry I'm so late. (4) _____ (you/wait) long?

Alex: Yes, I have! Where (5) _____ (you/be)?

Maria: I really am sorry. My watch is broken, and I didn't know what time it was.

Alex: Why didn't you ask somebody? I (6) _____ (stand) out here in the cold for at least forty minutes.

Maria: Oh, you poor thing! But we'd better hurry to get to the movie theater.

Alex: It's too late. The movie (7) _____ (start).

Maria: Really?

Alex: Yes. It (8) _____ (start) twenty minutes ago.

Use Your English

ACTIVITY 1 writing

You have just received a letter from the editor of your high school newspaper. She wants to include information about former students in the next edition of the paper. Write a letter to the editor, telling her what you have been doing recently. (Do not feel you have to use the present perfect progressive in every sentence! To make this letter sound natural think about all the other tenses you can use as well.)

ACTIVITY 2 speaking

The purpose of this game is to guess recent activities from their current results. Work in teams. Each team should try to think of four different results of recent activities.

Example: Recent Activity: *You have been exercising*

Present Result: *now you are exhausted*

When everyone is ready, each team takes turns acting out the results of the activities they have chosen. For example, Team A has chosen "being exhausted." Everybody in Team A gets up and acts out being exhausted. The rest of the class tries to guess what Team A has been doing. The first person to guess correctly, "You have been exercising, and now you are exhausted," scores a point for his or her team.

ACTIVITY 3 speaking

This is another team game. Each team presents a series of clues, and the rest of the class tries to guess what situation these clues refer to. For example, Team A chooses this situation: *A woman has been reading a sad love story.* The team tries to think of as many clues as possible that will help the other students guess the situation. When everyone is ready, Team A presents the first clue:

Team A: *Her eyes are red. (The other teams now make guesses based on this first clue.)*

Team B: *She has been chopping onions.*

Team C: *She's been crying.*

Team D: *She's been fighting with her boyfriend.*

Team C: *She's been reading a sad love story!*

Team A: *No. She feels very sad.*

Team A: *No. She's very romantic.*

Team A: *No. She was alone.*

You can choose one of the situations below or you can make up one of your own. The person who guesses the correct situation scores a point for his or her team.

1. He or she has been crying.
2. He or she has been watching old movies.
3. He or she has been working late every night.
4. He or she's been training for the Olympics.
5. He or she has been chopping onions.
6. He or she has been feeling sick.

ACTIVITY 4 listening

CD Track 22

Listen to the audio of a conversation between two old friends. These people haven't seen each other for several years, so they have a lot to talk about.

STEP 1

Make a list of the things that each speaker (Speaker 1 (man) / Speaker 2 (woman) has been doing or has recently done (or the things their family members and friends have done). Compare your list with a classmate's.

STEP 2

Look at the lists that you and your partner made. Together, write a sentence about each thing on your lists using either the present perfect or the present perfect progressive.

ACTIVITY 5 speaking/listening

STEP 1 Choose a goal: get healthy, learn a new skill, save money, or become famous. Imagine that you are trying to do this. What things have you been doing (or not doing) to achieve this goal? Make a list.

STEP 2 Interview your partner about his or her recent goal chosen from Step 1. Find out as much information as you can. Record your interview.

STEP 3 Listen to the recording of your interview in Step 2. Write down all the sentences that use the present perfect progressive. In each case, was it used correctly? Were there any cases where the present progressive could have been used but wasn't?

ACTIVITY 6 research on the web

Go on the Internet and use a search engine such as Google® or Yahoo® to research some news stories about what people have been doing recently. Look at an online newspaper or an online magazine and do another search there. For example, you could choose a local or favorite sports team, a celebrity, or a politician. Choose one story and explain what people have been doing and why. Give a summary to your class.

ACTIVITY 7 reflection

Make a list of five things that you have been doing recently to improve your English and five things you have not been doing.

UNIT 16

MAKING OFFERS WITH *WOULD YOU LIKE*

UNIT GOALS

- Make offers with *would you like*
- Choose correctly between *would you like* and *do you want*
- Use correct forms when accepting and refusing offers

OPENING TASK

At the Hotel Reception

STEP 1

Look at the picture. What do you think the hotel receptionist is saying to the guest?

STEP 2

Work in pairs. Chose your role as Student A or Student B. After each problem, switch roles as guest or receptionist. *Do not look at your partner's problems.* Student A look below. Student B turn to page 244.

Student A: You are a hotel guest. You have lost your voice, but you have some urgent problems. (See "Student A's Problems" below.) Go to the hotel reception and communicate your requests to the hotel desk clerk *without speaking or writing.*

Student B: Your job is to work out what Student A needs and to offer a solution. Close your book and guess what student A needs.

STUDENT A'S PROBLEMS	STUDENT B'S OFFER (STEP 3)
1. You are thirsty.	
2. You have a headache.	
3. You are hot. Your hotel room is very stuffy. You cannot open the window.	
4. You have lost your door key.	
5. You need a taxi right away.	

STEP 3

When you have finished, check the list to see if you correctly understood each other's problems. Then think of an appropriate offer for your partner's problems using *Would you like . . . ?* Write them in your notebook. Share your responses with your class.

FOCUS 1 Offers with *Would You Like*

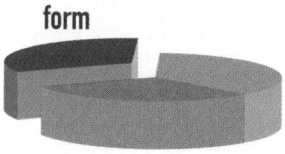

EXAMPLES	EXPLANATIONS
(a) **Would you like** some coffee? (b) **Would you like** some help? (c) **Would you like** to sit down? (d) **Would you like** to use the bathroom?	There are several ways to make offers. Use *Would you like* + noun phrase. Use *Would you like to* + verb phrase.
(e) **Would you like me to** open the window? (f) **Would you like me to** take your coat?	Use *Would you like me to* + verb phrase to make an offer about yourself.
(g) **Would you like** Sally **to** open the window? (h) **Would you like** Auntie Bev **to** help you wash your hands?	Use *Would you like* (person's name) *to* + verb phrase to make an offer about someone else.

EXERCISE 1

Think about the offers you made in the Opening Task on pages 239 and 244. Were your offers formed correctly? Change the ones that were not correct.

FOCUS 2 *Would You Like . . .?* or *Do You Want . . .?*

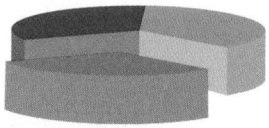

EXAMPLES	EXPLANATIONS
(a) **Would you like** a cup of tea? (b) **Do you want** a cup of tea?	Use *Would you like . . .?* if you want to be polite. Offers with *Do you want . . .?* are usually used with close friends and family. Example (a) is more polite or formal than (b).
(c) **Want** me to help you with your bags? (d) **Would you like** me to help you with your bags?	In informal situations "*Do you*" can be omitted from *Do you want . . .?* Example (c) is less formal than (d).

EXERCISE 2

Your new friend is having her first party in North America. She has invited some of her classmates, her teachers and their partners, and her neighbors: two elderly women. She has asked you to help her because she is nervous and does not know English very well. Change her commands and questions into polite offers, using *Would you like . . .* ? or *Do you want . . .* ?

	Make an offer to . . .
1. Come in.	everyone
2. Sit down.	the neighbors
3. Give me your coat.	the teachers and their partners
4. Want a chair?	the classmates
5. Want something to drink?	everyone
6. Cream in your coffee?	the classmates
7. Want the window open?	the teachers and their partners
8. Give me your cup. I'll get more coffee.	the neighbors

EXERCISE 3

Choose an item from the list below, but don't tell your partner which one. Try to get your partner to make an offer by hinting that you need him or her to help you. Continue by switching roles until you have practiced all the items in the list.

Example: **Student A:** Oh no! I left my dictionary at home and I need it for today's test.
Student B: Would you like to borrow my dictionary?
Student A: Thank you!

1. borrow a book
2. eat something
3. drink something
4. drive to the train station
5. use a cell phone
6. close the window
7. help me study
8. carry some boxes
9. _____ (make up your own offer)

FOCUS 3 Accepting and Refusing Offers

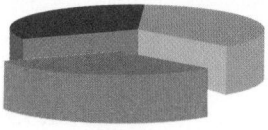

EXAMPLES	EXPLANATIONS
	ACCEPTING OFFERS
(a) A: Would you like something to drink? B: **Yes, please.**	Use *please* along with *yes* to politely accept offers.
(b) A: Would you like me to help you? B: Yes, please. **That's very kind of you.**	To be very polite, use an extra phrase to show that you appreciate the offer. (This is not usually necessary in informal situations.)
(c) A: Do you want the rest of my hamburger? B: **Sure. Thanks.**	In informal situations, words such as *sure, yeah,* and *thanks* show that you accept the offer.
(d) A: Would you like some coffee? B: **No, thank you.** OR **No, thanks.**	**REFUSING OFFERS** Use *thank you/thanks* with *no* to politely refuse offers.
(e) A: Would you like some coffee? B: No, thank you. **I've had enough.**	For polite refusals, you can tell why the offer cannot be accepted.
(f) A: Would you like me to help you? B: No, thanks. **That's nice of you, but I can manage.**	

EXERCISE 4

Match the offers with the appropriate responses. Where do you think each offer and response was made? Are they polite, or not very polite?

1. ___ Would you like to go to a movie?
2. ___ Another slice of pie?
3. ___ Would you like me to get you some more coffee?
4. ___ Do you want to have lunch together?
5. ___ Want some help with your homework?
6. ___ Would you like me to open the door for you?

a. Yes, please. It's delicious!
b. Thank you, but I can manage.
c. No, thanks. I have to go home early tonight.
d. That's very kind of you. Do you have time?
e. Sure. Here's my mug.
f. Good idea! When is your lunch break?

EXERCISE 5

Look at the following responses. What offer was probably made? Write it down in the blank.

1. **Offer:** _____
   Response: No, thanks. I've had enough.
2. **Offer:** _____
   Response: Yeah, sure. I haven't eaten a thing all day.
3. **Offer:** _____
   Response: Oh, no, thank you. I've seen it already.
4. **Offer:** _____
   Response: No, thanks. I'm warm enough.
5. **Offer:** _____
   Response: Yeah, it's really heavy. Thanks.
6. **Offer:** _____
   Response: Thanks, I'd love to. That sounds great.
7. **Offer:** _____
   Response: Thanks, but I've already got one of my own.

EXERCISE 6

For each of the following situations, write a short dialogue in which one person makes a polite offer (using *Would you like . . .*) and the other person either politely accepts or politely refuses the offer. Then find a partner and read your dialogues aloud, taking parts.

1. The English instructor, at the front of the classroom, is ready to show a video in class today. The switch to turn on the video player is right by Stefan, at the back of the room.
   Stefan says: _____?
   The instructor says: _____.
2. The dinner at Mrs. Zimunga's house is almost finished. Mrs. Zimunga notices that some of the guests ate their dessert—cherry pie—very quickly, and she thinks they might want another piece.
   Mrs. Zimunga says: _____.
   A guest says: _____.
3. Alfredo has a seat at the front of the city bus. He notices that an elderly woman has just gotten on, but there are no more seats left.
   Alfredo says: _____?
   The elderly woman says: _____.

4. As Mary is about to leave for the post office, she sees that there are several envelopes on the desk, stamped and addressed by her roommate Judith.

   Mary says: _____?

   Judith says: _____.

5. Just as Thomas starts to drive away to work, he sees that his neighbor Rob is walking down the sidewalk to the bus stop. Thomas knows that Rob's office is not far from where he works.

   Thomas says: _____?

   Rob says: _____.

6. Nyaradzo is jogging in the park, and she is about to cross a road. A stranger is waiting in his car, and he offers her a ride.

   The stranger says: _____?

   Nyaradzo says: _____.

It's not always necessary to refuse offers **politely!** Check with your classmates to see their answers for Nyaradzo's response in item 6.

Opening Task (continued from page 239)

STEP 2:

Student B: Your job is first to work out what Student A needs and to offer a solution. After that **you** become a hotel guest. You have lost your voice, but you have some urgent problems. (Look at "Student B's Problems" below.) Go to the hotel reception and communicate your requests to the hotel desk clerk (Student A) *without speaking or writing.*

STUDENT B'S PROBLEMS	STUDENT A'S OFFER (STEP 3)
1. There is no hot water in your bathroom.	
2. The light bulb is broken in your reading lamp.	
3. Your hotel room is very cold. You need an extra blanket.	
4. You are hungry. You would like some sandwiches sent to your room.	
5. You have a high fever. You need a doctor right away.	

Use Your English

ACTIVITY 1 speaking/listening

How do native speakers of English behave at parties? Is their behavior at formal parties different from their behavior at informal parties where the guests are all close friends or relatives?

Use the chart below to interview native speakers (or people who have spent a long time in an English-speaking country). There are blanks at the bottom for other topics you might want to find out about. Record your interview if possible.

WHAT DOES THE HOST DO OR SAY WHEN HE OR SHE . . .	FORMAL PARTIES	INFORMAL PARTIES
(a) invites the guests to sit down		
(b) offers the guests something to eat		
(c) encourages the guests to eat/drink more		
(d) invites the guests to start some activity (dancing/playing a game)		
(e)		
(f)		

ACTIVITY 2 writing

Your friend is coming to visit you this weekend. Write a short letter offering to meet him or her at the train station, and asking what activities he or she would like to do. Exchange your letter with a partner. Write a reply, accepting or refusing each offer politely. Exchange letters again. Were you polite enough?

ACTIVITY 3 listening/writing

CD Track 23

STEP 1 Listen to the audio of two people talking about giving parties. Divide a page in your notebook into two columns. Write some of the problems the man talks about in the first column below. Write the suggestions the woman makes about each problem in the second column.

STEP 2 Discuss the problems and suggestions with a partner. How did the man respond to the woman's suggestions?

STEP 3 Listen again once or twice. This time write down the exact words the woman suggested using for the three problems you listed in Step 1.

STEP 4 What might the people at the party say in response to each of these suggestions? Write down three sentences in your notebook.

STEP 5 Write three sentences they might use to refuse the offers.

ACTIVITY 4 speaking/listening

STEP 1 How can your classmate help you?
Think of two things that a classmate could do for you that would be helpful. Take two pieces of paper and write down one of those things on each piece. Do not write down your name.

Your teacher will collect the papers.

STEP 2 Your teacher will mix up the papers and give you two papers that other students wrote. (Make sure that you don't get your own!) Your job now is to guess who wrote each request for help. Go around the room to find the person. Make an offer to help each student you talk to using Would you like . . . ? or Do you want . . . ?

STEP 3 You must accept an offer if it is about the help you requested (the thing you wrote down on your piece of paper). You must refuse all other offers for help, even if they sound good.

ACTIVITY 5 speaking/writing

STEP 1 A good friend is at home in bed sick. You want to help out and make your friend feel better. Make a list of five things in your notebook that you might do to help. Then get together with a partner who will play the role of your friend. Make offers using Would you like . . .? and Do you want . . .? Your "friend" can accept or refuse your offers.

STEP 2 Copy the chart below in your notebook. Write down responses to the offers you made in Step 1. If your friend accepts your offer, the response will go in the Accept column. If your friend refuses your offer, the response will go in the Refuse column. For each column, rank these responses in order of politeness. (Which responses seemed most polite? Which seemed least polite?)

OFFER	RESPONSE TO YOUR OFFERS	
	Accept	Refuse

ACTIVITY 6 research on the web

Have you ever been annoyed by an email message? What kind of message was it? Why did you feel annoyed? Although email seems a fast and easy mode of communication, it also has rules of politeness which emailers have to learn. Find out about email etiquette by going to *InfoTrac® College Edition* and searching with keywords "email etiquette". Make notes of different types of advice that could make your emails more polite. Share them with your classmates.

ACTIVITY 7 reflection

Think of a situation where you offered to do something for someone. What was the person's response? Did you get the response you expected? Explain the situation to your partner and compare his or her response. Would you both have done the same thing in that situation?

Switch roles and listen to your partner's situation. Compare your offers to do something and the responses.

UNIT 17

REQUESTS AND PERMISSION

Can, Could, Will, Would, and *May*

UNIT GOALS

- Make polite requests
- Politely agree to and refuse requests
- Ask for permission
- Give or politely refuse permission

OPENING TASK

Babysitting

STEP 1

Your neighbors are going out for the evening and they ask you to babysit their two children, aged 4 and 7 years old. They have a list of things for you to remember. What kinds of things do you think you will have to do? Work with a partner and make a list.

STEP 2

Your neighbors have left you a note with instructions about what to do while they are gone. Unfortunately, their 4-year-old daughter drew all over the note after her parents left and you can't read all of it. Work with a partner and try to complete the missing parts of the note on the next page. The first one has been done for you.

We're so glad you're here to watch the kids while we're gone.

Here are some tips to help you.

C Will you please

1. [illegible] put them to bed by 8pm?

2. If they are hungry, [illegible]

3. [illegible] y brush their teeth before they go to bed?

4. They sometimes have trouble falling asleep, so would you mind [illegible]

5. If there are any phone calls, [illegible]

6. My cell phone is 356-555-5644. Please phone me if [illegible]

STEP 3

Now look at the choices for the missing parts of the note above. Write the appropriate letter in the spaces on the note. Were your "answers" to the missing parts similar to these?

a. . . . could you make them some toast—but no candy!

b. . . . there is an emergency.

~~c. Will you please~~ . . .

d. . . . reading them a story before they go to sleep?

e. Please could you make sure they . . .

f. . . . would you take a message and say we'll call back tomorrow?

FOCUS 1 Making Polite Requests

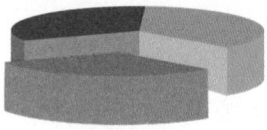

EXAMPLES	EXPLANATIONS
I left my notes at home. (a) **Would you mind** lending me your notes? (b) **Would** you **(please)** lend me your notes? (c) **Could** you lend me your notes **(please)**? (d) Will you lend me your notes **(please)**? (e) **Can** you **(please)** lend me your notes? (f) **Please** lend me your notes.	Most polite ↕ Least polite The degree of politeness depends on who you are talking to and the type of request you are making.

EXERCISE 1

Below are some situations in a supermarket. For each situation, make a polite request.

1. You want to know what time it is. You see another customer who is wearing a watch and you say: _____

   _____

2. You want to buy some tomato sauce but you cannot find the right aisle. You see a store assistant and you say: _____

   _____

3. You want to get a box of tissues from the top shelf, but you are not tall enough to reach it. You see another customer nearby and you say: _____

   _____

4. You cannot read the ingredients on a jar of jelly because you forgot your glasses. You find a store assistant and you say: _____

   _____

5. You are shopping with a friend but when you get to the checkout line, you suddenly remember that you forgot to get some milk. You turn to your friend and say: _____

   _____

6. When you are paying for your groceries, you remember that you need some change for the parking meter. You hand the cashier a dollar and say: _____

   _____

7. After paying for your groceries, you think there is a mistake on your bill. You go to the store manager and say: _____

   _____

FOCUS 2 Politely Refusing Requests

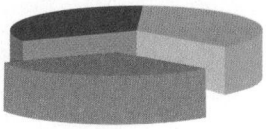

EXAMPLES	EXPLANATIONS
Can you lend me your notes? (a) **I'm sorry,** but I need them to study for the test. OR (b) **I'm afraid that** I didn't take any notes. OR (c) **I'd like to,** but I left mine at home, too.	If you have to refuse a request, it is polite to say **why** you are refusing. Phrases such as *I'm afraid that* or *I'm sorry* help to "soften" the *No*, and make it more polite.

EXERCISE 2

Walk around the classroom and ask a few classmates for the following things. If a classmate says *no*, write down the reason for refusing your request. Remember to write your classmates' names (or initials) in order to remember who you asked.

REQUEST	REASON FOR SAYING NO
1. lend you some money	
2. buy you a cup of coffee	
3. help you study for a test	
4. lend you a cell phone	
5. give you a ride home after class	
6. teach you how to dance	

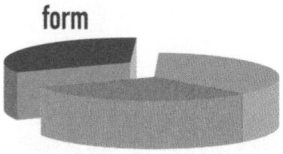

FOCUS 3 Responding to Requests

EXAMPLES	EXPLANATIONS
Can you lend me your notes? (a) I'd be glad to. (b) Sure, why not? (c) Yeah, no problem. (d) Yeah, I guess so.	You can respond to requests with short answers. Examples (b) and (c) are very informal. Example (d) shows that the speaker is uncertain.
Could you loan me five dollars? (e) Yes, I can. (f) NOT: Yes, I could.	*Could* and *would* are **not** used in responses to requests.
Would you go to the store with me? (g) Yes, I will. (h) NOT: Yes, I would.	

EXERCISE 3

Make polite requests for the following situations. Use *can, could, will, would*, or *would you mind* in these requests.

What is the response? How is the request politely accepted or refused?

1. You are carrying a large pile of books and aren't able to open the classroom door. You ask another student to open it.

You say: _____?

What does the student say? _____.

2. You are at a restaurant, and the people at the next table are talking loudly on a cell phone.

   You want them to stop, so you say: _____?

   What do they say? _____.

3. Your friend is helping you hang a picture on your wall. She is holding it up while you decide where it should go.

   You say: _____?

   What does your friend do or say? _____.

4. You are visiting a famous tourist spot, and a couple wants you to take their photograph together.

   One person of the couple says: _____

   _____

   What do you do or say? _____

   _____

5. You are trying to study for a test, and your neighbors are playing very loud music.

   You can't concentrate, so you say, _____?

   What do your neighbors do or say? _____.

EXERCISE 4

Below are some questions you might ask in the classroom. Copy the question in the appropriate box in the chart below. The first one has been done for you.

SOMETHING THE SPEAKER WANTS TO DO (REQUEST FOR PERMISSION)	SOMETHING THE SPEAKER WANTS SOMEBODY ELSE TO DO (GENERAL REQUEST)
1. Do you mind if I turn on the lights?	

1. Do you mind if I turn on the lights?
2. Can you open the window?
3. May I ask you a question?
4. Could you speak more slowly?
5. Would you mind lending me your dictionary?
6. Can I speak to you about the assignment?
7. Would you tell me the answer?
8. May we leave class early today?
9. Could you show us how to find the answers?
10. Could I borrow your textbook?
11. Would you mind if I handed in my assignment a day late?
12. Will you help me with my homework?

FOCUS 4 Asking for Permission

(a) **Would you mind** if I left early?
(b) **Do you mind** if I leave early?
(c) **May** I leave early?
(d) **Could** I leave early?
(e) **Can** I leave early?

Most polite
↕
Least polite

EXERCISE 5

For each answer, what was probably the question?

1. Question: _____?

   Teacher to student: No, I'd like you to hand it in on Friday. I announced the due date two weeks ago, so I'm afraid I won't be able to make any exceptions.

2. Question: _____?

   Friend to friend: Sure, it is a little cold in here.

3. Question: _____?

   Lecturer to member of the audience: Sorry, but I'm going to have to ask you to hold your questions until the end of my talk. We'll have fifteen minutes for questions.

4. Question: _____?

   Secretary (on phone): Yes, may I tell him who's calling?

5. Question: _____?

   Twelve-year-old child (on phone): Yes, hold on and I'll go and get him.

6. Question: _____?

   Mother (to child): OK, you can have one more. But only *one*, because we're going to eat soon, and I don't want you to spoil your appetite.

7. Question: _____?

   Hostess to guest: Oh, of course, please help yourself. I'm glad you like them.

8. Question: _____?

   Customer to salesperson: Yes, I want to look at the sweaters that are on sale—the ones that were advertised in the newspaper?

FOCUS 5 Responding to Requests for Permission

EXAMPLES	EXPLANATIONS
Would you mind if I left early? (a) No, not at all. (b) Sorry, but I need you to stay until 5:00.	Use short phrases to answer requests for permission. If you refuse a request, it is polite to give the reason.
May I leave early? (c) Yes, of course. (d) Sorry, but I'd rather have you stay until 5:00.	
Could I leave early? (e) Yes, you can. (f) NOT: Yes, you could.	*Could* is not usually used in responses to requests for permission.

EXERCISE 6

For each of the following situations, work with a classmate to make general requests or requests for permission, and then respond to these requests. Decide how polite you need to be in each situation and whether *can, could, will, would, may, would you mind*, or *do you mind* is the most appropriate to use. Use a variety of different possible responses.

1. You are at a friend's house, and you want to use the phone.
2. Your teacher says something, but you do not understand, and you want her to repeat it.
3. Your friend has asked you to pick her up at the airport. You want to know if her flight, #255 from Denver, is on time, so you call the airline.
4. You want to borrow your roommate's car.
5. Your roommate is going to the store, and you remember that you need some aspirin.
6. You are the first one to finish the reading test in class. You want to find out from your teacher if you are allowed to leave the room now.
7. It is very cold in class, and the window is open.
8. You see that your teacher is in her office with the door partly open. You want to go in to talk to her.
9. You are on the phone with the dentist's secretary because you want to change your appointment time.
10. You are at a close friend's house, and you would like a cup of tea.

Use Your English

ACTIVITY 1 listening/speaking

STEP 1 Go to a restaurant or cafeteria and pay attention to the different kinds of requests that are used. Try to observe five different requests. Take notes on these, using the chart below.

OBSERVATION SHEET		
PLACE:		
TIME:		
DAY:		
REQUEST:	WHO MADE IT:	RESPONSE:

STEP 2 Discuss the results of your observations with other classmates. Were their observations similar? What words were used most often in requests: *can, could, will, would*, or *would you mind?*

ACTIVITY 2 speaking

Play this game in a group of five or six students or with the whole class.

- **STEP 1** Pick a letter from the alphabet. Ask a classmate to buy you something at the mall that begins with that letter.
- **STEP 2** Your classmate must think of something to buy that begins with the letter you chose and then he or she must tell you what it is.
- **STEP 3** Your classmate then chooses another student.

Examples: Sara: *Bruno, would you please buy me something that begins with the letter S?*

Bruno: *Sure. I'll buy you sneakers. Sue, could you buy me something that begins with the letter M?*

Sue: *Ok. I'll buy you a magazine. Hartmut, would you mind buying me something that begins with the letter P?*

ACTIVITY 3 listening

How do people request permission to speak with someone on the telephone? Are these ways different depending on the situation?

Interview people about what they say in different situations. Some examples are: speaking with a doctor, speaking with a teacher, speaking with a close friend, and speaking with a family member.

SETTING	RELATIONSHIP	WHAT THEY SAY

ACTIVITY 4 writing

Congratulations! You have just won a certificate for Easy-Does-It Housecleaning Services. This entitles you to four hours of housecleaning service for your home. First make a list of what you want the housecleaner to do in your home (clean the windows, do the laundry, mop the floor, etc.). Then write these requests in a polite note to your housecleaner.

ACTIVITY 5 reading/speaking

STEP 1

What would you say in each of the following situations? Respond to each situation. Then compare your results with other students' results.

1. You are in the bookstore with a friend, standing in line to buy a textbook you need for class later that day. You realize you have left your wallet at home and you want your friend to lend you twenty dollars to pay for the book.

   You: _____

   _____

   Your friend: Sure. You can pay me back next week.

2. You have just heard about a new job and you feel that you are qualified. You need to ask your teacher for a letter of recommendation.

   You: _____

   _____

   Your teacher: I'd be happy to. When do you need it?

3. You are visiting a close friend at her house. You realize you are thirsty, but your friend hasn't offered you anything to drink.

   You: _____

   _____

   Your friend: Sure. Help yourself. You know where everything is, right?

4. You just made plans to study for a big test with your classmates, but suddenly you realize that you have a doctor's appointment at the same time—at 2:00 tomorrow. You decide that you want to change your doctor's appointment, so you call the doctor's secretary.

   You: _____

   _____

   The secretary: I *think* it's possible. When would you be available?

5. It's time to leave the house to meet your friend for a dinner date. But you can't find your car keys anywhere, and your friend has already left her house to meet you. You want to borrow your roommate's car and look for your car keys later.

   You: _____

   _____

   Your roommate: Yeah, no problem.

6. You are visiting a close friend's mother. She has made peach pie, and you'd love to have a second piece. Your friend has told you that her mother loves to feed people, so you know that it wouldn't be rude to ask for another piece.

   You: _____

   _____

   Your friend's mother: Oh, of course! Let me get it for you.

STEP 2

Ask at least three different people to respond to each situation. Record their answers.

ACTIVITY 6 listening/writing

CD Track 24

Now listen to the audio to hear what other speakers said in response to questions 1, 2, and 6 in Activity 5.

STEP 1

Compare the responses of the speakers on the audio with your responses in Activity 5, and also to the responses of the speakers you interviewed. Were you surprised at anything they said? Do you consider these polite responses? Do you think any of their requests would be refused?

STEP 2

For each situation, write down the exact requests that Agnes or Eliza made (if there were any). Then rate each request in terms of politeness on a 1 to 5 scale (1 = most polite; 5 = least polite/most informal). Are there any requests that are "off the scale" (not at all polite, or even rude)? Compare your ratings to other classmates' ratings, and discuss your results.

ACTIVITY 7 research on the web

Go on the Internet and use a search engine such as Google® or Yahoo® to find a site that can help you with writing a request letter. Type in keywords: "Writing a request letter". Use the information to write your own request letter.

ACTIVITY 8 reflection

Think of three ways your classmates could help you to improve your study skills. Write three requests to ask for help.

Example: *Could you show me how to organize my notes?*

In small groups, share your three requests and discuss the answers. What were the best ideas? Which ones can you use?

UNIT 18

USED TO WITH *STILL* AND *ANYMORE*

UNIT GOALS

- Use *used to* to compare past and present situations
- Form statements and questions with *used to*
- Use *still* and *anymore* correctly

OPENING TASK

Famous People Then and Now

STEP 1

Work with several other students. Look at the photographs of these movie stars. Which ones do you know? What kind of movies do you think they are in?

1.

2.

3.

4.

5.

6.

STEP 2

Look below at the photographs of the same people before they were famous. Match the old photographs with the current ones. Write the number and name next to each photo below.

a. _____ c. _____ e. _____

b. _____ d. _____ f. _____

STEP 3

In your opinion, who has changed a lot? Who hasn't changed much? Explain why you think so.

Example: I think Brad Pitt has changed a lot.
Why?
Because he used to _____ but
now he _____.

meaning

FOCUS 1 Comparing Past and Present with *Used To*

EXAMPLES	EXPLANATIONS
(a) Julia Roberts **used to** have curly hair (but now she doesn't).	***Used to*** can be used to show that something was true in the past, but now it isn't.
(b) Arnold Schwarzenegger **used to** make movies (but now he doesn't).	***Used to*** can also show that something happened regularly (often) in the past, but now it doesn't.

EXERCISE 1

Make statements with *used to* about Jennifer Lopez and Brad Pitt. Use the words in parentheses. You can add other ideas of your own.

1. Jennifer Lopez

   a. (live in New York City / Long Island) She used to live in New York but now she lives in Long Island.

   b. (have dark hair / light brown hair) _____

   c. (be on TV / make movies) _____

2. Brad Pitt

   a. (have long hair / short hair) _____

   b. (live in Missouri / Hollywood) _____

   c. (drive limousines / is a movie star) _____

Now make statements with *used to* about the other people in the Opening Task.

FOCUS 2 *Used To*

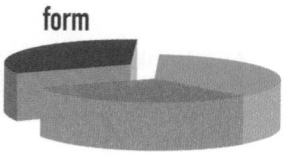

STATEMENT	NEGATIVE	QUESTION
I / You / We / They **used to** work.	I / You / We / They did not **use to** work. (didn't)	**Did** I / You / We / They **use to** work?
She / He / It **used to** work.	She / He / It did not **use to** work. (didn't)	**Did** She / He / It **use to** work?

FOCUS 3 *Anymore*

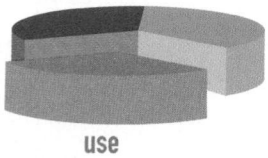

EXAMPLES	EXPLANATIONS
(a) Jennifer Lopez used to live in New York, but she doesn't live there **anymore.**	Use *anymore* to show a change in a situation or activity.
(b) Jennifer Lopez used to live in New York, but she doesn't **anymore.**	If the second verb phrase has the same verb, you can omit it.
(c) Jennifer Lopez doesn't live in New York **anymore.**	You can use *anymore* without *used to*. In (c) we understand that she used to live there.
(d) We **don't** go there anymore. (e) They **never** talk to me anymore. (f) **No one** likes him anymore. (g) Does he live there **anymore**?	Use *anymore* only with a negative statement or question.

EXERCISE 2

Interview your classmates about the changes in their lives. Then write short statements about these changes, using *anymore* and *used to*. (The word *but* may be helpful.)

Example: *Teresita used to live in Guam, but she doesn't anymore. She used to be single, but now she lives with a partner.*

FOCUS 4 *Still*

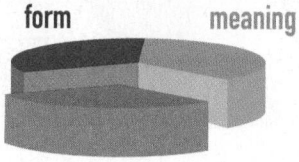

EXAMPLES	EXPLANATIONS
(a) She **still** lives in New Mexico. (She lived in New Mexico fifteen years ago; she lives there now.)	Use *still* to show that something or someone has NOT changed.
(b) He **still** runs five miles a day. (He ran five miles a day in the past; he runs five miles a day now.)	Use *still* to show that an activity or habit has NOT changed.
(c) He **still** lives in New Orleans.	Use *still* before the main verb.
(d) He is **still** crazy after all these years.	Use *still* after the verb *be*.
(e) She can **still** play the piano.	Use *still* after an auxiliary verb such as *can, may, should,* etc.

EXERCISE 3

Write statements using *still* about the people in the Opening Task on page 262 who have not changed very much. The following items will get you started, but you can add ideas of your own. Work with your classmates if you need more information.

1. Julia Roberts (very slim) _____.
2. Morgan Freeman (a beard) _____.
3. Jennifer Lopez (long hair) _____.
4. Arnold Schwarzenegger (very strong) _____.
5. Nicole Kidman (very pretty) _____.
6. Brad Pitt (handsome) _____.

EXERCISE 4

Look at the two descriptions of Jack in the past and in the present. Describe how his life has changed. Use *used to, still,* and *anymore.*

1996

- lived in Canada
- worked for a newspaper in Toronto
- went swimming every day
- weighed 190 pounds
- was single

2006

- lives in the United States
- works for a newspaper in Washington, DC
- goes running every day
- weighs 190 pounds
- is married

EXERCISE 5

Look at the maps of the island of Madalia. Work with a partner and use the information from the maps to complete the report below. Use *used to, didn't use to, still,* and *anymore* as appropriate. Use the verbs in parentheses. The first one has been done for you as an example.

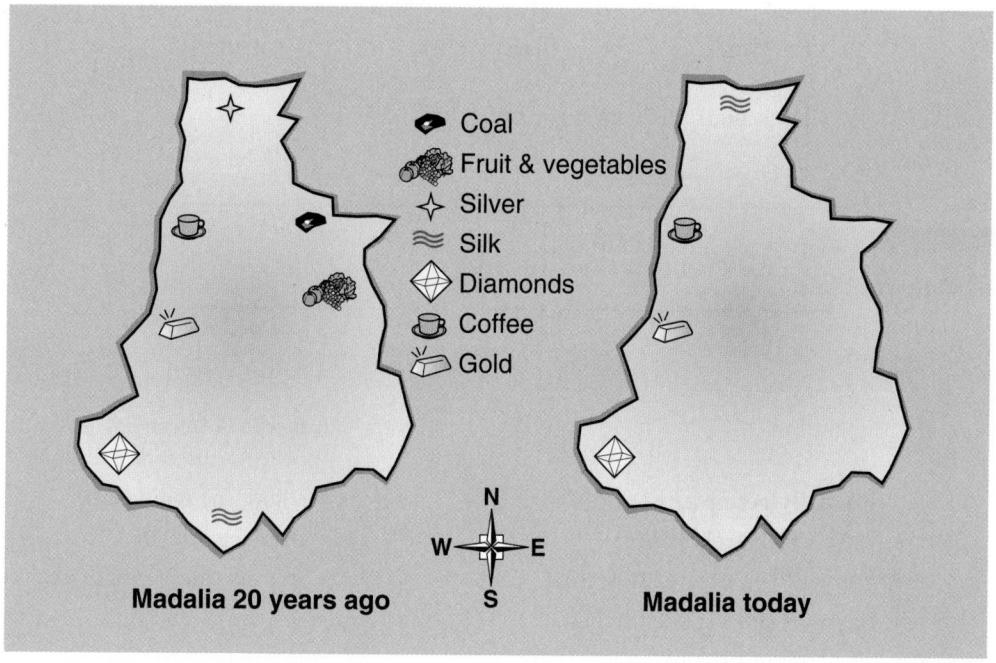

Madalia is a small country that is rich in natural resources, and Madalians have exploited those resources for many years. However, it is possible to note some changes in those resources in the last twenty years. For example, twenty years ago, Madalians (1) used to mine (mine) coal in the northeast. In addition, they (2) _____ (grow) _____ in the east. Also, they (3) _____, but today, they (4) _____ (not + mine) it _____. Furthermore, in the past, they (5) _____ (not + produce) _____ in the north; they (6) _____ (produce) it in the _____.

On the other hand, some things have not changed. They (7) _____ (mine) _____ in the southwest, and they (8) _____ (grow) _____ in the northwest. Finally, they (9) _____ (mine) _____ in the west.

EXERCISE 6

The words below tell how often something happens. Arrange these words in a list with **most frequent** at the top and **least frequent** at the bottom. Add any other similar words you can think of and put them in the appropriate place on the list.

often	always	never	seldom
sometimes	hardly ever	usually	rarely

Check your answers with Unit 1, Focus 3.

FOCUS 5 Adverbs of Frequency

EXAMPLES	EXPLANATIONS
	Adverbs of frequency (***always,*** etc.) can appear in different positions in a sentence:
(a) I **usually** get up at 6:00 A.M.	• before the main verb.
(b) They were **rarely** happy.	• after the verb ***be.***
(c) You will **sometimes** hear from them.	• after auxiliary verbs (***will, can, have,*** etc.).
(d) I have **seldom** spoken to her.	
(e) They **never** used to dance.	• before used to.
(f) He **always** used to call her.	
(g) **Sometimes** I go to bed at 9:00 P.M.	*Sometimes* can appear at the beginning or at the end of a sentence.

EXERCISE 7

Write a short article for your old high school magazine, reporting on your life and habits and how they have changed (or not) over the years since you left high school. Also describe your present life and habits and compare them with your past.

Try to include the following:

- something you used to do but don't do anymore
- something you used to do and still do
- something you didn't use to do but do now
- something you never, sometimes, often, or usually do

Don't forget to include changes (or not) in your physical appearance. We have begun the article for you:

I left high school in _____ (year). As I look back on my life since then, I realize that some things have changed, and some things have stayed the same. Let me start by telling you about some of the changes . . .

Use Your English

ACTIVITY 1 writing

STEP 1 If possible, find an old photograph of yourself (as a baby, a child, or one taken several years ago). If you cannot find a photograph, draw a picture. Attach the photo or picture to a large piece of paper and write several statements about yourself, showing things you used to do and don't do now, things you didn't use to do, and things you still do. Do not write your name on the paper. Your teacher will display all the pictures and descriptions.

STEP 2 Work with a classmate and try to guess the identity of each person. Who in the class has changed the most and who has changed the least?

ACTIVITY 2 writing

Think of a place you know well—the place where you were born or where you grew up. Write about the ways it has changed and the ways it has not changed.

ACTIVITY 3 speaking/listening

STEP 1 Interview a senior citizen. Find out about changes in the world or in customs and habits during his or her lifetime. What does he or she think about these changes? Record your interview, and then report on your findings to the class.

STEP 2 Listen to the recorded interviews. Did the speakers use *used to, still,* or *anymore* when talking about changes? If not, what did they use instead?

ACTIVITY 4 listening

CD Track 25

STEP 1

Listen to the audio of two senior citizens talking about the changes during their lifetimes. In your notebook, list each change that they discuss. Count the number of changes on your list.

Compare answers with your classmates.

STEP 2

Listen to the audio recording again, and pay attention to the way the senior citizens talk about changes. Did the speakers use *used to, still,* or *anymore* when talking about changes? If not, what did they use instead? Compare your findings again with another student.

ACTIVITY 5 speaking/writing

The women's movement has helped change the lives of many women in different parts of the world. However, some people argue that things have not really changed and many things are still the same for most women. Think about women's lives and roles in your mother's generation and the lives of women today in your country. Make an oral or written report on what has changed and what has stayed the same.

ACTIVITY 6 speaking

This activity gives you the opportunity to "become" a different person. Choose a new identity for yourself: Choose a new name, age, sex, profession, habits, occupation, personality, and appearance? How does your new person differ from the "real" you?

Create a full description of this person and introduce the "new" you to the class, comparing him or her with the person you used to be.

Example: *I want to introduce the new me. I used to be a college student, but now I am a movie star. I never used to leave home, but now I often travel to distant and exotic places. I used to wear practical clothes that I bought on sale. Now I wear designer clothes and expensive jewelry. . . .*

ACTIVITY 7 speaking/listening/writing

Write a profile of one of your classmates.

STEP 1 Interview your partner and find out something that he or she . . .

1. never does
2. seldom does
3. sometimes does
4. often does
5. usually does
6. always does

STEP 2 Write a report of your interview, without using your classmate's name. Begin with an introduction: (for example) "I am going to tell you some things about one of our classmates." End your report with a question: "Can you guess who this is?"

STEP 3 Read your report out loud, or display it along with all the other reports written by your classmates. Can you identify the people described?

ACTIVITY 8 research on the web

Go on the Internet and use a search engine such as Google® or Yahoo® to find out what famous stars used to do before they were famous. Type in keywords: "before they were famous" and the star's name. Collect some interesting facts to tell your classmates.

ACTIVITY 9 reflection

Think about how your learning styles and habits have changed since you were in high school. Write three sentences about how you used to study and learn then compared to now.

UNIT 19

PAST PERFECT

Before and *After*

UNIT GOALS

- Correctly use past perfect and simple past in a single sentence
- Correctly form past perfect sentences
- Understand the meanings of *before, after, by the time,* and *by*
- Use past perfect and the present perfect in the right situations

OPENING TASK

Family Changes

STEP 1

Family Tree A shows Tom's family when he left home in 1985 to travel around the world. Work with a partner to study *Family Tree A.* Note that ∞ = married.

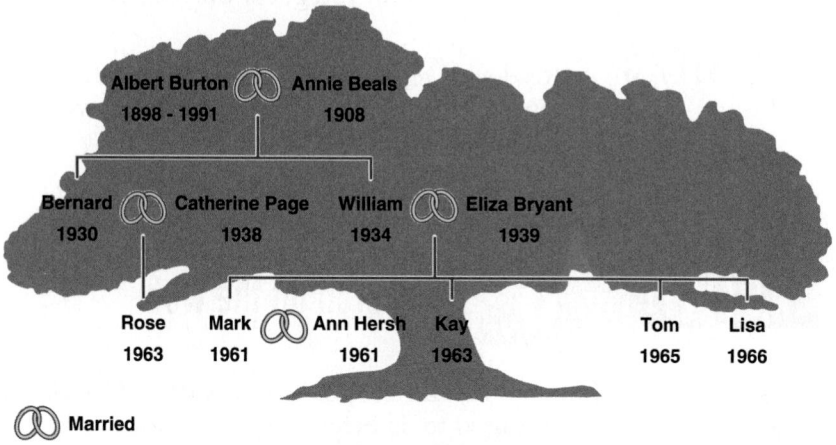

Family Tree A

STEP 2

Now look at *Family Tree B*, which shows Tom's family after he returned home from his world travels in 1993. What changes do you notice in Tom's family?

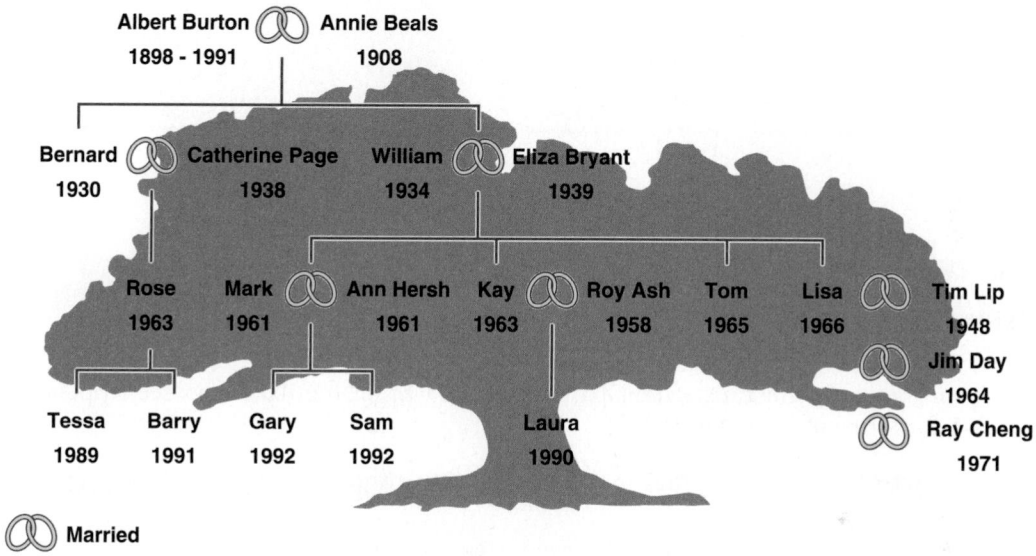

Family Tree B

STEP 3

Make at least five statements about changes that had taken place when Tom returned from his travels. Start these statements with:

When Tom returned, ...

OR *Tom returned after. . . .*

OR *By the time Tom returned, ...*

FOCUS 1 Past Perfect and Simple Past

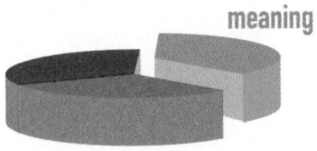

EXAMPLE	EXPLANATIONS
When I got there, he **had eaten** all the cookies. 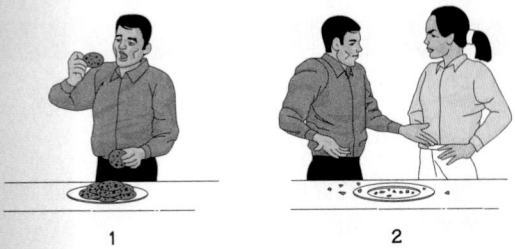 1 2 **First,** he ate the cookies; **then,** I got there. (I didn't see him eat the cookies.)	When two events both happened in the past: • use the past perfect for the first (earliest) event. • use the simple past for the second (most recent) event.

FOCUS 2 Past Perfect

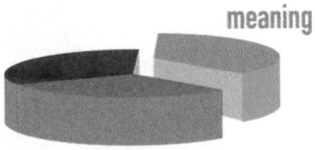

To form the past perfect, use *had* + past participle (*-ed* for regular verbs; see Appendix 5, p. A-5 for forms of irregular verbs).

STATEMENT	NEGATIVE	QUESTION	SHORT ANSWER
I / You / We / They **had** arrived. ('d)	I / You / We / They **had not** arrived. **(hadn't)**	**Had** I / you / we / they arrived?	Yes we **had.**
She / He / It **had** arrived. ('d)	She / He / It **had not** arrived. **(hadn't)**	**Had** he / she / it arrived?	No, she **had not** **(hadn't).**

EXERCISE 1

Look at the family trees in the Opening Task on page 272–273 to complete the statements. If there is a verb in parentheses, use it; otherwise, use any appropriate verb. The first one has been done for you.

1. When he returned home, Tom found that his grandfather (die) ___had died___.
2. When Tom returned, he learned that his cousin _____.
3. Tom arrived home to find that his sister Lisa _____.
4. When _____, his sister Kay _____; in addition, she and her husband _____.
5. On his return home, Tom found that his brother and sister-in law _____.
6. Tom learned that his grandmother had experienced both sorrow and joy. On the one hand, she (lose) _____, but on the other hand, she (gain) _____.
7. Sam and Gary have never met their grandfather, because he _____ before they _____.
8. By the time Tom got back home, his parents and his aunt and uncle (become) _____.
9. Tom also found that Rose _____ children, but she (not) _____. Lisa, on the other hand, _____ three times, but she (not) _____ any children.

EXERCISE 2

In the following pairs of statements, decide which event probably happened first. Write 1 beside the event you think happened first and 2 beside the one you think happened second. Then combine the statements to make one sentence using because. The first one has been done for you.

Example: My legs ached. 2
I played tennis. 1
My legs ached because I had played tennis.

1. His car broke down.
   He took the bus.

   _____

2. Charlotte was depressed.
   She failed her English exam.

   _____

3. Tanya sat in the sun all afternoon.
   Her skin was very red.

   _____

4. We didn't eat all day.
   We were really hungry.

   _____

5. Brenda's clothes were too tight.
   She didn't exercise for several months.

   _____

6. Neville couldn't sleep.
   He drank several cups of very strong coffee.

   _____

7. We studied hard for three weeks.
   We thought the test was easy.

   _____

8. I felt very tired yesterday morning.
   I didn't sleep well.

   _____

FOCUS 3 *Before, After, By the Time, By*

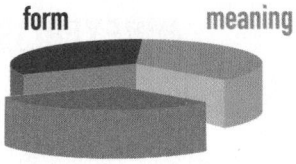

EXAMPLES		EXPLANATIONS
First Event	*Second Event*	
(a) She had left	**before** I arrived.	*Before, after,* and *by the time* show the order of events.
(b) She had left	**by the time** I arrived.	
(c) **After** she had left,	I arrived.	You can use the past perfect with *before* and *after,* but it is not necessary. You must use the past perfect in sentences with *by the time.*
(d) She left	**before** I arrived.	
(e) **After** she left,	I arrived.	
(f) He had finished all his shopping	**by** Christmas.	*By* + a noun phrase can also show order of events.
(g) **After** I had left,	he arrived.	**Punctuation note:** Use a comma after a clause with *before* or *after* if the clause comes first.

EXERCISE 3

Look at the following sentences; each one uses the past perfect. First, underline the event that happens first. Then check (✓) the sentences where it is **necessary** to use the past perfect to show the order of events.

1. Cathy went to her high school reunion ten years after she had graduated.
2. She had checked the map carefully before she started her journey.
3. She lost her way because so many things in her hometown had changed.
4. By the time she arrived, the party had almost finished.
5. Many of her old school friends had left before she got there.
6. She didn't recognize some of her friends because they had changed so much.
7. After she had talked to them for a while about the old days, she started to feel quite sad.
8. By the time she got home, she had decided not to go to any more high school reunions.

EXERCISE 4

Rewrite the following sentences in your notebook. Omit the underlined words and use the word in parentheses. Use the past perfect where necessary.

Example: First, Sue saw some photos of her grandmother's village, and then she decided to visit Italy. (after)
After Sue saw/had seen some photos of her grandmother's village, she decided to visit Italy.

1. Sue did some research on the Internet, and then she planned her trip. (after)
2. She bought an airline ticket, and then she booked a hotel in Palermo. (after)
3. She bought a guidebook and a map, and next she packed her bags. (before)
4. She arrived in Palermo, and next she called her mother's school friend. (after)
5. She walked around the city, and then she met her mother's friend in the main square. (before)
6. They drove to her grandmother's village, and then they visited her grandmother's old home. (after)
7. They spoke to many family members, friends, and other villagers, and then they returned to the city. (before)
8. Sue learned a lot about her grandmother's life before she got back at the end of the day. (by the time)
9. She went back to her hotel, and next she wrote some notes about her experience. (after)
10. She returned home, and six months later she wrote a successful book about her trip. (by the end of the year)

Were there any sentences where you **had to** use the past perfect?

FOCUS 4 Past Perfect versus Present Perfect

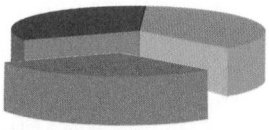

use

EXAMPLES	EXPLANATIONS
(a) She **was** tired yesterday because she **had taken** a long bike ride.	Use the past perfect to **contrast** two events in the past.
(b) She **is** tired (now) because she **has taken** a long bike ride.	Use the present perfect to **connect** the past with the present.

EXERCISE 5

Underline the mistakes in the following sentences and correct as necessary.

Example: *I wasn't tired yesterday because I ~~have~~ had slept for ten hours the night before.*

1. Nigel wasn't hungry last night because he has eaten a large sandwich for lunch.
2. Jan is really confused in class last Tuesday because she hadn't read the assignment.
3. Graham had gone home because he has a terrible headache today.
4. Howard is a lucky man because he had traveled all over the world.
5. Martha went to the hospital after she has broken a leg.
6. Before he has left the house, George locked all the doors and windows.
7. Professor Westerfield always returns our papers after she had graded them.
8. I didn't see you at the airport last night because your plane has left before I got there.
9. Matthew and James were late because they have missed the bus.

EXERCISE 6

In the story below, use the appropriate verb tense (simple past, past progressive, past perfect, present perfect) for the verbs in parentheses.

Richard (1) hasn't had (have, not) a vacation for several years. But last month he decided to go Florida for a week. He (2) _____ (drive) to the airport when he realized that he (3) _____ (forget) his passport. He immediately turned back. But when he (4) _____ (arrive) home, he found that he (5) _____ (have, not) his door keys. He (6) _____ (leave) them inside the house! He (7) _____ (climb) over the wall to get the keys that he (8) _____ (hide) under a plant pot in the backyard. But the keys (9) _____ (be, not) there because he (10) _____ (put, not) them back last time. He (11) _____ (open) the kitchen window, when a neighbor (12) _____ (see) him from her yard. "(13) _____ you _____ (lock) yourself out again?" "Yes, and I (14) _____ (leave) my passport inside!" The neighbor (15) _____ (help) Richard to get into his house. Finally, he (16) _____ (drive) back to the airport with his passport, but of course by then his plane (17) _____ (leave). Since then, Richard (18) _____ (try, not) to go on vacation again.

Use Your English

ACTIVITY 1 speaking/listening writing

The purpose of this activity is to compare different events and achievements at different times in our lives. You will need to get information from five of your classmates to complete this activity.

STEP 1

The left-hand column in the chart below shows different ages; your job is to find one interesting or surprising thing each classmate had done by the time he or she reached those ages. If you don't want to talk about your life with other students, feel free to invent things that you had done at those ages. Be ready to report on your findings. Copy this chart into your notebook so you have enough room to write.

	NAME	NAME	NAME	NAME	NAME
By the time, he or she was 5 years old . . .					
By the time he or she was 10 years old . . .					
By the time he or she was 15 years old . . .					
By the time he or she was 18 years old . . .					
By the time . . .*					
By the time . . .*					

* You choose an age.

STEP 2

Now choose the three most surprising pieces of information you found for each age. Tell the class what you found out.

ACTIVITY 2 speaking

STEP 1 Use the information from Activity 1 for a poster presentation. Take a large poster-sized sheet of paper and use this to make a poster that communicates the information you found. You can use graphics, pictures, and diagrams to make your poster interesting and eye-catching.

STEP 2 Display your poster so that your classmates can enjoy it and be ready to answer any questions they might have about it.

ACTIVITY 3 speaking/listening

STEP 1 Find out about someone's family history, preferably from someone 60 or older. You can help that person construct a family tree (as in the Opening Task), or you can use a chart like the one below to get information. Record your interview.

	BIRTHS, DEATHS, MARRIAGES, DIVORCES
1980–present	
1960–1980	
1940–1960	
1920–1940	

STEP 2 Report your findings to the class, either in a written or an oral report. (Record the report if it's done orally.) Be sure to use the past perfect and before, after, by, or by the time to contrast past events.

ACTIVITY 4 listening

Listen to the recordings of your oral reports from Activity 3 or from the actual interviews. Was the past perfect used? Were the time words *before*, *after*, *by*, or *by the time* used? Were there occasions where the past perfect or time words could have been used, but weren't?

ACTIVITY 5 speaking

Form groups of three or four students. Each student will think of a place that you visited in the past. It can be a place in your town or city, or in another country. Think of something special or interesting that happened to you there. Start the story with one sentence. Your group will interrupt your story with questions using *before* or *after.*

Example: A: *I went to Spain two years ago.*

B: *Had you been to Spain before?*

ACTIVITY 6 listening

CD Track 26

STEP 1

Listen to the audio of a senior citizen talking about her family history. Each time the speaker talks about an important family event—births, deaths, marriages, divorces—record the date (or the approximate date) on the chart below and write down who the event happened to. The first one is done for you.

BIRTHS	DEATHS	MARRIAGES	DIVORCES	RELATIONSHIP TO SPEAKER
	1940			mother

STEP 2

Work with a classmate to list the speaker's important family events in chronological order.

STEP 3

Listen to the audio for each usage of the past perfect. Write down the sentences in your notebook. Were the time words *before, after, by* or *by the time* used?

Then complete these sentences.

1. The speaker used the past perfect _____ times.
2. The interviewer used the past perfect _____ times.
3. The time words *before, after, by,* or *by the time* were used _____ times altogether (by both speakers).

Do your classmates agree with your answers?

ACTIVITY 7 research on the web

STEP 1

Choose a country that you know or would like to find out more about. Go on the Internet and use a search engine such as Google® or Yahoo® to find three or four important dates in the history of that country. These dates should mark important changes or turning points in the history of the country.

Here are some examples from American history:

DATE / EVENT	WHY IT WAS IMPORTANT
1492: Discovery of America by Europeans	Before 1492, Europeans had believed that the earth was flat.
1776: Independence from Great Britain	Before 1776, America had been a colony of Great Britain.
1920: Women got the right to vote.	Before 1920, American women had not been able to vote.

STEP 2

Work with a partner. Tell him or her about the dates and events you chose. Your partner will try to imagine what life was like before and after those events.

ACTIVITY 8 reflection

Think of one thing that changed your ideas about learning English. Was there a teacher, another student, or a book that helped you to see things differently? Talk with a partner. Explain how your ideas changed before and after this experience.

UNIT 20

ARTICLES

The, A/An, Some, and Ø

UNIT GOALS

- Understand the meaning of the articles *the, a, an,* and *some*
- Use articles correctly for first and second mentions of an item
- Know which articles to use with singular, plural, and noncount nouns
- Understand when to use Ø (no article)

OPENING TASK

Looking for the Perfect House

STEP 1

Look at the pictures. Describe each one. What is your ideal type of house?

1.

2.

3.

4.

5.

STEP 2

Put the following sentences in order so that they make a story. When you have finished, check to see if other students have the story in the same order.

a. _____ Esinam found a real-estate agent to help them.

b. _____ They finally decided to buy the little house and remodel the kitchen.

c. _____ The second place they saw was a pretty brick house by a lake, but the house was too expensive.

d. _____ Finally they saw a little one-bedroom house surrounded by trees at the end of a dead-end street.

e. _____ When I last talked to them, they had finished remodeling the kitchen, and they liked the house a lot.

f. _____ Esinam and Sunita decided to buy a house.

g. _____ The real-estate agent then showed them a house near some apartment buildings, but the house was too big, and the apartment buildings were too ugly.

h. _____ First they looked at a nice house in the suburbs, but there were no trees, and the house was too far away from work.

i. _____ They told the real-estate agent that they wanted to live in a quiet neighborhood. They also said that they preferred small houses.

STEP 3

Write the numbers of the pictures in Step 1 in the correct story order.

_____ _____ _____ _____ _____

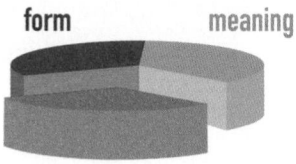

FOCUS 1 Definite and Indefinite Articles: *The*, *A/An*, *Ø* (no article), and *Some*

EXAMPLES	EXPLANATIONS
(a) *Father to Son:* Where did we park **the** car?	Use the definite article *the* to talk about a specific noun. In (a), the father and son are thinking about the same car—a car that they both can identify.
(b) Which car are they talking about? **The** family car.	With *the,* you can answer the question *Which . . . ?*
(c) Al needs a new notebook.	Use the indefinite article *a* or *an* to talk about one of a group of similar things, not about a specific thing. In (c), Al is thinking about notebooks in general. He's not thinking about a specific notebook that he can identify.
(d) What does Al need? **A** new notebook.	With *a/an*, you can answer the question *What . . . ?* (d) Use *a* or *an* with singular count nouns.
(e) Al needs **a** new computer, new software, and new instructional manuals.	Use the indefinite article Ø (no article) with noncount nouns or plural count nouns.
(f) Al needs **some** new software and **some** new instruction manuals.	Use the indefinite article *some* to talk about a nonspecific number or quantity with plural nouns or noncount nouns.

EXERCISE 1

Fill in the blanks in the story below with *the, a, an, Ø* (no article), or *some*.

1. I recently found _____ new job in New York City.
2. We spent the weekend looking at _____ apartments for rent.
3. Many apartments were very small, but _____ older apartments were quite large.
4. We finally chose _____ apartment in Brooklyn.
5. _____ apartment building we chose was made of wood and was about 100 years old.
6. We had lived in a new house before, but _____ old houses have more character.
7. One night, our daughter Sarah said she could hear _____ voices in the room upstairs.
8. She thought there were _____ ghosts up there.
9. But when we went to look, _____ room was empty.
10. We told ourselves it was our imagination playing _____ tricks on us.
11. Later we realized that _____ walls were very thin.
12. _____ voices that we heard were from the people next door.

FOCUS 2 Using Articles: First and Second Mention

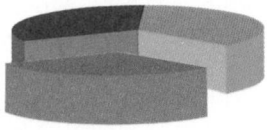

EXAMPLES	EXPLANATIONS
(a) I read **a** great book yesterday. (b) Martha just bought **a** new backpack. (c) I found **an** old dress of my mother's in the attic.	*A/an* is generally used to talk about a noun for the first time (first mention). Since the noun is introduced for the first time, it is not yet identified as a specific thing.
(d) I found an old dress of my mother's in the attic in the trunk. **The** dress was beautiful, with pearl buttons and lace sleeves.	Use *the* when the noun has been introduced and is now identified (sometimes called "second mention").

EXERCISE 2

Now look back at Exercise 1 and tell your partner why you used each article (*a/an, some, the* or Ø). Did you complete the exercise correctly? If not, go back and rewrite the sentences you missed.

EXERCISE 3

Read the following paragraph. For each underlined noun phrase, is the article usage correct? If the article usage is not correct, write the correct usage above the underlined words. These questions will help you:

- Is the writer talking about a noun for the first time?
- Is the writer talking about a specific noun?
- Is the writer talking about one of a group of similar things—**not** an identified/specific noun?

Since 1988, (1) a herd of deer has come to Pedro's apple orchard each October just after apple harvest for a feast. (2) An orchard is bordered by a forest, and Pedro and his family are able to watch (3) the herd come out of (4) a forest and walk directly to the nearest apple trees. Within minutes after the deer enter (5) the orchard, (6) the apples are gone, and (7) the deer return to the forest with their stomachs full. Watching the deer has become (8) an annual event for Pedro and his family. If Pedro could predict (9) the annual apple-eating event, he would invite his friends and have (10) the deer-watching party.

FOCUS 3 Indefinite Articles with Singular, Plural, and Noncount Nouns

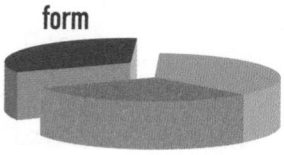

EXAMPLES	EXPLANATIONS
(a) I'd like to buy **a** piano and **an** organ. (b) **a** youngster (c) **a** university	Use *a* and *an* with singular count nouns. Use *a* before consonant sounds and *an* before vowel sounds. It is the **sound,** not the letter, that tells you whether to use *a* or *an*.
(d) **an** energetic woman (e) **an** unusual doll	If there is an adjective before the noun, then the first sound of the **adjective** tells you whether to use *a* or *an*, not the first sound of the noun.
(f) I'd like to buy **some** new CDs and tapes, and then I'd like to listen to **music** all day.	Use *some* or Ø (no article) with plural count nouns and noncount nouns.

EXERCISE 4

Fill in the blanks with *a, an,* or Ø (no article).

1. If I won the lottery, first I would buy _____ piece of land in the country.
2. Then I would build _____ unusual house and _____ huge barn.
3. Of course I would build _____ long fence, too.
4. Then I would buy _____ horses, _____ cows, and maybe _____ llama.
5. I would make sure to buy _____ hay for the winter, so that the animals would have plenty to eat.
6. I would probably hire _____ people to take care of the horses.
7. People say that you can't buy _____ happiness, but I think my ranch would certainly make me happy!

FOCUS 4 *Some* Instead of Ø (No Article)

EXAMPLES	EXPLANATIONS
(a) Al needs **some** new clothes. (b) I'd like to get **some** tickets to the concert on Friday.	Use *some* with plural count nouns and noncount nouns when you want to talk about quantity (amount).
(c) I'd like to listen to **some** jazz. (**s'm** jazz) (d) Can we get **some** cookies at the bakery? (**s'm** cookies)	When *some* is used instead of Ø (no article) in conversation, it is not stressed.
(e) I'd like to listen to (some) jazz. (f) Al needs (some) new clothes.	Usually *some* is optional (you **can** use it, but it's not necessary).
(g) Cookies are called biscuits in England. (h) NOT: Some cookies are called biscuits in England. (i) Spiders have eight legs. (j) NOT: Some spiders have eight legs.	Do not use *some* when you are talking about **all** members of a group of similar things.

EXERCISE 5

Look at your answers in Exercise 1. Mark with a check (✓) all the answers where Ø (no article) was used with either a plural count noun or a noncount noun. Could you use *some* instead? Discuss your answers with a partner.

1. _____
2. _____
3. _____
4. _____
5. _____
6. _____
7. _____
8. _____
9. _____
10. _____
11. _____
12. _____

form

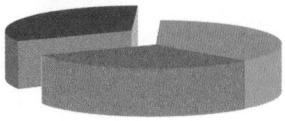

FOCUS 5 *The* with Singular, Plural, and Noncount Nouns

EXAMPLES	EXPLANATIONS
(a) *Son to Father:* Where did you put **the** keys?	Use *the* with all nouns that can be specifically identified:
	• plural count nouns: In (a) both speakers can identify which specific keys are being talked about.
(b) *Son to Friend:* Turn on **the** light, please.	• singular count nouns: In (b) they can both identify which specific light is being talked about.
(c) *Housemate to Housemate:* I can't find **the** sugar. Where did you put it?	• noncount (mass) nouns: In (c) they can both identify which sugar is being talked about.

EXERCISE 6

Fill in the blanks in the following story with *a/an, some, the,* or *Ø (no article).*

1. Last fall Anita worked in _____ apple orchard, picking apples.
2. _____ work was not easy.
3. She had sore muscles _____ first week of work, and every night she slept very soundly.
4. _____ first _____ orchard she worked in was considered small, with only fifty trees.
5. It was owned by _____ old, retired couple, who worked in the orchard as _____ hobby.
6. _____ next orchard Anita worked in was much larger, about twenty acres.
7. In this orchard, _____ trees had yellow apples, which were called "Golden Delicious."

8. Every day Anita ate _____ apples for breakfast and for lunch.
9. Even though _____ weather was beautiful, and _____ hard work made her feel very healthy, Anita was relieved when _____ apple-picking season was over.

Now work with a classmate and explain your choices.

FOCUS 6 Making General Statements with Ø (No Article)

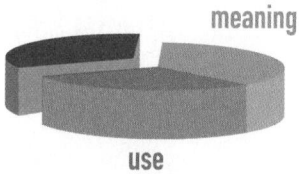

EXAMPLES	EXPLANATIONS
(a) **Al:** I need new clothes.	Use Ø (no) article to make general statements. In (a), Al needs new clothes **in general.** He's not thinking about specific clothes that he and his listener can identify. Use Ø (no article) to talk about plural count nouns that are not specific.
(b) I'd like to get **flowers** for my birthday.	In (b), you can't identify **which** flowers; you and the listener are not thinking about specific flowers.
(c) He is hoping to find **love.** (d) I like **jazz.**	Use Ø (no article) when you make a general statement using noncount (mass) nouns.
(e) Pencils are made with **graphite.** (f) **Rice** is eaten in Asia.	Use Ø (no article) when you make a general statement about a whole group or category.
(g) **Medical care** is very expensive in the United States. (h) Most people like **vacations.** (i) The university offers excellent classes in **art** and **music.**	Statements that use Ø (no article) can usually be paraphrased with *in general.* In (g): *In general,* medical care in the United States is expensive. (There may be some exceptions to the fact stated.)

EXERCISE 7

Circle the errors in article usage in the sentences below. Specifically, should you use *the* or Ø (no article)?

1. The love is a very important thing in our lives.
2. Without the love, we would be lonely and confused.
3. I believe that the money is not as important as love, although some people don't feel this way.
4. If the money is too important, then we become greedy.
5. When we get old, the health becomes as important as love.
6. My grandmother says, "Just wait and see. Work you do and the money you earn are important now, but when you're old . . .
7. . . . love that you feel for your family and friends, health of your loved ones—these are the things that will be most important."

FOCUS 7 *The* with Unique/Easily Identified Nouns

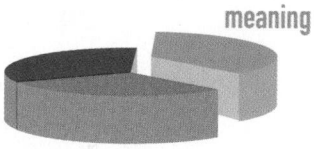

EXAMPLES	EXPLANATIONS
(a) In June, **the sun** doesn't set until 9:30.	The definite article *the* is used with nouns that are easily identified. Use *the* with nouns that are **universally** known (everyone in the world can identify it). In (a), everyone knows **which** sun they're talking about, since there's only one.
(b) Mary went to **the coast** on her vacation.	*The* is also used when the noun is **regionally** known (everyone in the region can identify it). In (b), everyone knows **which** coast they're talking about, since there's only one in the region.
(c) Did you feed **the cats**?	We can also use *the* when the noun is **locally** known (everyone in the immediate location can identify it). In (c), everyone in the immediate location knows **which** cats they're talking about, since they live together in the same house.

EXERCISE 8

For sentences 1–10 below, answer these three questions (answers may vary):

a. Where would you hear this sentence spoken?
b. Who do you think the speaker is?
c. What do you think happened or what was the conversation about **before** or **after** the sentence was spoken?

1. Please turn on *the* TV.
2. Could you change *the* channel?
3. We need some more chalk. Would you mind checking *the* blackboard in *the* back?
4. *The* rosebushes are lovely.
5. Could you pass *the* salt, please?
6. Excuse me, where's *the* women's restroom?
7. *The* sky is so blue today. I don't think you'll need *the* umbrella.
8. Have you seen *the* dog?
9. It's so romantic. See how bright *the* moon is?
10. Let's go to *the* mountains for our vacation instead of to *the* beach.

Use your answers to the three questions above to discuss in class why *the* was used in each sentence.

EXERCISE 9

Tell why *the* is used in each of the following sentences. (Some of these you will recognize from Exercise 8.) In the space at the left, write down **where** you think this statement was made. Then, on the right:

- If it is **universally** known, circle **U**.
- If it is **regionally** known, circle **R**.
- If it is **locally** known (because of the immediate location), circle **L**.

Setting

_____	1. Please turn on the TV.	U R L
_____	2. Could you change the channel?	U R L
_____	3. We need some more chalk. Would you mind checking the blackboard in the back?	U R L
_____	4. The rosebushes are lovely	U R L
_____	5. Could you pass the salt, please?	U R L
_____	6. Excuse me, please. Where's the women's restroom?	U R L
_____	7. The sky is so blue today. I don't think you'll need the umbrella.	U R L

_____ 8. Have you seen the dog? U R L

_____ 9. It's so romantic. See how bright the moon is? U R L

_____ 10. Let's go to the mountains for our vacation, insteadof to the beach. U R L

_____ 11. Son: Hey Dad, can I borrow the car?
Dad: Sure, if you can find the keys! U R L

_____ 12. I like your dress. Did you buy it at the mall? U R L

FOCUS 8 Using *The*: Second Mention, Related Mention, and Certain Adjectives

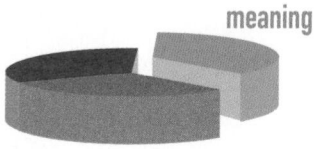

EXAMPLES	EXPLANATIONS
(a) She used to have a cat and a dog, but **the** cat died. (b) Last year I bought a guitar and a banjo. I decided to sell **the** banjo since I rarely play it.	Sometimes we use *the* with a noun because the noun has been talked about before (second mention). We can identify the cat in (a) and the banjo in (b) because they have been talked about before.
(c) He bought a suit, but **the** jacket had a button missing, so he had to return it. (d) I had a lock, but I lost **the** key for it.	In other situations we can identify a noun because it is *related* to something that has been talked about before (related mention). In (c), we know which jacket they're talking about, since *jacket* is part of *suit*.
(e) She had started to read a book when she noticed that **the** first chapter was missing. (f) She's **the** first person I met here and **the** only friend I have. (g) That's **the** hardest test I've ever taken. (h) You made **the** right choice.	Adjectives or phrases like *last, next, first, only,* and *right,* and superlatives like *best, hardest,* and *happiest* usually use the definite article *the* because they describe something that is "one of a kind." There's only one "first chapter" (in e), only one "first person" (in f), and only one "hardest test" (in g).
(i) It's **the** same old story. (j) We are taking **the** same class.	The definite article is always used with the adjective *same*.

EXERCISE 10

Read the story below. Decide why *the* is used each time it is underlined. If it is used because it has been talked about before, circle **S** (for **second mention**). If it is used because a **related** noun has been talked about before, circle **R** (for **related mention**).

1. Jerry was late for his appointment, so he went into a telephone booth near the bus stop to make a phone call. It looked like someone was living in the telephone booth. S R
2. There was a small blanket covering the window of the telephone booth like a curtain. S R
3. The floor of the telephone booth was swept clean with a broom. S R
4. The broom was hung on a hook in the corner of the telephone booth. S R
5. By the telephone, there was a pen and a notepad with a short list of names and telephone numbers. S R
6. Jerry also noticed that there was a coffee mug and a toothbrush sitting neatly by the telephone directory. S R
7. The coffee mug looked like it had recently been rinsed. There were still drops of water in it. S R
8. Jerry had such a strong feeling that he was in someone's living space that he decided to find another place to make the phone call. S R

EXERCISE 11

Look at the story in the Opening Task on page 285, making sure that it is in the right order. How many times is *the* used? Underline each *the* and explain why it was used.

		Reason *the* is used
Example: i.	*the* real-estate agent	second mention

EXERCISE 12

Underline and number each use of *the* in the following story. Then tell why each is used. The possible reasons for the use of *the* with a noun are:

a. It's universally known.
b. It's regionally known.
c. It's locally known—the immediate location makes it clear.
d. Second mention.
e. Related mention.
f. The adjective or phrase makes it "one of a kind."

Vocabulary:

levee—raised bank or wall to stop flooding

Hurricane Katrina, which hit Louisiana, Mississippi, and Alabama in August 2005, was the costliest and most destructive natural disaster the United States had ever seen. The hurricane resulted in damage to *levees* that protect New Orleans from Lake Pontchartrain and most of the city was flooded by the lake's waters. Large sections of the city lie at or below sea level, and over a million people lost their homes. Federal and state emergency services were criticized for their slow response to the disaster and nongovernmental agencies such as the Red Cross as well as many private individuals from all over the country volunteered their time and money to organize aid for the disaster victims. Oil-refining in the region was also severely hit, causing job losses and higher fuel prices. The government estimated that around $200 billion would be needed to rebuild New Orleans and other towns in the region.

1. _____
2. _____
3. _____
4. _____
5. _____
6. _____
7. _____
8. _____
9. _____
10. _____
11. _____
12. _____
13. _____

EXERCISE 13

In the following newspaper article, circle each *the* and *a*. Then explain why those articles are used.

Vocabulary:

relief—help for victims of a disaster
shelter—temporary accommodation
cot—temporary bed
disturbing—shocking
trailer—mobile home

Volunteers Head South to Help Victims of Hurricane Katrina

Matthew Toledo spent several days in Louisiana helping with relief efforts following Hurricane Katrina. Here are some of his observations of the experience.

"I felt I had to get on a plane and help in any way that I could. So I decided to buy a plane ticket and go down to Baton Rouge. I asked the Red Cross to place me where they had the greatest need. I told them I could do anything. They asked me if I had been trained as a shelter manager, and I said yes.

"I worked through the day getting people cots, blankets, and food, and then spent the evening sorting clothes and shoes that had been donated. One thing that impressed me was how compassionate the local residents were to the new 'residents' of their community. There was a constant stream of local people sorting clothes, serving meals, offering jobs—even their homes.

"Everybody had a story of survival. There were many disturbing stories, but there were also several stories of hope. A grandmother with three young children crawled out of their second story window to escape the rising waters. Just then, an empty fishing boat was floating towards them. They got on the boat and reached safety.

"Then there were two young men who drove their red Toyota pickup from New Orleans to Baton Rouge. They arrived at the shelter seeking food and a place to sleep. The next day they went out into the community and got jobs with a local building contractor. The next day they asked to be awakened by 5:30 so they could report to work on time. The day after that they went out and signed a two-year lease on a trailer to move into. "These guys, along with hundreds of volunteers that I was with, are the images that will stay with me—folks looking out for each other and committed to making things better."

Source: Adapted from *InfoTrac® College Edition* Article A137146366 *Los Angeles Business Journal*, September 12, 2005 v27 i37 p10 (1): http://infotrac-college.thomsonlearning.com (accessed 10/06/05).

Use Your English

ACTIVITY 1 speaking

TIC-TAC-TOE/Arranging Objects

Choose a small common object that can be moved around. It can be something that you are wearing (a ring, a watch) or carrying with you (a pencil, a book). It is all right if some people choose the same object. All of you will give your objects to one student. This student will then draw a big tic-tac-toe chart on the chalkboard

Now form two teams. Each team tells the student who has all the objects on a desk or table to arrange them according to their directions, one sentence at a time. (For example, "Put a book under the ring. Put the red pencil next to the book.") If the article usage in the sentence is correct (and the person is able to follow the directions), then the team gets to put an X or O in any of the tic-tac-toe squares. If it is not correct, then the team must pass. The first team to get three X's or three O's in a row or diagonally wins the game.

ACTIVITY 2 speaking/listening

Find a photograph or drawing to bring to class. Work in pairs. You have two minutes to look at your partner's picture. After the two minutes are up, give back the picture. Your partner can ask you ten questions about the picture to test your memory. The winner has the most correct answers. Concentrate on using articles correctly.

Example: Student A: What is the man wearing?
Student B: He's wearing a coat and a hat.

ACTIVITY 3 writing

Now without the help of your partner, write a short description of the picture that you described in Activity 2. Again try to use the articles correctly.

ACTIVITY 4 speaking/listening/writing

Here are some things that people say contribute to their happiness: love, romance, success, wealth/money, fame, popularity, health, religion. Interview three people about what they think is most important for their happiness. If possible, record their answers. Be sure to get information about the people you are interviewing, such as age group, gender, and occupation.

In an oral or written summary, give the results of your interviews and see if there is agreement in people's answers.

ACTIVITY 5 listening

CD Track 27

STEP 1 Listen to the audio of two people (Speaker 1 and Speaker 2) describing their homes. Write as many nouns as you can hear in your notebook.

STEP 2 Listen to the audio again and check which of these nouns are mentioned with definite or indefinite articles.

STEP 3 Compare your list with a partner. Discuss the reasons for the speakers' choice of articles.

ACTIVITY 6 speaking/listening

Ask a speaker of English and/or a classmate to describe their house, apartment, or other living space (for example, a dormitory) to someone who has never seen it. If possible, record their descriptions. How many rooms are there? Where are they located? How many doors and windows are there in each room? What kind of furniture is there? Are there curtains, or are there pictures on the wall?

After you share these descriptions with the rest of the class, listen carefully to the recording for article usage.

ACTIVITY 7 speaking/listening

A lot of people like to have nice quality or expensive possessions. What would you like? Describe five items to put on your "wish list" to someone. Explain how you would use each thing or how it would change your life. (Some examples are: a house, a swimming pool, a sports car, etc.) Record your description.

Listen carefully to your recording. Did you use articles correctly?

ACTIVITY 8 research on the web

Go on the Internet and use a search engine such as Google® or Yahoo® to find at least four headlines from recent online newspapers. Copy them or print them out and bring them to class. Put in articles (*the,* Ø article, *a/an,* or *some*) wherever you think they are appropriate in order to make the headlines into more complete statements. (Note: You might need to add main verbs or auxiliaries too, such as a form of *be* or *do*.)

Example: Powerful Storm Threatens Gulf Coast

Adding articles: *A* powerful storm threatens *the* Gulf Coast.

Explanation: *A* is used with *storm* because it is not a specific storm. It has not been mentioned before. *The* is used with *Gulf Coast* because this is the name of a specific identifiable region of the United States.

ACTIVITY 9 reflection

Look back at the rules for using articles in this unit. Compare the use of articles in English with another language that you know. Explain the differences to a partner or your class. Can you identify any common errors that you or a speaker of that language might make when using articles in English?

UNIT 21

ARTICLES WITH NAMES OF PLACES

UNIT GOALS

- Use articles with names of places
- Use articles with names of institutions

OPENING TASK

Geography Quiz

STEP 1

Look at the pictures. How many of these places can you identify?

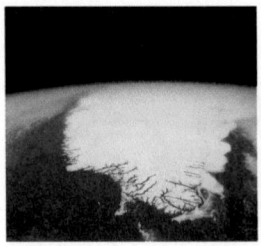

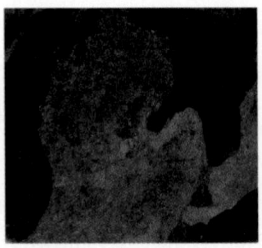

STEP 2

Form groups of five. In your group, complete the chart. If you have different opinions in your group, write down all the different answers. Which ones can you match with the photos from Step 1?

WHAT IS . . . ?	ANSWER
the largest continent in the world	
the longest river	
the largest country (in size, not population)	
the biggest island	
the highest mountain range	
the highest mountain	
the biggest desert	
the largest ocean	
the largest lake	
the largest planet	

STEP 3

When you have finished, compare your answers with those of other groups. Write the final answers on the board. (If you cannot agree, you may want to research the answer for homework.)

STEP 4

Take turns making complete statements based on the information in your chart.

Example: *The Amazon is* _____.

FOCUS 1 Articles with Names of Places

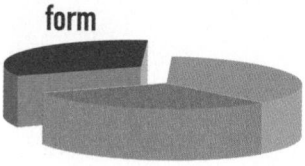

EXAMPLES	EXPLANATIONS
	Use Ø (no article) with names of:
South America	• continents
Zimbabwe	• countries
New York	• cities
First Avenue	• streets and highways
Interstate 90	
Mars	• planets
Jamaica	• islands
Mount Shasta	• single mountains
Lake Champlain	• lakes
Yosemite National Park	• parks
	Use *the* with names of:
the Yellow River	• rivers
the Gobi Desert	• deserts
the Arctic Ocean	• oceans
the Caspian Sea	• seas
the Andes	• mountain ranges
the Hawaiian Islands	• groups of islands
the Great Lakes	• groups of lakes
the Middle East	• most regions
the United States	• countries that are collections take *the*

EXERCISE 1

Look at the categories below. For each category (1–10), put the correct answers from the Opening Task on pages 302–303 in either Column A or B. For example, the largest continent is Asia, which does not use *the,* so this would go in Column B for #1.

CATEGORY	(A) USE *THE*	(B) DON'T USE *THE*
1. the largest continent in the world		Asia
2. the longest river		
3. the largest country (in size, not population)		
4. the biggest island		
5. the highest mountain range		
6. the highest mountain		
7. the biggest desert		
8. the largest ocean		
9. the largest lake		
10. the largest planet		

EXERCISE 2

Read the conversation. Underline all the names of places. Explain why *the* is used or **not** used in each case.

A: Have you ever been to Canada?

B: Yes, I went there with my friend a couple of years ago during the winter vacation.

A: Where did you go?

B: Well, we stayed in Vancouver most of the time and went skiing on Mount Whistler. Then we took a train up to Lake Louise. It's really high up in the mountains and the train ride is spectacular. Oh yes, and we also visited Victoria, which is the capital of British Columbia.

A: I thought Vancouver was the capital?

B: Vancouver is the largest city, but the capital is actually a smaller city on Vancouver Island. It's very pretty there.

A: Did you like Vancouver?

B: I think it's an amazing place—wherever you go you can get marvelous views of the Pacific Ocean and of the Rockies. Next time I want to take a boat trip to the Queen Charlotte Islands or maybe up the western coast to Alaska.

Write and practice a conversation with your partner about a place that you have visited. Include as many names of countries, islands, cities, mountains, lakes, and other places as you can.

EXERCISE 3

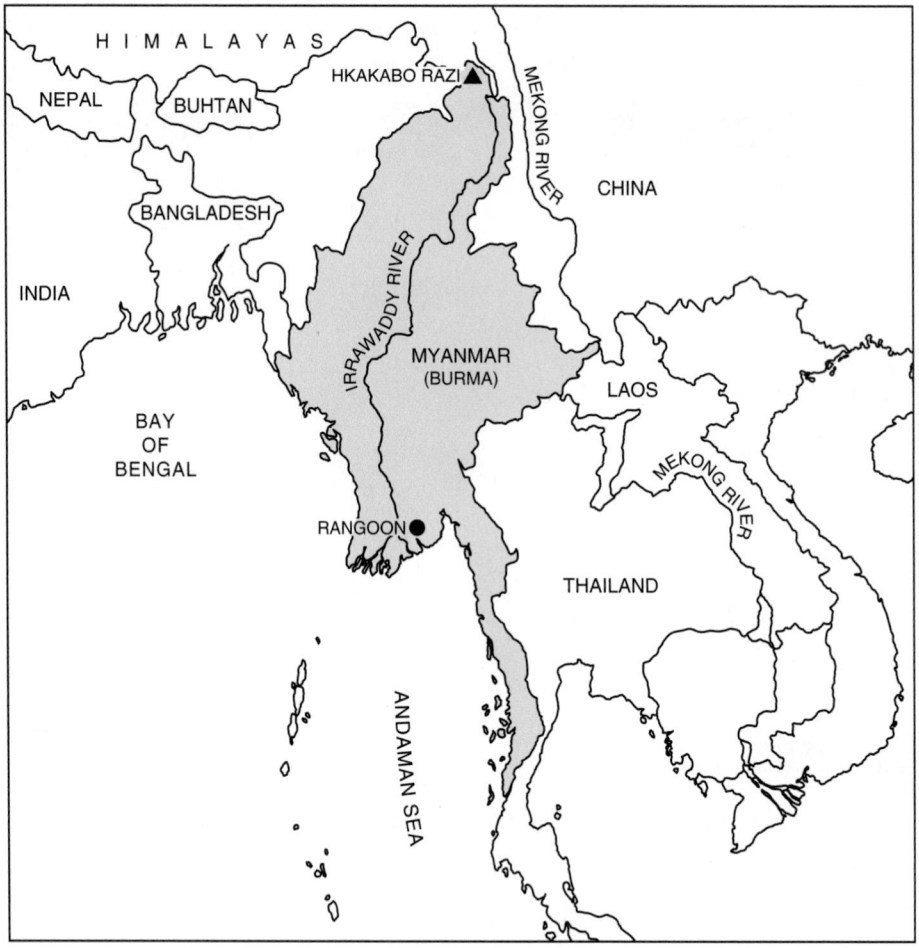

Fill in the blanks with *the* or Ø (no article).

(1) _____ Burma is sandwiched between (2) _____ India and (3) _____ Bangladesh on one side and (4) _____ China, (5) _____ Laos, and (6) _____ Thailand on the other. To the south is (7) _____ Andaman Sea and (8) _____ Bay of Bengal. Burma has several important river systems including (9) _____ Irrawaddy, which runs almost the entire length of the country and enters the sea in a vast delta region southwest of (10) _____ Rangoon, the capital. (11) _____ Mekong River forms the border between Burma and Laos. (12) _____ Himalayas rise in the north of Burma, and (13) _____ Hkakabo Razi, on the border between Burma and Tibet, is the highest mountain in southeast Asia, at 5881 meters (19,297 feet).

Adapted from *Burma, A Travel Survival Kit*, by Tony Wheeler. Lonely Planet Publications, 1982

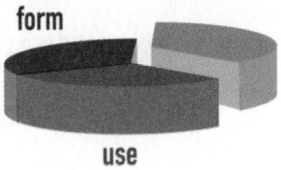

FOCUS 2 Articles with Names of Institutions

EXAMPLES	EXPLANATIONS
(a) Summit Elementary School (b) Children's Hospital and Medical Center (c) Boston College (d) Louisiana State (University)	**Use Ø (no article):** • for schools, hospitals, and prisons • when the place name comes **before** *College* or *University*
(e) **the** Eiffel Tower (f) **the** University of Northern Iowa	**Use *the*:** • for most tourist attractions • when *University of* comes before the place name

EXERCISE 4

The following conversation is between Sheryl Smith, a real estate agent, and the Joneses, who want to buy a house. Fill in the blanks with *the* or Ø (no article).

Sheryl Smith: I'm sure you'd like the area. It borders (1) _____ Discovery Park, which has free outdoor concerts at (2) _____ Rutherford Concert Hall, and also there's (3) _____ Whitehawk Native American Art Museum, which you've probably heard of. It's quite well known.

Mike Jones: Yes, yes.

Donna Jones: What about schools?

Sheryl Smith: Well, there's (4) _____ Smith College of Architecture, of course . . .

Donna Jones: I mean public schools for our children.

Sheryl Smith: Oh, well, (5) _____ Golden Oaks Elementary School is only a few blocks away, on (6) _____ First Avenue. And there's a high school about a mile north of the park.

Mike Jones: (pointing) Aren't those (7) _____ White Mountains?

Sheryl Smith: Yes. On clear days, you can even see (8) _____ Mt. Wildman, the tallest mountain in the range.

Mike Jones: Oh, yes. I heard about a good fishing spot there, on (9) _____ Blue Lake.

Sheryl Smith: Yes, my husband goes there and to (10) _____ Nooksack River to fish. He could tell you all about it.

Mike Jones: Ms. Smith, I think you might have made a sale today.

EXERCISE 5

Fill in the blanks with *the* or Ø (no article). The first two have been done for you.

1. ___ø___ Hawaii
2. ___the___ Hawaiian Islands
3. _____ Saudi Arabia
4. _____ Harvard University
5. _____ Himalayas
6. _____ Museum of Modern Art
7. _____ First Avenue
8. _____ Mississippi River
9. _____ University of Miami
10. _____ Turkey
11. _____ United States
12. _____ Pyramids
13. _____ West
14. _____ Africa
15. _____ Lake Wenatchee
16. _____ Saturn

EXERCISE 6

For each underlined place name, check to see if the article is used correctly. If it is wrong, correct it: Add *the* or cross out *the*. The first one has been done for you.

WHERE TO GO IN SAN FRANCISCO

Situated on (1) the West Coast of the United States, (2) the city of San Francisco is a popular tourist destination with a variety of unique sightseeing opportunities for every visitor. No visit to San Francisco is complete without crossing (3) the Golden Gate Bridge. You can walk, cycle, or drive across this 1.7-mile-long bridge, which offers a fantastic view of the city on one side and (4) Pacific Ocean on the other. Try a taste of Chinese food in (5) the Chinatown, the largest Chinese community outside (6) the Asia. A short ferry ride will take you to (7) the island of Alcatraz, the famous island prison in the middle of (8) the San Francisco Bay. Visit (9) the Golden Gate Park for more exciting views of the city and across the Bay to (10) Marin Headlands. Other places of interest around the city include (11) Asian Art Museum and (12) California Academy of Sciences, which has a planetarium and an aquarium.

Use Your English

ACTIVITY 1 speaking/writing

Form groups of five students. Think of five famous places in the world—for example, mountains, lakes, islands, or buildings. With your group, write a quiz to find out how many people in your class know where these places are. Your quiz should have five questions and each question should have three possible answers. Exchange quizzes with the other groups in your class and answer their questions.

Example: Where is Madagascar?
a. in the Pacific Ocean b. in the Atlantic Ocean c. in the Indian Ocean

ACTIVITY 2 speaking

With the help of your teacher, form two teams. Each team will have five minutes to think of as many names of islands, mountains, and lakes as possible and write them on a sheet of paper (or on the blackboard). Each name with correct article use will be worth one point. The team that has the most correct names + articles wins.

ACTIVITY 3 writing

Think of a city or region you know and like. What places are the top tourist sights for first-time visitors? Write a short description of the tourist attractions and special features. Draw a map showing the locations of these places. Display your work in the classroom

ACTIVITY 4 listening

CD Track 28

Listen to the audio of a person talking about where she lives.

1. Work with a partner. Discuss the place the woman is talking about. Where is it? Why does she like it?
2. Listen again. Circle the names of the places the woman mentions.

_____ Leblon Beach	_____ North America	_____ Pacific Ocean
_____ Sugar Loaf Mountain	_____ Santa Marinha Street	_____ South America
_____ City Historic Museum	_____ City Park	_____ Rio de Janeiro
_____ Museum of Brazil	_____ Ipanema Beach	

3. In front of the names of the places you wrote, write the word the or leave the space blank. Compare your answers with a classmate's and discuss why Ø (no article) or *the* was used with each place name. If you disagree on any answers, look back at Focus 1 and Focus 2 for help in deciding on the correct answer.

ACTIVITY 5 speaking/writing/listening

STEP 1

You have been asked by a travel company to design a poster to attract overseas visitors to the region where you are living. Or, if you prefer, you can make a poster about another place you know and like (See Activity 3), especially if there are other students interested in the same place.

Get together with a group of students to brainstorm local areas of interest. Your poster should have pictures and labels about the area and also short written descriptions. Display and compare your posters.

STEP 2

The poster that you made in Step 1 in Activity 5 was so successful that you have been asked to talk about the region to a group of tourists and travel guides. Record your short talk. Listen to the recording and check to see if you used *the* and Ø (no article) correctly.

ACTIVITY 6 reading

Read the information about two vacation destinations. Work with a partner.

Student A will ask questions about each place. (Example: Where should I go for the weekend?)

Student B will use the information to help Student A decide where to spend the vacation.

Example: Well, I just went to Boston, Massachusetts. There's a lot to see there. . . .

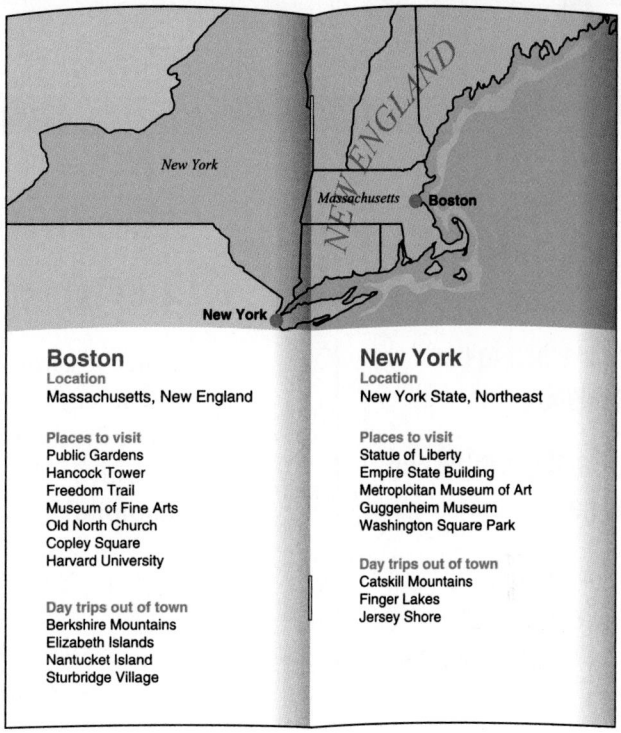

ACTIVITY 7 research on the web

***InfoTrac® College Edition* Option:** What are the seven wonders of the world? What are some different ways of interpreting this title? Go to *InfoTrac* to find the answers. Search for the keywords 'seven wonders of the world'. Compare your answers with a group and make a list of your choices for the top seven most amazing sights in the world.

ACTIVITY 8 reflection

Which rule for using articles with place names do you find most difficult to remember? Is there a name of a place that you often get wrong? Think of a memory tip that will help you to remember the correct article usage for this place. Share your ideas with a partner.

Example: No article needed with names of three things that begin with 'c': continents, countries, cities.

UNIT 22

THE PASSIVE

UNIT GOALS

- Know when to use passives
- Correctly form *be* and *get* passives
- Know the difference between the *be*-passive and the *get*-passive
- Know when to include the agent in the sentence

OPENING TASK

The Island of Campinilea

You are gathering information for a book on the fictional island of Campinilea, an island located somewhere off the west coast of South America. The first chapter will be called "The Products and Natural Resources of Campinilea."

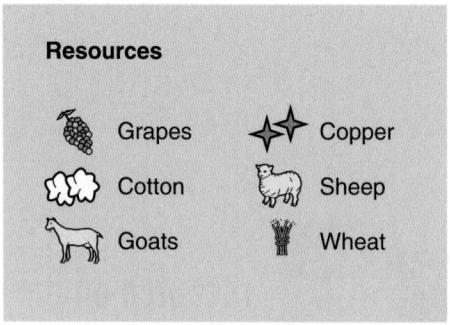

STEP 1

Use the key to interpret the information on the map on the next page. Discuss the island's resources with a partner.

Examples: Where are grapes cultivated? . . . in the north.
Where is cotton grown?

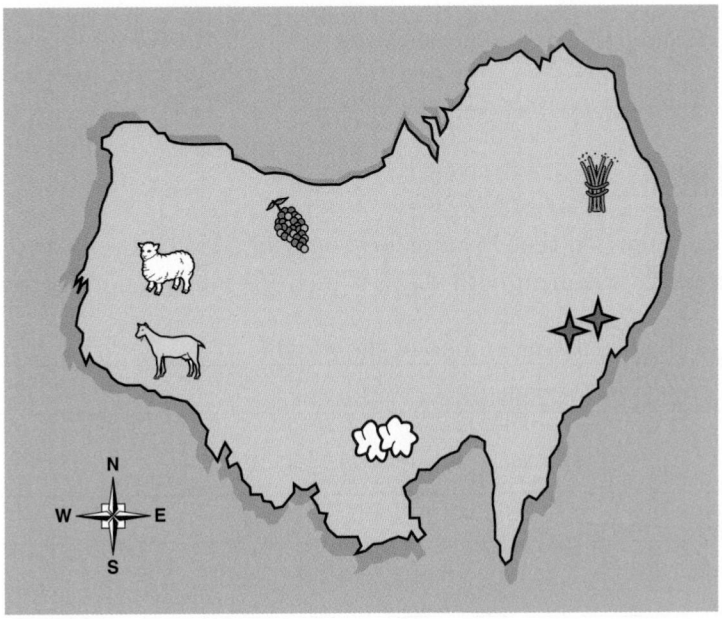

STEP 2

Use the map to match the activities to the appropriate location. The first one has been done for you.

ACTIVITIES	LOCATIONS
cultivate grapes	in the east
raise sheep	in the southeast
grow cotton	in the northwest
grow wheat	in the north
mine copper	in the west
raise goats	in the south

STEP 3

Using this information, make five sentences about the products and natural resources of Campinilea for the first chapter of your book.

meaning

FOCUS 1 Active and Passive

EXAMPLES	EXPLANATIONS
(a) Farmers **cultivate** grapes in the north.	Use the **active** to focus on the person who performs the action.
(b) Grapes **are cultivated** in the north.	Use the **passive** to focus on the result of the action, not the person who performs it.
(c) NOT: Sheep are lived in the northwest.	Passives are only used with transitive verbs (verbs that take an object in the active voice).

EXERCISE 1

Look at Step 3 of the Opening Task on page 313. Did you use the passive or the active? Write each statement both ways. Which statement sounds better? Why?

1. a. They cultivate grapes in the north
   b. Grapes are cultivated in the north.

2. a. _____
   b. _____

3. a. _____
   b. _____

4. a. _____
   b. _____

5. a. _____
   b. _____

FOCUS 2 Forming the *Be* Passive

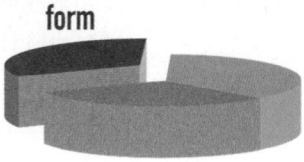

To form the passive, use the appropriate tense of be, followed by the past participle (pp):

EXAMPLES	TENSE	FORM	
(a) Wool **is produced** here.	Simple Present	am/is/are	+ pp
(b) Wool **is being produced** here right now.	Present Progressive	am/is/are being	+ pp
(c) Wool **was produced** here.	Simple Past	was/were	+ pp
(d) Wool **was being produced** here ten years ago.	Past Progressive	was/were being	+ pp
(e) Wool **has been produced** here since 1900.	Present Perfect	have/has been	+ pp
(f) Wool **had been produced** here when the island was discovered.	Past Perfect	had been	+ pp
(g) Wool **will be produced** here next year.	Future (*will*)	will be	+ pp
(h) Wool **is going to be produced** here.	Future (*be going to*)	am/is/are going to be	+ pp
(i) Wool **will have been produced** here by the year 2025.	Future Perfect	will have been	+ pp

EXERCISE 2

The second chapter of the book on Campinilea is called "The People of Campinilea and Their Customs." Look at the following statements about Campinilea; write 1 beside those you think belong to Chapter 1 (Products and Resources) and 2 beside those you think belong to Chapter 2 (People and Customs).

_____ 1. In the west, unmarried women leave their family homes at the age of 25 and raise goats in the mountains.

_____ 2. Miners mined silver throughout the island during the last century.

_____ 3. They will plant the first crop of rice in the south next year.

_____ 4. In the southeast, fathers take their oldest sons to the copper mines on their twelfth birthday in a special ceremony to teach them the legends and rituals associated with Campinilean copper.

_____ 5. Easterners are more traditional than southerners; for example, farmers in the east have harvested wheat in the same way for hundreds of years, while those in the south are constantly exploring new techniques for growing cotton.

_____ 6. They have produced grapes in Campinilea for only a few years.

Do you think it would be appropriate to use the passive in any of these statements from Exercise 2 on page 315? Why do you think so? Rewrite those statements here:

_____

_____

_____

_____

EXERCISE 3

Complete the following, using the verb tense that fits best.

Adventurous tourists are beginning to discover Campinilea, and the island is hard at work getting ready to welcome more visitors. A new airport (1) _____ (build) last year, and at the moment, hotels (2) _____ (construct) along the southern beaches. A new road (3) _____ (finish) next year so visitors will be able to reach the northern region. Five years ago, very little (4) _____ (know) about Campinilea; but last year, three books (5) _____ (write) about the island, and several guide books (6) _____ (publish). At the moment, these books (7) _____ (translate) into different languages. English (8) _____ (teach) in schools so many Campinileans know a little English, but not many other foreign languages (9) _____ (speak).

Tourism has brought many changes to this small island, and people are afraid that it will have a negative effect on the traditional customs and culture of the people. For example, last month in the capital, several young Campinileans (10) _____ (arrest) for being drunk in public, and some tourists (11) _____ (rob) near the beach. However, if you leave the tourist areas and go up to the mountains, you will find that life is still the same as it was hundreds of years ago. For example, since the sixteenth century, the same tribal dances (12) _____ (perform) to celebrate the Campinilean new year, and the same type of food (13) _____ (serve). For centuries, visitors (14) _____ (invite) to join Campinileans in the celebration of festivals, and you will find traditional Campinilean hospitality in these regions has not changed at all.

FOCUS 3 The Passive

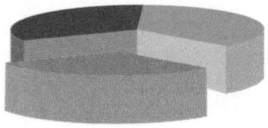

EXAMPLES	EXPLANATIONS
(a) All the cookies **were eaten** last night.	Use the passive when you don't know who performed the action.
(b) Wheat **is grown** in the east.	Use the passive when the person who performed the action is obvious. In example (b), it is obvious that farmers are the people who grow the wheat.
(c) A mistake was **made.**	Use the passive when you don't want to tell who performed the action.
(d) The computer **is protected** from electrical damage by a special grounding plug. (e) The proposal **was rejected** by the people of King County in last night's vote.	The passive is more formal than the active. It is more common in writing, especially in scientific and technical reports, and in newspaper articles. It is less common in conversation.

EXERCISE 4

The Campinilean police are currently investigating a robbery that took place in a hotel room a few nights ago. Work with a partner. One of you should look at Picture A below; the other should look at Picture B on page A-18. One of you has a picture of the room **before** the robbery, and the other has a picture of the room **after** the robbery. Seven different things were done to the room. **Without looking at your partner's picture,** ask each other questions and find what these seven things were and complete the report below.

ROBBERY AT HOTEL PARAISO

Last night the police were called to investigate a robbery that took place at the Hotel Paraiso. The identity of the thief is still unknown. The police took note of several unusual occurrences. For example,

_____

_____

_____

_____

The public has been asked to contact the police with any information about the identity of the thief. Any information leading to an arrest will be rewarded.

Picture A

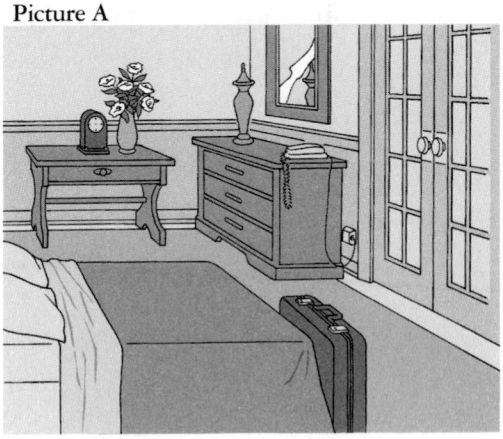

FOCUS 4 Including the Agent in Passive Sentences

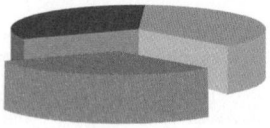

EXAMPLES	EXPLANATIONS
(a) Wheat is grown in the east. (b) NOT: Wheat is grown in the east by farmers.	In most situations where the passive is used, the *by*-phrase (the agent) is understood and therefore is *not* used.
(c) Wheat is grown in eastern Campinilea. It is planted **by men,** and it is harvested **by women and children.** (d) *Hamlet* was written by **William Shakespeare.** (e) Several South American countries were liberated **by Simon Bolivar.** (f) I can't believe it! This novel was written **by a 14-year-old.**	You can include the agent (the person who performs the action) with a *by*-phrase if that information is important. It is important to include the agent: • when new information is added, (Example c, second sentence) • with proper names or famous people (Examples d and e) • when the agent's identity is surprising or unexpected (Example f)

EXERCISE 5

Decide if each italicized phrase (*by* + agent) is necessary in the sentences below. Cross out the *by*-phrases that you think are unnecessary.

Passage 1

Campinilea was described (1) *by Jules Verne* in one of his early novels. It was seen (2) *by people* as an exotic yet stable society. Recently, it was rated (3) *by Travel Magazine* as one of the top ten tourist spots in the world. One of the reasons for the country's popularity is that the products produced (4) *by Campinileans* in Campinilea are excellent.

For example, rugs have been produced (5) *by Campinilean people* for centuries. They are woven (6) *by women from the mountain tribes* and are then transported to the capital (7) *by mule* and are sold in the markets (8) *by relatives of the weavers.*

Another excellent product is the mineral water of Campinilea. In restaurants in the capital city, bottled water is served (9) *by waiters*. It is interesting that this water is rarely drunk (10) *by Campinileans,* but it is much appreciated (11) *by foreign tourists.*

Passage 2

Dear Janette,

I've been working hard this whole week on my book. In some ways, I wish that I hadn't gotten paid an advance (1) by the publishers, since now I feel a lot of pressure to finish quickly. I guess that's the purpose of an advance! I really hope, though, that when the book is finally finished (2) by me, it will be appreciated (3) by people. I am hoping that I can finish soon, because it means that I will soon be paid in full (4) by the publishers! Even if it's done soon, the book won't actually be published (5) by the publishers until at least six months after the manuscript is received (6) by them.

Did I tell you that Scout got hurt (7) by another dog? She was playing with Patches, the neighbor's dog, like she always does, and her ear got bitten pretty severely (8) by Patches. I had to take her to the vet's and get it stitched up (9) by the vet. The vet asked me if Scout got attacked (10) by Patches, and I had to explain that no, she and Patches just like to play rough. Luckily, Scout's fine. And of course she and Patches are playing together again, just as hard as ever, so it's clear that their friendship hasn't been damaged (11) by the experience.

Gotta run! Back to work on the book . . .

Love,

Dean

form

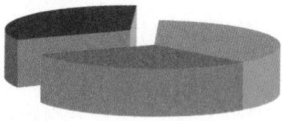

FOCUS 5 Forming the *Get*-Passive

To form the *get*-passive, use the appropriate tense of *get*, followed by the past participle (pp):

EXAMPLES		TENSE	FORM	
(a)	Her cookies always **get eaten.**	Present Simple	*get/gets*	+ pp
(b)	Her cookies **are getting eaten.**	Present Progressive	*am/is/are getting to get*	+ pp
(c)	Her cookies **got eaten.**	Past Simple	*got*	+ pp
(d)	Her cookies **were getting eaten.**	Past Progressive	*was/were getting*	+ pp
(e)	Her cookies **have gotten eaten.**	Present Perfect	*have/has gotten*	+ pp
(f)	Her cookies **had gotten eaten.**	Past Perfect	*had gotten*	+ pp
(g)	Her cookies **will get eaten.**	Future (*will*)	*will get*	+ pp
(h)	Her cookies **are going to get eaten.**	Future (*be going to*)	*am/is/are going to get*	+ pp
(i)	Her cookies **will have gotten eaten** by the time we get home.	Future Perfect	*will have gotten*	+ pp

Questions: Simple present and past:

EXAMPLES	QUESTION FORM
(a) Do her cookies **get eaten**?	*Do/does* + subject + *get* + pp
(b) Did her cookies **get eaten?**	*Did* + subject + *get* + pp

Negative: Simple present and past:

EXAMPLES	NEGATIVE STATEMENT FORM
(a) Her cookies do not get eaten.	subject + *do/does* + *not* + *get* + pp *(don't/doesn't)*
(b) Her cookies did not get eaten.	subject + *did not* + *get* + pp *(didn't)*

EXERCISE 6

Read the following situations. What do you think probably happened before each one? Match the situation with one of the previous events in the box below.

Situation	Previous Event
1. Oh, no! Not my clean white shirt!	_____
2. We're finally able to pay our bills.	_____
3. It's so exciting to see my name in print.	_____
4. I told you not to leave it outside at night!	_____
5. When I came back to the parking lot, I found these dents on the side.	_____
6. They took him straight to the hospital by ambulance.	_____
7. Thank you for all your support. Now that I am mayor, I will work to improve our schools.	_____
8. The packet's empty, and there are only a few crumbs left!	_____

a.	They got paid.	e.	All the cookies got eaten.
b.	His car got hit.	f.	She got elected.
c.	Someone got injured.	g.	His book got published.
d.	Some coffee got spilled.	h.	Her bike got stolen.

EXERCISE 7

Complete the following with the *get*-passive and the appropriate tense.

A: You're late! What happened?

B: I had to take the bus, because my car (1) is getting fixed (fix).

A: Oh? What's wrong with it?

B: It (2) _____ (break into) last week and a window on one of the doors (3) _____ (damage).

A: That's terrible! How did it happen?

B: Well, I went into the bank on Thursday and when I came out, I saw that the side window (4) _____ (smash). Some thieves had broken into the car. Not only that, but I (5) _____ (fine) too, because I hadn't put enough money in the meter.

A: _____ anything (6) _____ (steal) from inside the car?

B: Yes, the CD player and some CDs. I reported it to the police.

A: _____ anyone (7) _____ (arrest)?

B: No, but they found the CDs later. They (8) _____ (throw) into a trash can!

A: At least they found something! When will your car be ready?

B: I hope the work (9) _____ (finish) by next Monday. That's just as well because I (10) _____ (pay) by the insurance company until next week and I can't afford to pay for it until then.

FOCUS 6 *Be*-Passive versus *Get*-Passive

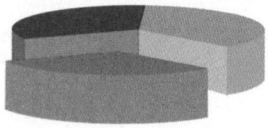

use

EXAMPLES	EXPLANATIONS
(a) They **are married.** (b) They **got married** last year.	In most situations, the *be*-passive emphasizes a continuing state, while the *get*-passive emphasizes a change in the situation.
(c) The answer **was known.** (d) NOT: The answer **got known.** (***know*** = an unchanging state) (e) She **was wanted** by the police for shoplifting. (f) NOT: She **got wanted** by the police for shoplifting.	Because the *get*-passive emphasizes a change in a situation, it is only used with action or process verbs. It cannot be used with stative verbs (verbs that refer to situations, or "states," that do not change). Some common stative verbs: *own* *like* *hate* *see* *love* *know* *feel* *want*
(g) *To a friend:* Have you heard the news? Isao's car **got stolen!** (h) *In a police report:* A white Honda Civic **was stolen** last night.	*Get*-passives are often used in conversation and rarely in writing or formal speaking. *Be*-passives are more formal than *get*-passives. *Get*-passives often describe actions with negative effects.

EXERCISE 8

Where possible, change the underlined verbs to *get*-passives. If it is not possible to use the *get*-passive, explain why.

Passage 1

Steve is usually very punctual, but yesterday was a really bad day. First, the elevator in his apartment building broke down, and he (1) got ~~was trapped~~ on the 5th floor for 20 minutes. Next, his car (2) was hit by a motorbike on the way to work. Luckily, the driver (3) wasn't injured, but the back of his car (4) was damaged, so he had to stop and exchange insurance information. When he finally arrived at work, he found that his computer (5) was infected by a virus, and he wasn't able to prepare his report on time. A few minutes later, he (6) was called to the manager's office. The manager (7) was disliked by everyone for being so strict. Steve explained how he (8) had been delayed by the elevator, the motorbike, and the computer virus, but the manager was not amused. "How can we (9) be respected by our customers if our reports (10) are not delivered on time?" Steve thought he would (11) be fired on the spot, but instead the manager just told him to stay late until the report (12) was finished.

Passage 2

"Fake" Jewel Robbery

A pearl and ruby necklace, which (1) was once owned by Queen Marie Antoinette, (2) was stolen from the National Museum on Monday night, a museum spokesperson said. For security reasons, however, the jewels on display at the museum (3) had been replaced by copies. "Luckily, the real jewels (4) weren't taken," said a museum guard. "I guess we (5) were all fooled," said one visitor to the museum.

EXERCISE 9

Tabloid newspapers present sensational, but usually untrue, stories. Look at the following tabloid newspaper headlines and rewrite each one as a complete sentence. Use a *get*-passive wherever possible; use a *be*-passive where you cannot use a *get*-passive. Remember to add articles when necessary.

Example: *TEEN EATEN BY GIANT COCKROACHES*
A teenager got eaten by giant cockroaches.

1. ELVIS SEEN IN SUPERMARKET LINE

_____

2. VICE-PRESIDENT KIDNAPPED BY SPACE ALIENS

_____

3. WORLD'S WORST HUSBAND MARRIED 36 TIMES

_____

4. FALSE TEETH STUCK IN MAN'S THROAT FOR SIX MONTHS

_____

5. THREE-YEAR-OLD ARRESTED DRIVING TRUCK

_____

What do you think each headline is about? Why?

Find some of your own examples from other newspapers. Read them to your classmates. Your classmates will try to guess what the story is about.

Use Your English

ACTIVITY 1 reading/speaking/listening

Look at the following tabloid headlines and ask three friends to explain what he or she thinks each headline means. Record the conversation and then listen to the recording to see if he or she uses any passive forms in his or her explanations. Share your findings with the rest of the class.

WOMAN HYPNOTIZED BY ALIENS
MAN'S LIFE SAVED BY HITCHHIKING GHOST
SUITCASE DROPPED 5,000 FEET BY AIRLINE
BIGFOOT FOUND IN NEW YORK CITY
WOMAN PREGNANT WITH DAUGHTER'S BABY

ACTIVITY 2 speaking/listening

In this activity, you will make a chain story about somebody's bad day—a day when everything went wrong. One student will start the story and will continue until he or she uses a *get*-passive. When he or she uses a *get*-passive, the next person will continue.

Example: Student 1: *Andy had a really bad day. First, he overslept. When he got dressed, he forgot to put his pants on.*

Student 2: *He ran out of the house, but was embarrassed to realize he had forgotten his pants. Before he could get back inside, he got bitten by the neighbor's dog.*

Student 3: *The dog . . .*

ACTIVITY 3 writing or speaking/listening

Have **you** ever had a really bad day? A day when everything went wrong, through no fault of your own? Describe the day, either in an informal letter to a friend, or, if you prefer, out loud to a classmate. If you tell your story rather than write it, record it. Listen to the recording for the use of the passive, especially the *get*-passive.

ACTIVITY 4 listening

Ask someone (a native speaker of English, if possible) to tell you about a really frightening experience he or she has had. Find out what happened, and how it happened. Record the conversation.

Listen to the recording. Was the passive used? If so, was it the *be*-passive or the *get*-passive? Was the agent (the *by*-phrase) used?

ACTIVITY 5 listening

CD Track 29

STEP 1 Listen to the audio of two people talking about bad experiences they have had. What experiences did the speakers have? What is similar and different about their experiences?

STEP 2 Listen to the audio again. Write down all the statements that use the passive. For each statement, was the *be*-passive or the *get*-passive used? Was the agent (the *by*-phrase) used?

ACTIVITY 6 reading

ACHIEVEMENT SNAP

STEP 1

a. Work in pairs. Try to think of twenty different achievements (discoveries, inventions, or works of art), as well as the name of the person(s) who created them. Here are a few examples:

ACHIEVEMENT	PERSON
The telephone	Alexander Graham Bell
Hamlet	William Shakespeare
Mona Lisa	Leonardo da Vinci
Psycho	Alfred Hitchcock

b. Write each name on an index card and then write each achievement on a different index card. You should have a total of forty cards. Now you are ready to play Achievement Snap. The object of the game is to make a correct match between Achievement and Person.

STEP 2

1. Get together with another pair. Put all your "People Cards" in one deck and all your "Achievement Cards" in another deck. Shuffle each deck carefully.
2. Put the deck of Achievement Cards face down on a table.
3. Deal the People Cards to the players. Each player should have several cards. Do not look at your cards.
4. The dealer turns over the first Achievement Card and puts down his or her first People Card.
5. Keep taking turns at putting down People Cards until a match is made. The first person to spot a match shouts "Snap" loudly and explains the match: "The telephone was invented by Alexander Graham Bell." If everyone agrees that the match is factually and grammatically correct, the player takes the pile of People Cards on the table.
6. The winner is the person who collects the most People Cards.

Remember to use an appropriate verb in matching the person and the achievement. Common verbs include: *compose, write, discover, invent, direct, sing, paint.*

NOTE: It is possible to continue playing after you lose your People Cards. If you correctly spot a "match," you can collect the cards on the table.

ACTIVITY 7 speaking or writing

Make a presentation (oral or written) about your country or a place that you know well. Bring in pictures or maps to illustrate your talk. Describe the resources and products, any changes over time, and any predictions for the future.

ACTIVITY 8 research on the web/writing

Choose one famous invention discovery, or creation such as one of those in Activity 6. Go
on the Internet and use a search engine such as Google® or Yahoo® to search for information about your topic.

When, where, and how was it invented discovered, or created?

Who was it invented or discovered or created by?

Write a short summary of your research and tell the class.

What was the most interesting thing that you learned?

Which Web site was most useful in helping you with your research?

What kind of research could this Web site be useful for?

ACTIVITY 9 reflection

Choose one tense of the passive that you find difficult to remember. Choose a sentence from your story in Activity 3 that could use this tense. Draw a picture to illustrate your sentence.

UNIT 23

PHRASAL VERBS

UNIT GOALS

- Know when to use phrasal verbs
- Know which phrasal verbs take objects and which phrasal verbs do not take objects
- Correctly form sentences containing phrasal verbs and objects
- Know which phrasal verbs are separable and which are inseparable

OPENING TASK

School Routines

STEP 1

Look at the pictures. What do you think is happening in each one?

STEP 2

Work with a partner. Read the clues and complete the crossword.

Clues across:

1. Use the new words to _____ up your own story.
3. Please _____ up the new words in a dictionary.
4. Read the answers and _____ out the incorrect choices.
5. At the end of the lesson, please _____ up the classroom.
6. Look at the answer key and _____ out if your answers are correct.

Clues down:

2. At the end of the test, you must _____ in all your papers.
3. Don't _____ out any questions. Try to answer everything.
6. Use your pencil to _____ in the blanks.
7. You can use your calculator to _____ out the answers.
8. Please _____ up when the teacher says your name.

STEP 3

Check your answers with your classmates. How many of these things have you done today? Tell your partner.

(Solution to Opening Task Puzzle on page A-18)

FOCUS 1 Phrasal Verbs

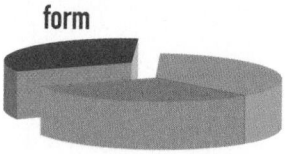

EXAMPLES				EXPLANATIONS
	Verb	*Particle*		Phrasal verbs have two parts: a **verb** and **particle**. Common particles are *off, on, in, out, up.*
(a) Please	**take**	**out**	your books.	
(b) You can	**look**	**up**	the new words.	
(c) Don't	**hand**	**in**	your papers until the end of the exam.	

EXERCISE 1

With a classmate, use the phrasal verbs to make a list of instructions for each task.

Example: Take a test: put away/fill in/leave out/hand in
First, put away all your textbooks and notes.
Then fill in your name and student ID on the test sheet.
Don't leave out any questions.
Finally, hand in your papers at the end of the test.

1. Take out a library book: look up/take down/check out/give back
2. Use a CD player: take out/switch on/put in/turn up
3. Get cash from an ATM: put in/key in/take out/take back
4. Drive a car: get in/put in/switch on/press down
5. Your idea: .....

FOCUS 2 When to Use Phrasal Verbs and How to Learn Them

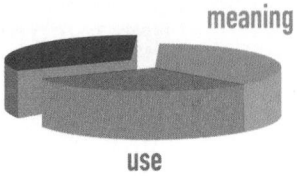

EXAMPLES	EXPLANATIONS
(a) **Look out!** There's a car coming! (b) The movie starts at 8:00. Please don't **show up** late or we won't get good seats.	Phrasal verbs are very common, especially in informal spoken English. It is often difficult to guess the meaning of a phrasal verb, even when you know the meaning of each part. In some situations, however, the context can help you make a guess. In (a), *look out* means be careful. In (b), *show up* means arrive.
(c) You should **look over** your homework before you give it to the teacher. (d) My friend David **looks after** my cats when I go on vacation.	When you use the same verb with a different particle, the meaning usually changes. In (c), *look over* means to check or examine something. In (d), *look after* means to take care of. To remember the meanings of phrasal verbs, learn the two parts together as one vocabulary item, in the same way that you learn new words.

EXERCISE 2

Get together with a classmate and match each verb in the diagram below with a particle from the list to the left of the diagram to create a set of phrasal verbs to describe typical school activities. (Notice that some verbs can take different particles to express different meanings.) Check that you understand the meaning of the phrasal verbs you create (your teacher or a good English/English dictionary can help). Remember, in this exercise, we are only thinking about phrasal verbs that are often used to talk about "school."

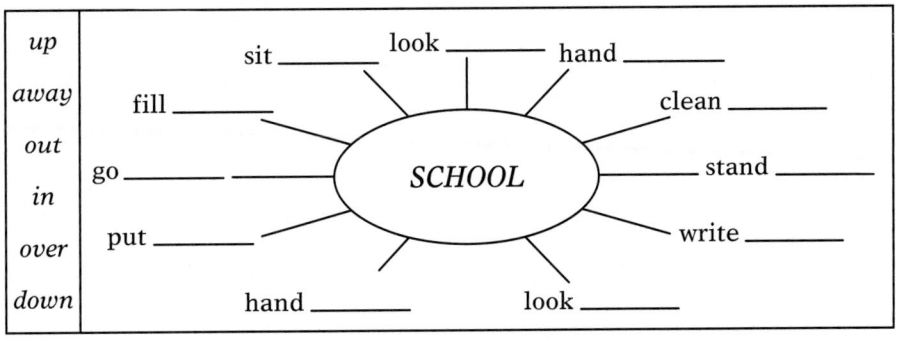

EXERCISE 3

Use the phrasal verbs from Exercise 2 to complete the text below.

French Lessons

I will never forget my first French lessons many years ago in high school. Our teacher was very strict and rather old-fashioned, even for that time. When she entered the classroom, we all had to (1) stand _____ and say "Bonjour, Madame Morel," and we couldn't (2) sit _____ until she gave us permission. Every class followed exactly the same routine, with absolutely no variation. First, we always had "dictée." The teacher read a passage, sentence by sentence, and we had to (3) write _____ exactly what she said, word for word. We weren't allowed to use dictionaries in class, so we couldn't (4) look _____ the meanings of any words we didn't know. Then, she always gave us precisely five minutes to (5) look _____ our papers to check the spelling and punctuation. This was very important because if we (6) handed _____ work that had more than one mistake in it, we had to stay behind after class. Next, she always (7) handed _____ a list of vocabulary words for us to memorize. Then after exactly ten minutes, she gave us a quiz that always told us to (8) "fill _____ the blanks with the appropriate vocabulary word." Finally, she (9) went _____ the vocabulary words from the previous day's lesson to make sure that we hadn't forgotten them. How I hated French lessons! Even when the bell rang at the end of the day, we couldn't leave until we (10) had cleaned _____ the classroom and (11) put _____ all our books.

EXERCISE 4

Use as many of the phrasal verbs from Exercises 1, 2, and 3 as you can to describe a class you have taken or are taking now. Make a list and then describe the class to a classmate.

FOCUS 3 Phrasal Verbs That Take Objects

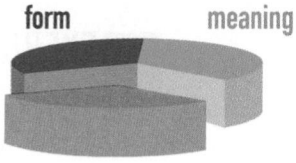

EXAMPLES	EXPLANATIONS
	Like other verbs, many phrasal verbs take objects.
(a) We had to **call off** the meeting because everyone was sick.	In (a), the object of the sentence is *the meeting.*
(b) We're trying to sleep. Please **turn down** that radio!	In (b), the object of the sentence is *that radio.*

Some common phrasal verbs that take objects:

PHRASAL VERB	EXAMPLE	MEANING*
Call off	We had to **call off** the meeting because everyone was sick.	Cancel
Put off	Let's **put off** our meeting until next week.	Change to a later time or date
Pick up	Please **pick up** your towel! Don't leave it on the bathroom floor.	Lift or take from a particular place
Set up	We need to **set up** a time to discuss this.	Arrange a meeting or appointment
Talk over	It's important for couples to **talk over** their problems and misunderstandings.	Discuss a problem

PHRASAL VERB	EXAMPLE	MEANING*
Throw out	I **threw out** all my old school books and papers when we moved.	Put in the garbage, get rid of
Turn down	We're trying to sleep. Please **turn down** that radio!	Lower the volume of radio, TV, etc.
Turn off	I'll **turn off** the TV as soon as this program ends.	Stop a machine, engine or electrical device
Turn on	She always **turns on** the radio to listen to the news.	Start a machine, engine or electrical device

*Some of these phrasal verbs may have different meanings in different situations.

EXERCISE 5

Respond to the following situations using as many of the phrasal verbs discussed so far in this unit as possible. (Some of the language from Unit 10, *Giving Advice and Expressing Opinions,* and Unit 17, *Requests and Permission,* might also help you here.)

1. You are trying to talk on the phone but your roommate is listening to some very loud music.
   You say: Please turn down that radio!!
   _____
   _____

2. A friend is applying for a job and has just written a letter of application.
   He asks you to check the letter for grammatical errors.
   He says: _____
   _____
   _____

3. A family member is sick and you need to leave town for a few days to take care of her. You call a colleague and explain the situation. Then you ask him to telephone your clients and delay all the meetings you had arranged with them until the following week.
   You say: _____
   _____
   _____

4. It is the first class meeting of the school year. Your new teacher is explaining his policy about grading and homework. He expects students to give him their homework on time.
   He says: _____
   _____
   _____

5. You have helped organize a foreign film festival on campus. You ask some of your classmates to help you distribute fliers about the movies to students in the cafeteria during the lunch break.
   You say: _____
   _____
   _____

6. Your friend's roommate leaves papers and clothes all over the floor. She asks for your advice.
   You say: _____
   _____
   _____

FOCUS 4 Separating Verbs and Particles

EXAMPLES	EXPLANATIONS
subject *verb* *particle* *object (noun)* (a) She **turned** **on** the light. OR *subject* *verb* *object (noun)* *particle* (b) She **turned** the light **on.**	Many phrasal verbs are **separable**: When the object is a noun, you can: Put the object **after** the particle. OR Put the object **between** the verb and the particle.
subject *verb* *object (pronoun)* *particle* (c) She **turned** **it** **on.** (d) NOT: She **turned on** it. (e) He **cleaned** it **up**. (f) NOT: He **cleaned up** it.	When the object of a separable phrasal verb is a pronoun, you must put the object **between** the verb and the particle. This is because the pronoun gives information that is known to both speaker and listener (here, the speaker and listener both know what *it* refers to). Known information does not usually come at the end of a sentence in English.

EXERCISE 6

Replace the underlined words with a phrasal verb from the list below. For now, only separate the verb and the particle when the object is a pronoun.

try on	find out	take off	call up	throw out	set up	take back
	go over	put on	get off	put off		

taking your shoes off

Shirley: Why are you (1) removing your shoes? I thought you were going to go for a walk.

Julia: I decided to (2) wear my boots. It's raining outside.

Shirley: I thought those boots were too small. You said you wanted to (3) return them to the store. Did you (4) discover if they have a larger size?

Julia: I guess I (5) delayed it too long. When I (6) phoned the store, the salesperson said I'd have to wait at least a month for the next delivery, so I decided to keep these after all.

Shirley: That's crazy! Don't wear them if they're too small. Why don't you borrow my hiking boots?

Julia: I thought you (7) put those in the garbage when we moved.

Shirley: No, they're somewhere in my closet if you want to (8) wear them to see if they fit you.

Get together with a classmate. Compare your answers and then read the new dialogue aloud to each other. Change roles and read the dialogue again.

FOCUS 5 Inseparable Phrasal Verbs

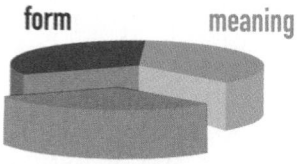

EXAMPLES	EXPLANATIONS
(a) Yesterday I **ran into** my friend Sal. OR (b) Yesterday I **ran into** her. (c) NOT: Yesterday I ran my friend into. (d) NOT: Yesterday I ran her into.	Not all phrasal verbs can be separated. Some phrasal verbs are **inseparable:** With these verbs you cannot put the object between the verb and the particle, even when the object is a pronoun. It is difficult to guess which phrasal verbs are separable and which are inseparable. It is a good idea to learn if a phrasal verb is separable or inseparable when you learn its meaning. A good dictionary will give you this information.

Some common inseparable phrasal verbs:

PHRASAL VERB	EXAMPLE	MEANING*
Come across	You never know what you'll find at a yard sale! Last week, I **came across** a valuable old Beatles record.	Find something or someone
Run into	Colleen was really surprised to **run into** her ex-boyfriend at the supermarket.	Meet someone unexpectedly
Get off	Don't **get off** the bus until it stops.	Leave a bus, train, or plane
Get on	You can't **get on** a plane without a boarding pass.	Enter a bus, train, or plane
Go over	Our teacher always **goes over** the main points in a unit before she gives us a test.	Review
Get over	Jeb has gone to bed early because he's still **getting over** the flu.	Recover from illness or sadness

*Some of these phrasal verbs may have different meanings in different situations.

EXERCISE 7

Replace the underlined words with phrasal verbs from the list below. Separate the verb and particle where necessary.

pass away find out came across cheer up put off run into call on get on

came across

1. Yesterday Sally finally <u>found</u> Marie's phone number. She tried to call her, but the line was busy.
2. So, she decided to <u>visit</u> her <u>at home</u>.
3. Earlier that day, Sally <u>met</u> their friend Ron <u>unexpectedly</u> as he was leaving the apartment building.
4. He was ready to <u>enter</u> the bus to go to his sister's house.
5. He told Sally that his grandfather had <u>died last week</u>.
6. Of course, Sally was sorry to <u>hear</u> the sad news.
7. She suggested to Marie that the three friends should <u>postpone</u> the dinner party they had been planning.
8. Marie agreed, and she also thought they should visit Ron to help him <u>recover</u> from his loss.

EXERCISE 8

STEP 1 **Where do you think the following were probably said? Match the sentences with the pictures.**

1.

2.

3.

4.

Example: 4 *Please hand in your papers now.*
Please hand them in now.

a. ___ Let's go over last week's quiz.

_____

b. ___ Can I try on this shirt?

_____

c. ___ Let's set up a meeting for next week.

_____

d. ___ You can't check out these books without a current ID.

_____

STEP 2 **Underline the phrasal verbs. Rewrite each sentence using a pronoun, moving the particle if is possible to do so.**

STEP 3 **Now think of other phrasal verbs that could be used in each context. Make sentences as in Step 2. Exchange sentences with your partner, and rewrite them using pronouns.**

FOCUS 6 When and When Not to Separate Phrasal Verbs

EXAMPLES	EXPLANATIONS
(a) Last week Sharifah organized her closet and **threw out** all her old clothes. OR (b) Last week Sharifah organized her closet and **threw** all her old clothes **out.**	You can separate the verb and the particle when the object consists of just a few words.
(c) Last week Sharifah organized her closet and **threw out** all the clothes that were several years old. (d) NOT: Last week Sharifah organized her closet and **threw** all the clothes that were several years old **out.**	Do not separate the verb and particle when the object is longer than three or four words.

EXERCISE 9

Are the underlined phrasal verbs correct in the following sentences? In sentences where the verb and the particle are incorrectly placed, circle the particle and draw an arrow to show its correct position.

Example: *I have a meeting at 4:00 tomorrow, but I'm trying to put off it until the next day.*
Put it off. Correct

1. Cherie always shows up for work on time. She has to get the bus on at 7:00 A.M., but yesterday she overslept and didn't get up until 8:00. She was late for work!

2. Last month, Sunny went through her file cabinets and threw all the papers she had been keeping since her time in graduate school out.

3. When Nina ran Tim into, he pointed out that they had not been in touch for over a year. They promised to call each other up more often in the future.

4. When Sandra called, Graham was out. He tried to call back her, but he couldn't get through because the line was busy.

5. Eli's mother passed last year away. Since she died, he has put the decision about what to do with her house in Brooklyn off.

6. When Sally and the other children arrived at camp, the camp counselor went the rules over. The boys had to wash the dishes and the girls had to put away them.

EXERCISE 10

Go over the sentences you wrote in Exercise 5 on pages 334 and 335. Underline the phrasal verbs you used and separate the particles where you think it is possible.

FOCUS 7 Phrasal Verbs That Do Not Take Objects

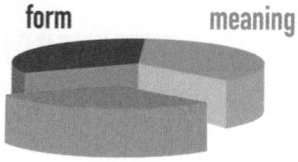

EXAMPLES	EXPLANATION
(a) My roommate's gone on vacation, and I have no idea when he's going to **come back.** (b) Cyril waited for his friends for over an hour but they didn't **show up.**	Some phrasal verbs do not take objects. Because they do not take objects, they are inseparable.

Some common phrasal verbs that do not take objects:

PHRASAL VERB	EXAMPLE	MEANING*
Break down	My car **broke down,** so I walked.	Stop working (machine, engine etc.)
Catch on	Some fashions **catch on** right away.	Become popular
Come back	Goodbye, please **come back** soon.	Return
Come to	When I **came to,** I was in the hospital.	Regain consciousness
Eat out	Darlene is too busy to cook, so she usually **eats out.**	Eat in a restaurant
Get by	He doesn't earn much, but he seems to **get by.**	Survive satisfactorily, with limited money
Grow up	His mother **grew up** in Vancouver.	Become an adult
Pass out	When Pat broke her leg in a skiing accident, she **passed out.**	Faint, lose consciousness
Show up	It isn't a good idea to **show up** late for a job interview.	Arrive, appear at a place

*Some of these phrasal verbs may have different meanings in different situations.

EXERCISE 11

Use phrasal verbs to complete the letter from Nancy to her housemate, Mary.

Replace the underlined words with phrasal verbs from the list below. You may need to change the form of the phrasal verb.

If the phrasal verb can or must be separated, put the particle in the appropriate position. (See the example.) You will need to use some of the phrasal verbs more than once; you may not need to use some of them at all.

run into	talk over	turn down	show up
come over	find out	pick up	get off
hang up	come back	grow up	put on
catch on	pass out	eat out	put off

Mary and Nancy have recently moved to a new city and have just bought a house together. Mary is currently overseas on a business trip, so Nancy has written her a letter, telling her all the news.

Dear Mary,

I miss you! Being alone in this new house is a good experience for me, but at the end of the day I wish you were here to (1) discuss talk things over with me. I've been very busy painting the kitchen—you won't recognize the place when you (2) return _____! However, at the moment it's a terrible mess and there's no way I can cook here yet, so I (3) eat in restaurants _____ every night. You'll be glad to know that there are several excellent Thai restaurants in our neighborhood. It's amazing how Thai food has (4) become popular _____ everywhere in the last few years, isn't it?

Guess what? The other day I (5) met unexpectedly _____ Ruth and Maureen. What a surprise! They (6) were leaving/departing _____ the bus at the bus stop right by our house. It turns out they were on their way to visit Ruth's grandmother, who lives just around the corner. Ruth's son, Sam, was with them. Actually it was a bit embarrassing because I didn't recognize him at first; you really won't believe how much he (7) has matured/become an adult _____ since we last saw him.

I (8) am discovering _____ lots of new things about our neighborhood . . . and our neighbors! We'll have to (9) lower _____ the volume on our CD player by 7:30 each night. The neighbors in the green house (10) arrived here/at this place _____, to complain about the noise the other day. They have a 3-month-old baby, so they need it to be quiet so the baby can sleep. We (11) discussed _____ it in a very "neighborly" way. I told them, though, that you're a night owl, and that night time is the time you like to listen to music. Loud! We decided you'll have to start (12) wearing _____ headphones!

There's a lot more I could say. I can't wait for you to (13) _____ return. This time I promise (14) I'll arrive _____ on time at the airport. See you soon. . . .

Love,

Nancy

EXERCISE 12

STEP 1 **Work with a classmate or a small group. Can you fill in the missing words in this word puzzle to create phrasal verbs? Sometimes the missing word is a particle that can combine with all the attached verbs to make different phrasal verbs; other times, the missing word is a verb that can combine with all the attached particles to make different phrasal verbs. (A good English/English dictionary may help you.)**

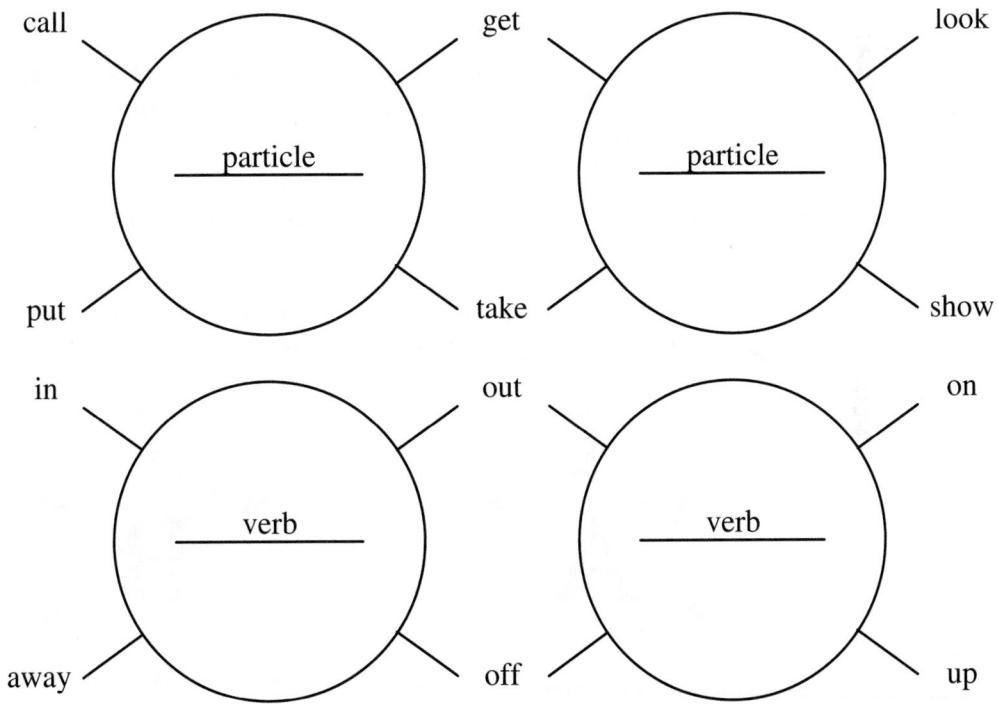

STEP 2 **Use each phrasal verb in a sentence, showing that you understand its meaning. State whether the phrasal verb is separable or inseparable.**

Use Your English

ACTIVITY 1 speaking

You can either play this game with a classmate or in teams. You need a die/dice to play.

STEP 1 Player (or team) 1 throws the die/dice and selects the verb from circle A that corresponds to the number thrown. For example, if she throws 3, then the verb is *turn.*

STEP 2 Player (or team) 2 throws the die/dice again and selects the particle from circle B that corresponds to the number thrown. For example, if she throws 1, the particle is *off.*

STEP 3 The first player (or team) to come up with a sentence containing the verb + particle, scores a point. For example, the player who comes up with a sentence using *turn off* correctly scores the point. If the combination of verb + particle does not create a meaningful phrasal verb, the first player to say "Impossible" scores the point.

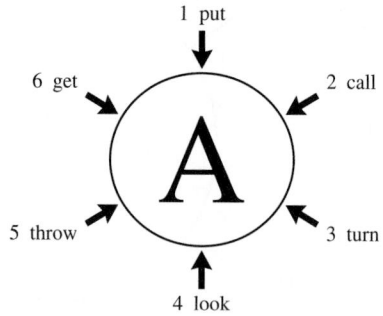

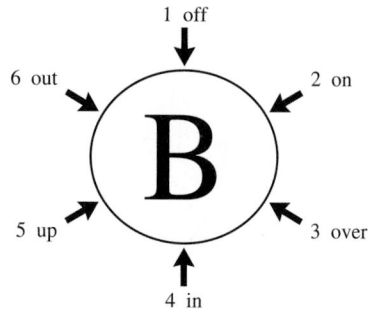

Variation: After you have played this game a few times, get together with some classmates to make your own version. Choose six verbs and six particles. Draw two circles and write the verbs and particles in each circle. Try out your game on your classmates.

If you are playing in a team, you could copy the two circles onto a big piece of paper and stick it on the wall so that everyone can see.

ACTIVITY 2 speaking/listening

STEP 1 Interview three different people. Ask them to describe their typical morning routines, from the moment they wake up until they leave the house to go to work or school. Record their responses.

STEP 2 Listen to what they say. What differences and what similarities do you find? Write down any phrasal verbs that they use. Share your findings with your classmates and your teacher.

ACTIVITY 3 listening

CD Track 30

Listen to the audio of native speakers of English describing their early morning routines. What differences and similarities do you find among the speakers? Make a list of the phrasal verbs that the speakers used. Compare your list with a classmate.

ACTIVITY 4 listening

Your teacher is going to give you a set of instructions. Listen to each instruction; if the instruction contains a phrasal verb, do what your teacher tells you to do. If the instruction does **not** contain a phrasal verb, do nothing. For example, if your teacher says "Stand up," you stand up because *stand up* is a phrasal verb. If your teacher says "Turn to your right," you do nothing at all because *turn* is not a phrasal verb.

Variation: Anyone who follows a command that does not contain a phrasal verb drops out of the game. The last person to remain in the game is the "winner." After a while, give your teacher a rest and take turns giving the commands to the rest of the class.

ACTIVITY 5 writing/reading

The purpose of this activity is to write a set of instructions for somebody who doesn't know how to make a peanut butter and jelly sandwich. First, look at the bag of supplies that your teacher has brought to class. Then, work with your group to write your instructions, trying to use as many phrasal verbs as possible. When you are ready, read the instructions to your teacher, one step at a time, and he or she will try to follow your instructions exactly as you give them.

ACTIVITY 6 writing/reading

STEP 1 Choose one of the contexts below. What phrasal verbs do you associate with these contexts? Think of as many phrasal verbs as you can for each context and write them in the outer circle around each context. Redraw these context circles with a larger white band in your notebook.

STEP 2 Exchange notebooks with a classmate. Choose one of the contexts and write a dialogue on a piece of paper. Include many of the phrasal verbs he or she has written down.

STEP 3 Exchange your paper with a different classmate. Read the dialogue. Can you guess the context he or she has chosen?

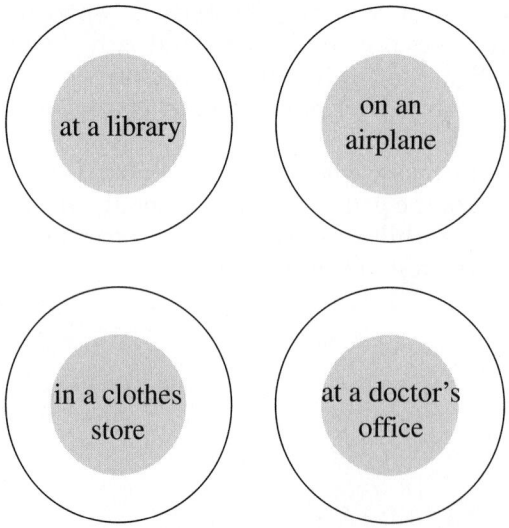

ACTIVITY 7 writing

Think about everything you have done in the last week. Write a letter to your teacher, telling him or her about your week, **trying to use as many phrasal verbs as possible.** Before you hand your letter in, look it over carefully to find out how many phrasal verbs you were able to use. Write the number of phrasal verbs you used at the end of the letter.

ACTIVITY 8 research on the web

Go on the Internet and use a search engine such as Google® or Yahoo® to find a Web site where you can test your knowledge of phrasal verbs. Enter keywords "test phrasal verbs". Choose one Web site to recommend to your classmates.

ACTIVITY 9 reflection

Choose five phrasal verbs from this unit that you find difficult to remember. Think of a sentence that explains the meaning of each verb. Write each sentence on a card, using a blank instead of the phrasal verb. Write the verb on the back of the card. Use the cards to test yourself or a classmate.

Example:

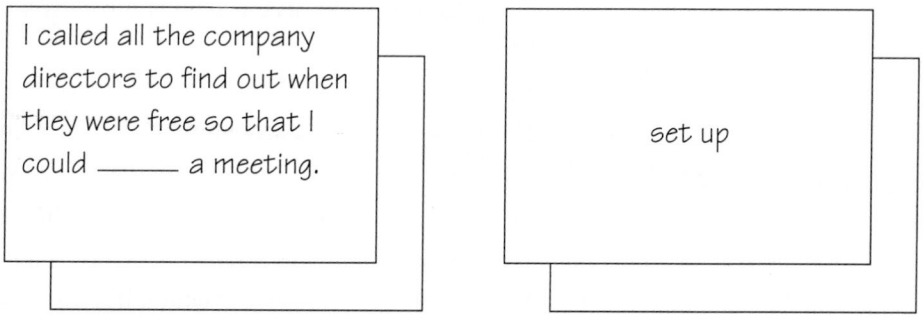

UNIT 24

ADJECTIVE CLAUSES AND PARTICIPLES AS ADJECTIVES

UNIT GOALS

- Form correct adjective clauses with *who* and *that* to describe people
- Use adjective clauses with *which* and *that* to describe things
- Understand how to use participles as adjectives
- Know the difference between *-ed* and *-ing* participles

OPENING TASK

Who Do They Love?

STEP 1

Look at the people in the picture. What are their relationships? Who likes whom?

STEP 2

Lee, Tracy, Sid, and Kit are in love. Can you find who belongs together? Get together with a partner to read the clues, complete the chart, and solve the puzzle.

CLUES:

1. Lee loves the person who speaks Swahili.
2. Tracy loves the person who tells amusing stories.
3. The teacher loves the writer.
4. The pilot loves the person who is interested in history.
5. Sid loves the person that plays the piano.
6. The person who tells amusing stories is a pilot.
7. The person that runs three miles a day is a doctor.
8. The person who plays the piano is a teacher.
9. The person who is interested in history is a doctor.
10. The doctor loves the person who tells amusing stories.
11. The person who speaks Swahili is a writer.
12. The pilot loves the person who runs three miles a day.

Information about Lee:

- _____
- _____

LEE
loves...

- *the person who speaks Swahili*
- _____

Name _____

Information about Tracy:

- _____
- _____

TRACY
loves...

- _____
- _____

Name _____

Information about Kit:

- _____
- _____

KIT
loves...

- _____
- _____

Name _____

Information about Sid:

- _____
- _____

SID
loves...

- _____
- _____

Name _____

STEP 3

Complete the sentences. Read them to a partner. Compare answers.

The person _____ loves Lee is _____. The person _____ loves Kit is _____.

The person _____ Sid loves is _____. The person _____ Tracy loves is _____.

(Opening Task, Step 3 solution found on page A-18)

FOCUS 1 Adjective Clauses: Using *Who* and *That* to Describe People

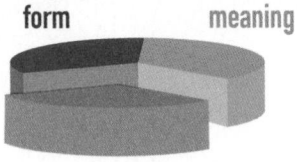

EXAMPLES	EXPLANATIONS
(a) The person **who speaks Swahili** is a writer. (b) The pilot loves the person **who runs three miles a day.**	Restrictive adjective clauses (also known as relative clauses) give identifying information about a noun.
(c) The person **who** plays the piano is a teacher. OR (d) The person **that** plays the piano is a teacher.	Adjective clauses begin with a relative pronoun. To refer to people, you can use the relative pronouns *who* or *that*. *That* is more commonly used in informal conversation than in writing.
(e) Sid loves the person who **plays** the piano. OR (f) Sid loves the person that **plays** the piano.	Every adjective clause contains a verb.
Subject (g) **The person** who tells amusing stories is a pilot. *Object* (h) Lee loves **the person** who speaks Swahili.	An adjective clause can describe the subject or object of the main clause.

EXERCISE 1

Go back to the clues in the Opening Task on page 349.

a. Underline every adjective clause you find.

b. Circle every relative pronoun.

c. Draw an arrow to connect the relative pronoun with the noun it describes.

d. Write "S" if the adjective clause describes the subject of a sentence. Write "O" if it describes the object.

Example: The pilot loves the person who runs three miles a day. O

EXERCISE 2

Get together with a partner and look over the information in the chart below. The owners of the houses on this block of Upham Street are all women.

HOUSE	HABITS	LIKES	DISLIKES	PLACE OF BIRTH	OCCUPATION
1.	swims three times a week	dogs	TV	Manchester	lawyer
2.	eats out every night	fast cars	baseball	Madrid	marketing manager
3.	lifts weights	music	politics	Miami	marketing manager
4.	drinks five cups of coffee a day	cats	ballet	Mexico City	lawyer
5.	sings in the shower	art	baseball	Montreal	marketing manager
6.	walks to work	movies	basketball	Moscow	lawyer

Use the information in the chart to make as many true statements as you can about the owners of these houses, using adjective clauses. We have started the first ones for you.

1. The woman who likes dogs lives next to the woman who _____.
2. The lawyer that dislikes ballet lives between the marketing manager who _____ and the marketing manager who _____.
3. The marketing manager who _____ lives between the lawyer that _____ and the marketing manager who _____.
4. The woman _____

5. The lawyer _____

6. The marketing manager _____

7. _____

_____

8. _____

_____

9. _____

_____

10. _____

_____

Look back at the sentences you have written. Underline the adjective clauses, circle the relative pronouns, and draw arrows to the appropriate nouns (as you did in Exercise 1).

FOCUS 2 *Which* and *That*

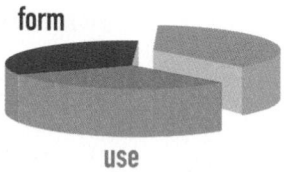

EXAMPLES	EXPLANATIONS
(a) I bought a book **which** I really wanted to read. OR (b) I bought a book **that** I really wanted to read. (c) The book **which** he wrote is excellent. OR (d) The book **that** he wrote is excellent.	To refer to things in adjective clauses, you can use *which* or *that*. *That* is more common in informal conversation than in writing.

EXERCISE 3

Do this exercise with a group of five or six classmates. Complete the chart below. This chart is like the one in Exercise 2, except for the first category. Decide on who will be Student #1. Then use your positions in the group seating arrangement to finish writing your names in column 1.

STUDENT NAME	HABITS	LIKES	DISLIKES	PLACE OF BIRTH	OCCUPATION OR DESIRED OCCUPATION
1.					
2.					
3.					
4.					
5.					
6.					

STEP 1 **Interview each other to fill in the blanks on the chart. Feel free to make up your answers, just for fun.**

STEP 2 **When you have filled in your charts, make clues about each person in the chart using adjective clauses in your statements. The other students will guess who you are talking about.**

Example: *She is sitting between the person who likes ice cream and the person who wants to be a doctor.*

EXERCISE 4

STEP 1 **Complete the following to make true statements about yourself. Try to describe both people and things in your statements. Circle the appropriate relative pronouns. (More than one relative pronoun may be possible.)**

1. I am bored by people that / which / who _____.
2. I am interested in _____ that / which / who _____.
3. I am frightened of _____ that / which / who _____.
4. _____ that / which / who _____ are really annoying.
5. _____ that / which / who _____ is/are often interesting.

STEP 2 **Get together with a partner and compare your statements. Be ready to share the most interesting or surprising statements with the rest of the class.**

EXERCISE 5

Edit the following story. Use relative pronouns whenever possible to avoid repeating words, as in the example. After you have finished editing the passage, compare your suggestions for changes with a classmate's. (There is sometimes more than one way to make improvements and avoid repetition.)

1. It's interesting talking with women. ~~These women~~ who have had experiences. ~~Their experiences~~ which are similar to mine. There are a lot of things to talk about.
2. For example, *balance* is a topic. Most of my women friends are interested in this topic.
3. Achieving balance is a challenge for many women. Many women have jobs and family responsibilities.
4. Some women don't have jobs outside their homes. These women sometimes feel criticized. They feel criticized by other people.
5. These people think that women should have careers. This is an attitude. More and more people share this attitude.

6. Some women work at jobs and have young children. These women also feel criticized. They feel criticized by other people.
7. Other people think that all women should stay at home with their children. They should never be sent to a day care center. Day care is a business, not a loving home. This is a belief. This belief makes some women feel a lack of balance in their lives.
8. Some women never have children. These women may feel pressure from their own parents. Their own parents worry that their children won't provide them with grandchildren.
9. These are examples. These examples show how it can be difficult for women to feel sure they are doing the right thing for themselves and for their children.

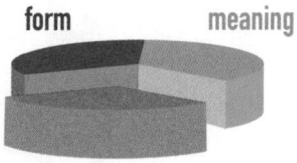

FOCUS 3 Participles as Adjectives

EXAMPLES	EXPLANATIONS
(a) People who have traveled to many different countries are often very **interesting.** (b) We were very **amused** by the jokes that Bruce told us.	*Interesting* and *amused* are participles formed by adding *-ing/-ed* to a verb. These participles act like adjectives when they modify nouns.
(c) Professor Rand is very knowledgeable, but his lectures are **boring.**  (source/boring)	Adjectives that end with *-ing* usually describe the source (the thing or person that makes us feel a certain way).
(d) Many students were **bored** during Professor Rand's lecture.  (emotion/bored)	Adjectives that end with *-ed* usually describe the emotion (how we feel about something)

EXERCISE 6

STEP 1 In the pictures below, draw arrows that start at the source (the reason for the feeling) and that point to the emotion (the way the person feels).

STEP 2 Then use the word (on the right) to label the pictures with *-ing* adjectives (which describe the source) and *-ed* adjectives (which describe the emotion). The first one has been done for you.

EXERCISE 7

Circle the correct adjective for each of the following sentences.

1. Melanie likes the family in the apartment above her, but sometimes she feels that their teenage boy is annoying/annoyed, especially when he plays his stereo too loudly.
2. However, she usually finds their presence upstairs very comforting/comforted.
3. Once she heard a frightening/frightened noise outside. She thought it was a prowler, so she called up her neighbors.
4. They invited her to their apartment for a relaxing/relaxed cup of tea and a soothing/soothed conversation.
5. This helped her to calm down until she was no longer frightening/frightened.
6. Melanie especially likes Jane, the mother. Jane tells Melanie amusing/amused stories about herself and her family members' daily life.
7. Jane's husband Bob is a shoe salesperson. Even though this may sound like a boring/bored job, it's not.
8. Lots of surprising/surprised things happen to shoe salespeople. Just last week, for example, a real prince came into the store with his bodyguards and bought twenty pairs of Italian leather shoes.
9. The prince thought Bob was such a polite and amusing/amused person that he gave him a fifty-dollar tip.
10. Of course, Bob thought that this was very exciting/excited, and he took Jane and the family out to dinner that night.
11. Jane works part-time in a pet store as a dog groomer. She says that some of the customers never give their dogs baths. These dogs are sometimes so dirty and uncomfortable that it is shocking/shocked.
12. Jane's stories are so entertaining/entertained that Melanie usually doesn't mind the noise that Jane's teenage son makes.
13. In fact, Melanie was very disappointing/disappointed when she heard that Jane and her family might move.

EXERCISE 8

Circle all the *-ed* and *-ing* adjectives in the following passage. Then decide whether the correct form has been used. In other words, are there cases where the *-ing* adjective is used when the *-ed* adjective should be used (or vice versa)?

SHELLEY'S ANCESTORS

Shelley had an interested day yesterday. Three of her favorite cousins dropped in for an unexpected visit, and they had a very stimulating conversation. They told each other surprised stories about some of their relatives. Shelley was shocked by some of these stories. For example, when their great aunt—their grandmother's sister—was quite young, she traveled around the world, fell in love with a Dutch sailor, and had a baby but did not get married. Her embarrassing parents disowned her, but many years later they helped her raise the child. Another distant member of the family was a drug addict in New York in the thirties, and according to Shelley's cousins' mother, he was quite a rude and disgusting fellow. This man's brother was a horse of a different color, though. Apparently he was an inspired and talented artist, who also created amused illustrations for children's books. After hearing all of these stories, Shelley realized that her family history was certainly not bored!

Use Your English

ACTIVITY 1 speaking/listening/writing

CAN YOU TOP THAT?

STEP 1 Look at the list of adjectives below and choose one that describes an experience you have had (for example, an embarrassing moment, a boring day, an exciting date). Try to remember how you felt as a result.

embarrassing	disgusting	frightening	boring
horrifying	rewarding	exciting	entertaining
disappointing	surprising	relaxing	shocking
annoying	amusing	exhausting	inspiring

STEP 2 Circulate for fifteen minutes and exchange experiences with classmates to find out if they have had an experience that "tops" yours—that is, an experience that is even more embarrassing, more boring, or more exciting than yours.

STEP 3 Report to the rest of the class on what you found. Vote on who has had the most embarrassing, boring, exciting (etc.) experience.

STEP 4 Choose two of the experiences that your classmates told you about and describe them in writing.

STEP 5 When you finish writing, read your work and circle any participles used as adjectives. Underline any adjective clauses that you used.

ACTIVITY 2 writing/reading

STEP 1

Think of a person that everyone in your class knows (someone famous or someone in your class!). Or think of a thing or object that is familiar to everyone. Write three statements using adjective clauses that describe this person or thing.

I'm thinking of something that I drink every day. It's something that is more expensive now than it used to be. It's something that helps me feel more awake. (Answer: coffee)

STEP 2

Read your statements one at a time and have others guess what or who you are describing. Work in pairs or in teams if you prefer.

ACTIVITY 3 speaking

Think of someone that you know. Choose someone who is quite a character. In other words, think of someone who stands out in some way or is easy to remember. Describe this person, using some adjective clauses and some *-ed* or *-ing* adjectives to describe him or her.

ACTIVITY 4 listening

CD Track 31

STEP 1

Make a list of all the characteristics you would like to find in the ideal partner (spouse, girlfriend, boyfriend, companion).

STEP 2

Listen to the audio. You will hear three friends talking about their ideal partners. Take notes about their ideas.

STEP 3

Look at the list you made in Step 1 and compare it with the notes you made from the tape. How many differences and similarities can you find?

STEP 4

Listen to the audio again. Write down any examples of adjective clauses and participle adjectives that you hear in your notebook.

ACTIVITY 5 listening/speaking

First think of as many -ing adjectives as possible. Your teacher will write each of these on a separate sheet of paper. As your game goes on, your group may add more to the list as needed. You will use these words to play Password in teams or in pairs. In this game, one person (or team), the Clue-Giver, looks at the word on the piece of paper without letting the other person (or the other team) see it.

Then the Clue-Giver gives a one-word clue that describes this word to the other person (or the other team), the Clue-Guesser. The Clue-Giver can continue to give as many clues as needed in order for the word to be guessed. The goal is to have the Clue-Guesser guess the word as soon as possible with as few clues as necessary.

ACTIVITY 6 speaking

Think of as many *-ed* adjectives as possible. Then "mime" (act out) these words and phrases, which are written on separate sheets of paper. You can use gestures and facial expressions, or you can invent a silent story, but you cannot speak. The goal is to have the other person (or the other team) guess the word or phrase as quickly as possible.

ACTIVITY 7 research on the web

InfoTrac® College Edition: Choose a pair of participle adjectives (an *–ed* adjective and an *–ing* adjective)—for example, *frightened / frightening* (see p. 356 for some other examples). Search *InfoTrac®* for articles containing these words in the title or in the article content. Choose five different examples. Write down the sentence where the adjective occurred and the topic of the article. Compare answers with your classmates.

ACTIVITY 8 reflection

Choose three pairs of participle adjectives (an *–ed* adjective and an *–ing* adjective) that you find difficult to remember. Make up one sentence using both adjectives.

Example: *The new movie was interesting and my friends were all interested in my opinion of it.*

UNIT 25

CONDITIONALS

UNIT GOALS

- Know when to use hypothetical conditionals
- Form correct conditional sentences for present, past, and future situations
- Know the difference between future conditionals and hypothetical conditionals
- Understand the meaning of *would*, *might*, and *may* in conditionals

OPENING TASK

Imaginary Situations

STEP 1

Imagine you are on a desert island. What things would you need to survive? Discuss with a partner and make a list.

STEP 2

Get together with a partner and look at each object very carefully. What would you do with them on a desert island?

Example: *If I had a knife, I would.....*

IF I ...	I WOULD ...
have / a knife	
see / ship	
find / human footprints	
not have / water	
meet / another survivor	

STEP 3

Share your ideas with the rest of the class. Vote on the most interesting and creative ideas.

(Opening Task Step 2 Solution found on page A-18)

FOCUS 1 Hypothetical Conditionals

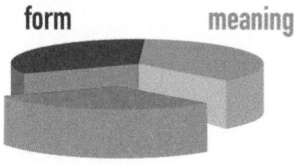

EXAMPLES	EXPLANATIONS
(a) **Ann:** What **would you do if you were** on a desert island by yourself?	Use hypothetical conditionals to talk about an imaginary situation. This is not a real situation, but one that you are picturing in your mind.
(b) **Shin:** First, **I'd look** for food and water, and then **I'd build** a shelter. (c) **Ann:** What **if there wasn't** any food on the island?	Use *was* or *were* for verbs with *be* and the simple past for other verbs in the *if* clause. Use *would* + base form of the verb in the main clause.
(d) **Shin:** I think **I'd try** to make a signal for a boat or a plane.	Use an *if* clause to introduce the topic. After that, it is not necessary to repeat the *if* clause in every sentence. *Would* + base form of the verb shows that you are talking about a hypothetical situation that has already been introduced.

EXERCISE 1

Write the sentences from the Opening Task. Be sure to use *if* clauses and *would* correctly.

1. If I had a knife, I would use it to cut some wood for a fire.

2. If I saw a ship, I would

3. _____

4. _____

5. _____

EXERCISE 2

What would you do if you were in these situations? Which situation would you prefer to be in and why? Discuss with a partner. Write two or three sentences with *If*. Then share your ideas with the rest of the class.

_____

_____

_____

EXERCISE 3

STEP 1 **Choose one of your classmates to be the "leader" for this exercise.**

STEP 2 **The leader will finish this sentence: "If I were a millionaire, ..."**

Example: *If I were a millionaire, I would buy a big house in the country and retire.*
(*If* clause) (Main clause)

STEP 3 **The next person will change the main clause into an if clause and add a new main clause.**

Example: If I bought a big house in the country and retired, I would write poetry all day long.

STEP 4 **Go around the room so that everyone has a chance to add to the "chain" of events.**

FOCUS 2 Past Hypothetical Conditionals

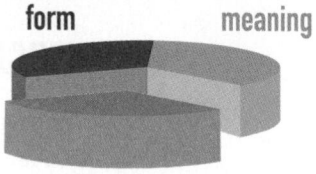

EXAMPLES	EXPLANATIONS
past perfect (a) If you **had called** me last night, I *would* + *have* + past participle **would have come** to see you. (b) If we **had known** it was Marianne's birthday, we **would have had** a surprise party for her. (c) If Bonnie **hadn't robbed** a bank, she **wouldn't have gone** to jail.	Past hypothetical conditionals talk about imagined situations in the past. It is not possible for these situations to happen because they refer to the past. To express these situations, use past perfect in the *if* clause and *would* + *have* + past participle in the main clause. We know that it is impossible to change the past, but we often think about how things might have been different in the past. In (a), I *didn't* come to see you because you *didn't* call me. In (c), Bonnie *did* go to jail because she *did* rob a bank.
past perfect (d) If Dominica **had passed** her exam, she *would* + base verb **would be** a doctor now. (e) If Pia **hadn't been born** in Egypt, she **would not speak** fluent Arabic. *past perfect* (f) If we **had won** last week's lottery, we *would* + *be* + verb + *-ing* **would be lying** on a beach in the South of France today.	Some hypothetical conditionals make a connection between the past and the present. They show an imagined change in a present situation, caused by an imagined change in a past situation. These are untrue situations because it is impossible to change the past. You usually use past perfect in the if clause and *would* + base form of the verb or *would* + *be* + verb+ *-ing* in the main clause.

EXERCISE 4

Read the following:

Ilene hates parties, so just over ten years ago, she was surprised to receive an invitation to a New Year's party from somebody that she didn't know very well. She didn't really want to go by herself, so she asked her friend Diana to go with her. Before the party, Ilene and Diana had a nice dinner together at Diana's house. It was a cold, snowy night and when it was time to leave for the party, all Ilene wanted to do was stay home and watch a video. Diana persuaded her to change her mind, however, and after they had driven all the way across town, Ilene realized that she had left the party invitation at home. Diana wanted to go back and get it, but Ilene thought she could remember the address. They found the right street, but Ilene wasn't sure about the number of the house, so they drove around until they came to a house where there was a party going on. They decided this was the right place. They didn't recognize anybody there and Ilene wanted to leave right away. However, Diana, who wasn't as shy as Ilene, persuaded her to stay. Feeling very uncomfortable, Ilene stood in a corner by herself, watching Diana have a good time. After about an hour, she decided to go home. As she was leaving, she tripped and fell down some icy steps outside the house. Luckily just at that moment, somebody was coming up the steps on his way to the party and he caught her in his arms. And that's how Ilene met her husband. . . .

Ilene and Jeff have now been together for ten years, and they are still amazed at the way they met. For a start, Ilene had gone to the wrong party. The one she had been invited to was a couple of blocks away. And then it turned out that Jeff hadn't been invited to that party either. In fact, he was only in town because his sister was very sick and he had flown in from out of state to visit her. His sister lived next door, and when he ran into Ilene, he was on his way to ask the neighbors if they could turn the music down. Jeff, who is an anthropologist, was supposed to leave the next day to spend two years in West Africa, but that night, there was a terrible snowstorm and the airport was closed for three days. It was during those three days that Jeff and Ilene first got to know each other. But that's not all; when Jeff got to West Africa, there was a great deal of political unrest in the region where he was working. After two months, he was forced to abandon his research project. The first thing he did when he got back to the United States was call Ilene.

Now, every New Year's Eve, Jeff and Ilene laugh about how they almost never met. "What if . . . ?" Jeff always asks. "Don't even think about it," Ilene always replies.

Get together with a partner and think about how Jeff and Ilene met (and how they almost didn't meet). How many statements containing hypothetical conditionals can you make about their story? For example: *If Ilene hadn't received a party invitation, she wouldn't have gone out on New Year's Eve. If Jeff had been gay, he wouldn't have been interested in Ilene.*

Share your statements with the rest of the class. Who was able to make the most?

FOCUS 3 Word Order in Conditionals

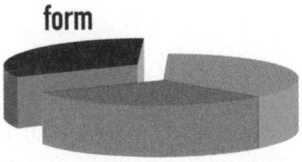

EXAMPLES	EXPLANATIONS
(a) If we were on a desert island, we would use string to make a fishing line. OR We would use string to make a fishing line if we were on a desert island.	Differences in word order do not change the meaning.
(b) If we had known how to build a boat, we would have escaped. OR We would have escaped if we had known how to build a boat.	Use a comma after the *if* clause when it comes first.

EXERCISE 5

How would **your** life be different now if things had been different in the past? Use the headings below to make a list of important events in your life.

Example: *If I hadn't gone to the ballet when I was 5 years old, I wouldn't have studied dancing. I wouldn't be a dancer now if I had studied art instead of ballet.*

1. Something you did when you were young

_____

2. Something you didn't study when you were young

_____

3. A person you met or a place you visited

_____

4. An opportunity you decided not to take

_____

5. A book that you read

_____

6. An important decision that you made

_____

When you have made your list, get together with another student and tell him or her how your life would be different if these things had (or hadn't) happened. Then tell the rest of the class what you found out about your partner.

EXERCISE 6

For each situation, complete the following hypothetical conditionals, using the given verb in your answers.

Situation A

Example: 1. Eloise's husband has always been a thin man in good physical condition. If he suddenly _____ (become) fat, Eloise _____ (be) shocked.

This is a hypothetical situation which will probably **not** happen because Eloise's husband has always been a thin man.

Answer: Eloise's husband has always been a thin man in good physical condition. If he suddenly *became* (become) fat, Eloise *would be* (be) shocked.

2. Eloise started seeing a doctor about her cholesterol problem three years ago. If she _____ (knew) about her problem earlier, she _____ (change) her diet years earlier.

Situation B

3. Ali's doctor says that one of the reasons Ali has high blood pressure is that he never expresses his anger. His doctor says that it is not healthy to "bottle it up." He says that if Ali _____ (get) angry once in a while, his blood pressure _____ (not + be) so high.

4. Ali never gets angry with his family. His children _____ (run away) from him if he ever _____ (yell) at them.

Situation C

5. Dan, who doesn't earn very high wages, has been shopping at discount stores for years. Even if he _____ (have) a lot of money to shop with, he _____ (buy) from discount stores.

6. When Dan graduated from college, his father gave him a used truck. Together they worked on the truck until it was in excellent condition. If Dan _____ (not + learn) how to repair trucks, he _____ (be) more enthusiastic about new trucks.

Situation D

7. People who live in this area have forgotten how to conserve water. If it _____ (not + rain) so much last year, people _____ (remember) water conservation practices.

8. People _____ (be able) to water their lawns every day if it _____ (rain) more this summer. However, the forecast is that this area is going to experience a drought this summer.

EXERCISE 7

STEP 1 **On one sheet of paper, write the following words and complete the hypothetical *if* clause.**

If I were _____.

Now, on another sheet of paper complete the main clauses.

I would _____.

STEP 2 **Your teacher will collect and scramble your *if* clauses and your main clauses, and then you will take one of each. Read your sentence aloud to the rest of the class. Does it make sense?**

STEP 3 **After hearing everyone read their sentences, find the person who has the main clause that matches the *if* clause you have now.**

STEP 4 **Now find the person who has the *if* clause that matches your main clause.**

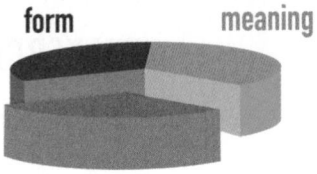

FOCUS 4 Future Conditionals

EXAMPLES	EXPLANATIONS
simple present — *will/be going to* + base verb (a) If you **study** hard, you **will get** a good grade. (b) If it **rains** tomorrow, I'm **going to bring** my umbrella. (c) Steve **will give** you a ride if you **ask** him.	Future conditionals make predictions about what will happen in the future. You usually use simple present in the *if* clause and *will be* or *be going to* + base form of the verb in the main clause.

EXERCISE 8

Most countries have superstitions. Here's a common North American superstition: If a black cat crosses your path, you will have bad luck.

Match A and B below to create some other common North American superstitions. Check your answers with other students and with your teacher.

A	B
1. If you break a mirror,	a. if you knock on wood.
2. If you find a four-leaf clover,	b. you will bring bad luck to all the people in the house.
3. You will have bad luck	c. you will have seven years of bad luck.
4. You will prevent something bad from happening	d. if you carry one in your pocket.
5. If you open an umbrella indoors,	e. you will be the next person to get married.
6. A rabbit's paw will bring good luck	f. if you walk under a ladder.
7. If you catch the bride's bouquet at a wedding.	g. you will be very lucky.

Do you have any of these superstitions in your country? Do any of these superstitions have a different meaning in your country? (For example, in Great Britain, if a black cat crosses your path, you will have **good** luck.) Think of some common superstitions from your country and tell them to the rest of your class. How many people in your class believe in these superstitions?

EXERCISE 9

Go around the room and ask the other students the questions in the chart below. Change partners after every question. Write the answers you receive in your notebook.

When your chart is complete, compare your answers with your classmates. In your opinion, what was the most interesting or surprising answer to each question? Write it in the chart.

Example: *Question:* What will you do if you get an A in this class?
Answer: I'll hug my teacher and say, "Thank you! Thank you!"

WHAT WILL YOU DO . . .

QUESTION	ANSWER	MOST INTERESTING ANSWER
1. . . . . if you get an A in this class?		
2. . . . . if your pants rip in tomorrow's class?		
3. . . . . if I give you $10 right now?		
4. . . . . if there is a fire drill?		
5. . . . . if you don't see me tomorrow?		
6. . . . . if our teacher is sick tomorrow?		
7. . . . . if it's raining when class is over?		
8. . . . . if you lose this book?		

EXERCISE 10

Think of three ways in which you would like to change your life.

Example: *I'd like to exercise more.*

Tell your partner how your life will change if these things happen.

Example: *If I exercise more, I'll be fitter and healthier.*

HOW WOULD YOU LIKE TO CHANGE YOUR LIFE?	WHAT WILL HAPPEN?
1.	
2.	
3.	
4.	
5	

FOCUS 5 Future Conditionals or Hypothetical Conditions?

EXAMPLES	EXPLANATIONS
Future Conditional: (a) If a woman **runs** for president of the United States one day, more women **will go into** politics.	Future conditionals talk about possible situations and show what you think will happen in those situations.
Hypothetical Conditionals: (b) If I **ran** for president, nobody **would vote** for me. (c) If Elvis **had run** for president, a lot of his fans **would have voted** for him. (d) If Al Gore **had become** president in 2000, American politics **would be** quite different today.	Hypothetical conditionals talk about improbable situations: situations that are not likely to happen (b), or impossible situations (c and d).

EXERCISE 11

Say whether the situations in the *if* clauses are future (possible) or hypothetical (improbable). Compare your answers with a partner's.

1. If it rains, I will not have to water the garden. _____
2. If it rained, I would be very happy. _____
3. Marcy would quit her job if she got pregnant. _____
4. If I won the lottery, I would travel around the world. _____
5. Aunt Shira will give us a wedding shower if we decide on a wedding date. _____
6. If Laurel gets hurt again, her father will make her quit the girl's soccer team. _____
7. If the baby slept through the night without waking up, his parents would finally get a good night's sleep. _____
8. Jasmine would buy a big house if she were rich. _____

EXERCISE 12

Work with a partner to complete the following. In each sentence, decide if the situation is possible or hypothetical and write an appropriate form of the verb.

Situation A

1. Gao is a doctor, but if he ___were___ (be) a truck driver, he ___would have___ (have) very different skills. (This situation is hypothetical because Gao is not a truck driver.)
2. Gao's wife is a doctor, too, but she is planning to change her career. If she _____ (change) her career, she _____ (study) to become a lawyer.

Situation B

3. Antonieta is Brazilian, but she has lived in the United States and New Zealand, so she speaks excellent English. If she (stay) in Brazil, her English _____ (not) (be) so good.
4. However, Antonieta _____ (speak) French too if she _____ (move) to France next year.

Situation C

5. Mary's car is old. If it _____ (break down), she _____ (buy) a new one.
6. Because Mary has a car, she has driven to school every day this term. But if she _____ (not) (have) a car, she _____ (take) the bus.

Situation D

7. Marcia has applied to graduate school. She _____ (start) school next fall if she _____ (get) accepted.
8. When Marcia was 21, she quit school for several years to get married and raise a family. If she _____ (continue) her studies instead of raising a family, she _____ (begin) graduate school a long time ago.

FOCUS 6 Factual Conditionals

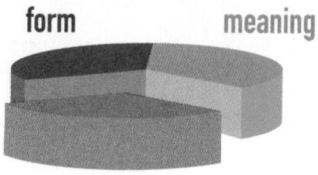

EXAMPLES	EXPLANATIONS
simple present (a) If you **leave** milk in the sun, it **turns** sour. (b) I **eat** yogurt and fruit for breakfast if **I have** time	Factual conditionals talk about what is always true or what usually happens in certain situations. You really expect these things to happen. Use simple present in the *if* clause and simple present in the main clause.
(c) **When** you leave milk in the sun, it turns sour. (d) I eat yogurt and fruit for breakfast **whenever** I have time.	Because you expect these situations to happen, you can use *when* or *whenever* (every time that) instead of *if*. The meaning does not change.

EXERCISE 13

Get together with a partner and complete the following statements to make factual conditionals with *if*, *when*, and *whenever*. Check your answers with your classmates and your teacher.

Example: If you heat water, it boils.

1. An ice cube melts if _____.
2. If you heat metal, _____.
3. Red wine stains when _____.
4. Cats purr if _____.
5. Rain changes to snow if _____.
6. If you press the "Power" button on a computer, _____.
7. Wool shrinks _____.
8. At the end of a play, people usually applaud _____.

Discuss each of the sentences above with your partner. Decide if they are always true or usually true.

FOCUS 7 *Would, Might, May,* and *Will* in Conditionals

EXAMPLES	EXPLANATIONS
Hypothetical Conditions: (a) If I were on that desert island, **I would** definitely try to get away as soon as possible. (b) If I were on that desert island, I **might** try to get away or I **might** wait for someone to rescue me. (c) If Americans got more exercise, they **might** be healthier.	Use *would* in the main clause to show the most probable result of the *if* clause. Use *might* in the main clause to show other possible results of the *if* clause. When you use *might*, you are less certain of the result.
Past Hypothetical Conditionals: (d) If John Lennon hadn't died, the Beatles **might have** reunited. OR If John Lennon hadn't died, the Beatles **may have** reunited. (e) If we had arrived at the airport ten minutes earlier, we **might have** caught the plane. OR If we had arrived at the airport ten minutes earlier, we **may have** caught the plane.	In past hypothetical conditionals, you can use *might have* + past participle or *may have* + past participle. The meaning does not change.
Future Conditionals: (f) If it rains tomorrow, we **will** stay home. (g) If it rains tomorrow, we **might** stay home or we **might** go to the movies. OR If it rains tomorrow, we **may** stay home or we **may** go to the movies.	In future conditionals, use *will* in the main clause to show that you strongly expect this result to happen. Use *might* or *may* in the main clause to show that this result is possible, but you are not so certain that it will happen.

EXERCISE 14

Complete the following conversations with will, would, may, might, would have, might have, or may have.

Conversation A

Abel: Have you and Ken decided what you're going to do over Labor Day weekend?

Miles: Not really. It all depends on the weather. If it's nice, we (1) _____ (go) camping, that's for sure. But if it rains, we (2) _____ (visit) my folks in Oakland or we (3) _____ (stay) here and catch up on our reading. I'm really not sure yet. I guess we'll just wait and see.

Conversation B

Mother: Don't drop that glass!

Child: Why not?

Mother: If you drop something made of glass, it (4) _____ (break).

Child: Oh.

Mother: Watch out! Don't turn it upside down.

Child: Why not?

Mother: Because if you do that, it (5) _____ (spill).

Conversation C

Janette: Did you hear about the guy who found an old Lotto ticket in a trash can?

Dean: Yeah, the guy who won eight million dollars? The guy with four grown kids and a bunch of grandchildren?

Janette: Yeah. He bought the ticket six months ago and he found it just two days before it was due to expire.

Dean: If he had found it two days later, he (6) _____ (not) (win) the eight million dollars.

Janette: Yeah, and his children (7) _____ (not) (be) rich now.

Dean: And his grandchildren (8) _____ (not) (have) college funds.

Janette: And the eight million dollars (9) _____ (go back) into the next Lotto!

Dean: And we (10) _____ (win) it!

Use Your English

ACTIVITY 1 speaking

STEP 1 Work in groups of four.

STEP 2 Read the following questions. Without showing anyone else your paper, write down what you think you would be and what each person in your group would be in the following situations:

a. If you were an animal, what would you be?

b. If you were a color, what would you be?

c. If you were food, what would you be?

Example: *If I were an animal, I would be a cat. If Terri were an animal, she would be a deer. I also think that Rachel would be a mouse, and Peter would be a flamingo.*

STEP 3 When you have all finished, share your ideas and compare what **you** think your group members would be with what **they** think they would be.

	a. ANIMAL	b. COLOR	c.FOOD
You			
Name:			
Name:			
Name:			

Remember that it is not necessary to repeat the *if* clause in every sentence.

ACTIVITY 2 writing

In a paragraph or two, describe the most interesting results about **yourself** from Activity 1. First tell why you described yourself the way you did. Then tell why you think your group members described you the way they did.

For example, if you said, "If I were a color, I would be purple," but everyone else said you would be yellow, give us the possible reasons for these opinions.

Remember that it isn't necessary to repeat the *if* clause in every sentence.

ACTIVITY 3 writing

Form teams. Together write an imaginary future situation on a piece of paper. For example, *What would happen if* . . . everyone in the world were ten feet taller? . . . everyone lived the same number of years? . . . all children studied at home?

After you write down one situation, work together to describe the results. Then your team will tell some of your ideas to the other teams. They will try to guess the situation and tell what the *if* clause is. The team that guesses the situation most often wins.

ACTIVITY 4 listening/speaking

Your school is about to build a new library. The president of the student union wants to celebrate the event by placing a time capsule inside the walls of the new building. (A time capsule is a box containing a number of objects that represent the culture of a community at that point in time. You put into the time capsule objects that you feel reflect the ideas, culture, and values of the community. If people find the time capsule one hundred years from now, they will have an idea of what life was like in the past.)

If the president asked you about what to put in the time capsule, what would you say? Get together with two or three other students and decide on a list of five objects that you would put in the time capsule because you believe they represent American culture now. Share your ideas with the rest of the class and explain why you chose these objects. When you have heard everybody's ideas, vote on the five objects that you, as a class, would put in a time capsule to represent current American culture.

ACTIVITY 5 speaking/listening

The purpose of this activity is to find out what Americans would put in a time capsule like the one in Activity 4.

STEP 1 Interview three different native speakers of English by asking the question: If you had to put three things in a time capsule to reflect American culture right now, what would you choose and why? Record your interviews.

STEP 2 Listen to your recording and report your findings to the rest of your class. As a class, make a list of the objects that everyone interviewed would put in the time capsule. What does this tell you about American culture today? Compare this list with the one that your class made in Activity 4. How many differences and similarities are there in these lists? Do your ideas about what represents American culture differ from Americans' ideas?

STEP 3 Listen to your recording again. How many times do the speakers use *would*? Write down any sentences containing *would*. How many times do the speakers use full *if* clauses? Why do you think this is so? Write down any sentences containing *if* clauses. What does this tell you about the use of *if* clauses in real conversations?

ACTIVITY 6 listening

CD Track 32

Listen to the audio of three different Americans talking about what they would put in a time capsule.

STEP 1 What would they put in the capsule? List the objects.

STEP 2 Listen to the audio again. How many times do the speakers use **would**? Write down any sentences containing **would**. How many times do the speakers use full if clauses? Why do you think this so? Write down any sentences containing *if* clauses. What does this tell you about the use of *if* clauses in real conversations?

ACTIVITY 7 speaking/listening or writing/reading

If you had to put five objects representing **your** culture into a time capsule, what would you choose and why? Make a report (either written or oral) on your choices. If you make a written report, read your or another student's work carefully and check to see if you or he or she were able to use any of the language from this unit. If you choose an oral report, record yourself as you make the report. Listen to your recording and write down any sentences containing language from this unit.

ACTIVITY 8 research on the web

Peter, Paul, and Mary were a popular folk group in the sixties. The title of one of their famous songs was, "If I had a hammer . . ." Go on the Internet and use a search engine such as Google® or Yahoo® to find the words to this song. Find a recording online if possible. Can you sing it? What do you think the words mean?

ACTIVITY 9 reflection

Think of three ways in which you could make more time to study English. Write your ideas as sentences starting with '*If . . .*' Example: *If I stopped watching TV, I'd read more English books or newspapers.*

APPENDICES

Appendix 1 Forming Verb Tenses A-1
A. Simple Present A-1
B. Present Progressive A-2
C. Simple Past A-3
D. Past Progressive A-3
E. Present Perfect A-4
F. Present Perfect Progressive A-4
G. Past Perfect A-5
H. Future (*Will*) A-5
I. Future (*Be Going To*) A-6

Appendix 2 Forming the Passive A-7
A. The *Be* Passive A-7
B. The *Get* Passive A-7

Appendix 3 Forming Conditionals A-8
A. Factual Conditionals A-8
B. Future Conditionals A-8
C. Hypothetical Conditionals A-8
D. Past Hypothetical Conditionals A-8

Appendix 4 Overview of Modal Auxiliaries A-9
A. Probability and Possibility A-9
B. Giving Advice and Expressing Opinions A-11
C. Necessity and Obligation A-12
D. Prohibition and Permission A-12

Appendix 5 Common Irregular Verbs A-13

APPENDIX 1 Forming Verb Tenses

Appendix 1A Simple Present (verb/verb + –*s*)

Statement	Negative	Question	Short Answers
I / You / We / They work.	I / You / We / They do not/ don't work.	Does I / you / we / they work?	Yes, I / you / we / they do.
He / She / It works.	He / She / It does not/ doesn't work.	Does he / she / it work?	Yes, he / she / it does.
			No, I / you / we / they don't.
			No, he / she / it doesn't.

Appendix 1B PRESENT PROGESSIVE (*am/is/are* + verb + *–ing*)

Statement	Negative	Question	Short Answers
I am (I'm) working.	I am not (I'm not) working.	Am I working?	Yes, I am. No, I'm not.
You are (you're) working.	You are not (aren't) working.	Are you working?	Yes, you are. No, you aren't. OR You're not.
She/He/It is (She's/He's/It's) working.	She/He/It is not (isn't) working.	Is she/he/it working?	Yes, she/he/it is. No, she/he/it isn't. OR She's/He's/It's not.
We are (We're) working.	We are not (aren't) working.	Are we working?	Yes, we are. No, we aren't. OR We're not.
They are (They're) working.	They are not (aren't) working.	Are they working?	Yes, they are. No, they aren't. OR They're not.

Appendix 1C Simple Past (verb + *–ed* or irregular form)

Statement	Negative	Question	Short Answers
I You We They He She It } worked.	I You We They He She It } did not/ didn't work.	Did } I / you / we / they / he / she / it work?	Yes, } I / you / we / they / he / she / it did. No, } I / you / we / they / he / she / it didn't

Appendix 1D Past Progressive (*was/were* + verb + *–ing*)

Statement	Negative	Question	Short Answers
I She He It } was sleeping.	I She He It } was not sleeping. (wasn't)	Was } I / she / he / it sleeping?	Yes, } I / she / he / it was.
We You They } were sleeping.	We You They } were not sleeping. (weren't)	Were } we / You / they sleeping?	No, } we / You / they weren't.

Appendix 1E Present Perfect (*has/have* + verb + past participle)

Statement	Negative	Question	Short Answers
I, You, We, They have gone. ('ve)	I, You, We, They have not gone. (haven't)	Have I, you, we, they gone?	Yes, I, you, we, they have.
She, He, It has gone. ('s)	She, He, It has not gone. (hasn't)	Has she, he, it gone?	Yes, he, she, it has.
			No, I, you, we, they haven't.
			No, he, she, it hasn't.

Appendix 1F Present Perfect Progressive (*has/have* + *been* + verb + *–ing*)

Statement	Negative	Question	Short Answers
I, You, We, They have been ('ve) sleeping.	I, You, We, They have not been (haven't) sleeping.	Have I, you, we, they been sleeping?	Yes, I, you, we, they have been.
She, He, It has been ('s) sleeping.	She, He, It has not been (hasn't) sleeping.	Has she, he, it been sleeping?	Yes, he, she, it has been.
			No, I, you, we, they haven't been.
			No, he, she, it hasn't been.

Appendix 1G Past Perfect (*had* + verb + past participle)

Statement	Negative	Question	Short Answers
I / You / We / They / She / He / It had ('d) arrived.	I / You / We / They / She / He / It had not (hadn't) arrived.	Had I / you / we / they / she / he / it arrived?	Yes, I / you / we / they / he / she / it had. No, I / you / we / they / he / she / it hadn't.

Appendix 1H Future: *will* (*will* + verb)

Statement	Negative	Question	Short Answers
I / You / We / They / She / He / It will leave. ('ll).	I / You / We / They / She / He / It will not (won't) leave.	Will I / you / we / they / she / he / it leave?	Yes, I / you / we / they / he / she / it will. No, I / you / we / they / he / she / it won't.

Appendix 1I Future: *be going to* (*am/is/are* + verb)

Statement	Negative	Question	Short Answers
I am going to leave. ('m)	I am not going to leave. ('m)	Am I going to leave?	Yes, I am.
You, We, They are going ('re) to leave.	You, We, They are not going (aren't) to leave.	Are you, we, they going to leave?	Yes, you, we, they are.
She, He, It is going ('s) to leave.	She, He, It is not going (isn't) to leave.	Is she, He, it going to leave?	Yes, he, She, it is.
			No, I am not. ('m not.)
			No, you, we, they are not. (aren't)
			No, he, she, it is not. (isn't)

APPENDIX 2 Forming the Passive

Appendix 2A The *Be* Passive

To form the passive, use the appropriate tense of *be,* follwed by the past participle (pp).

	Tense	Form of *Be*	
(a) Wool **is produced** here.	Simple Present	*am/is/are*	+ PP
(b) Wool **is being produced** here right now.	Present Progressive	*am/is/are being*	+ PP
(c) Wool **was produced** here.	Simple Past	*was/were*	+ PP
(d) Wool **was** being produced here ten years ago.	Past Progressive	*was/were being*	+ PP
(e) Wool **has been produced** here since 1900.	Present Perfect	*have/has been*	+ PP
(f) Wool **had been produced** here when the island was discovered.	Past Perfect	*had been*	+ PP
(g) Wool **will be produced** here next year.	Future (*will*)	*will be*	+ PP
(h) Wool **is going to be produced** here.	Future (*be going to*)	*am/is/are going to be*	+ PP
(i) Wool **will have been produced** here by the year 2010.	Future Perfect	*will have been*	+ PP

Appendix 2B The *Get* Passive

	Tense	Form of *Get*	
(a) Her cookies always **get eaten**.	Simple Present	*get/gets*	+ PP
(b) Her cookies **are getting eaten**.	Persent Progressive	*am/is/are getting*	+ PP
(c) Her cookies **got eaten**.	Simple Past	*got*	+ PP
(d) Her cookies **were getting eaten**.	Past Progressive	*was/were getting*	+ PP
(e) Her cookies **have gotten eaten**.	Present Perfect	*have/has gotten*	+ PP
(f) Her cookies **had gotten eaten**.	Past Perfect	*had gotten*	+ PP
(g) Her cookies **will be eaten**.	Future (*will*)	*will get*	+ PP
(h) Her cookies **are going to get eaten**.	Future (*be going to*)	*am/is/are going to get*	+ PP
(i) Her cookies **will have gotten eaten** by the time we get home.	Future Perfect	*will have gotten*	+ PP

APPENDIX 3 Forming Conditionals

Appendix 3A Factual Conditionals

If Clause	Main Clause
[*If* + simple present] If you heat water,	[simple present] it boils.

Appendix 3B Future Conditionals

If Clause	Main Clause
[*If* + simple present] If you study hard,	[*will/be going to* + base verb] you will get a good grade.

Appendix 3C Hypothetical Conditionals

If Clause	Main Clause
[*If* + simple past] (a) If we had lots of money, [*If* + Be very → subjunctive *were*] (b) If I were rich,	[*would* (*'d*) + base verb] we'd travel around the world. [*would* + base verb] I'd travel around the world.

Appendix 3D Past Hypothetical Conditionals

If Clause	Main Clause
[*If* + past perfect] If you had called me,	[*would*+ *have* (*'ve*) + *verb* + past participle] I would have come to see you

APPENDIX 4 Overview of Modal Auxilliaries

Appendix 4A Probability and Possibility (Unit 5)

	Possible (less than 50% certain)	Probable (about 90% certain)	Certain (100% certain)
Present Forms	less certain He *could* play golf. He *might* play golf. He *may* play golf. more certain	He *must* play golf.	He plays golf.
Present Forms	less certain She *could* be a doctor. She *might* be doctor. She *may* be a doctor. more certain	She *must* be a doctor.	She is a doctor.
Question Forms	less certain *Could* he play golf? *Might* he play golf? more certain	—	*Does* he play golf?
Question Forms	less certain *Could* she be a doctor? *Might* she be a doctor? more certain	—	*Is* she a doctor?
Negative Forms	less certain He *might not* play golf. He *may not* play golf. He *couldn't* play golf. more certain	He *must not* play golf.	He *does not/doesn't* play golf.
Negative Forms	less certain She *might not* be a doctor. She *may not* be a doctor. She *couldn't/can't* be a doctor. more certain	She *must not* be a doctor.	She *is not/isn't* a doctor.

Continued on next page

Continued from previous page

	Possible (less than 50% certain)	Probable (about 90% certain)	Certain (100% certain)
Past Forms	less certain He *could have* played golf. He *might have* played golf. He *may have* played golf. more certain	He *must have* played golf.	He played golf.
Past Forms	less certain She *could have* been a doctor. She *might have* been a doctor. She *may have* been a doctor. more certain	She *must have* been a doctor.	She *was* a doctor.
Past Forms	less certain *Could* he *have* played golf? *Might* he *have* played golf? more certain	—	*Did* he play golf?
Past Forms	less certain *Could* she *have* been a doctor? *Might* she *have* been a doctor? more certain	—	*Was* she a doctor?
Progressive Forms	less certain He *could be* playing golf. He *might be* playing golf. He *may be* playing golf. more certain	He *must be* playing golf.	He *is* playing golf.
Progressive Forms	less certain He *could have been* playing golf. He *might have been* playing golf. He *may have been* playing golf. more certain	He *must have been* playing golf.	He *was* playing golf./ He *has* been playing golf.
Future Forms	less certain It *could* rain tomorrow. It *may (not)* rain tomorrow. It *might (not)* rain tomorrow. more certain	It *will probably* rain tomorrow. It *probably won't* rain tomorrow.	It *will/will/not/won't* rain tomorrow.

Appendix 4B Giving Advice and Expressing Opinions (Unit 10)

WEAK ↕ STRONG	You	*might* *could* *should/should not/shouldn't/ought to* *had better/'d better not* *must*	call him.

Appendix 4C Necessity and Obligation (Unit 11)

PRESENT	PAST	FUTURE
Necessary and Obligatory		
She *must* go.	—	She *must* go.
She's/*has got to* go.	—	She's/*has got to go.*
She *has to go.*	She *had to* go.	She *has to* go./ She'*ll/will have to* go.
Not Necessary and not Obligatory		
She *doesn't/does not have to* go.	She *didn't/did not have to* go.	She *doesn't/does not have to* go. She *won't/will not have to* go.

Appendix 4D Probihition and Permission (Unit 11)

PRESENT	PAST	FUTURE
Prohibited and not Permitted		
We *can't/cannot* smoke in here.	We *couldn't/could not* smoke in here.	We *will not/won't be able to* smoke in here.
We *mustn't/must not* smoke in here.	—	
Permitted		
We *can* smoke in here.	We *could* smoke in here.	We *will be able to* smoke in here.

APPENDIX 5 Common Irregular Verbs

BASE FORM	PAST-TENSE FORM	PAST PARTICIPLE	BASE FORM	PAST-TENSE FORM	PAST PARTICIPLE
be	was	been	leave	left	left
become	became	become	lend	lent	lent
begin	began	begun	let	let	let
bend	bent	bent	lose	lost	lost
bite	bit	bitten	make	made	made
blow	blew	blown	meet	met	met
break	broke	broken	pay	paid	paid
bring	brought	brought	put	put	put
build	built	built	quit	quit	quit
buy	bought	bought	read	read*	read
catch	caught	caught	ride	rode	ridden
choose	chose	chosen	ring	rang	rung
come	came	come	run	ran	run
cost	cost	cost	say	said	said
cut	cut	cut	see	saw	seen
dig	dug	dug	sell	sold	sold
do	did	done	send	sent	sent
draw	drew	drawn	shake	shook	shaken
drink	drank	drunk	shoot	shot	shot
drive	drove	driven	shut	shut	shut
eat	ate	eaten	sing	sang	sung
fall	fell	fallen	sit	sat	sat
feed	fed	fed	sleep	slept	slept
feel	felt	felt	speak	spoke	spoken
fight	fought	fought	spend	spent	spent
find	found	found	stand	stood	stood
fly	flew	flown	steal	stole	stolen
forget	forgot	forgotten	swim	swam	swum
get	got	gotten	take	took	taken
give	gave	given	teach	taught	taught
go	went	gone	tear	tore	torn
grow	grew	grown	tell	told	told
hang	hung	hung	think	thought	thought
have	had	had	throw	threw	thrown
hear	heard	heard	understand	understood	understood
hide	hid	hidden	wake	woke	woken
hit	hit	hit	wear	wore	worn
hold	held	held	win	won	won
hurt	hurt	hurt	write	wrote	written
keep	kept	kept			
know	knew	known			
lead	led	led			

* Pronounce the base form: /rid/; pronounce the past-tense form: /red/.

ANSWER KEY
(for puzzles and problems only)

UNIT 1

Answers to Exercise 10 (page 12)

- Horses sleep standing up.
- Bats use their ears to "see."
- Scorpions have twelve eyes.
- Elephants sometimes go for four days without water.
- Swans stay with the same mates all their lives.
- Antelopes run at 70 miles per hour.
- Bears sleep during the winter months.
- Spiders live for about two years.

UNIT 2

Student B Opening Task (page 18)

Picture B

Answers to Exercise 5 (page 25)

1. (example) See you later
2. I hear you
3. Know what I mean?
4. I love you
5. I don't think so
6. I don't know
7. Believe it or not
8. You are (You're) welcome

UNIT 4

Answers to Exercise 10 (page 62)

1. A	5. M	9. E	13. O	17. K
2. P	6. R	10. B	14. F	18. D
3. G	7. Q	11. I	15. C	19. S
4. J	8. N	12. L	16. H	

UNIT 5

"Official" Answers to Activity 1 (page 84)

1. A giraffe passing a window. 2. A pencil seen from the end. 3. A cat climbing a tree.

UNIT 6

Solution to the Opening Task (pages 88–89)

Mrs. Meyer killed her husband. She entered the bathroom while he was brushing his teeth, and she hit him over the head with the bathroom scale. Then she turned on the shower and put the soap on the floor.
How do we know this?

- From the toothbrush: He was brushing his teeth, not walking out of the shower.
- From the footprints: The shoe prints indicate a woman's high heeled shoes leading from the shower.
- From the bathroom scale: The scale does not indicate zero.

Pair Work Task: Activity 1 (page 99)

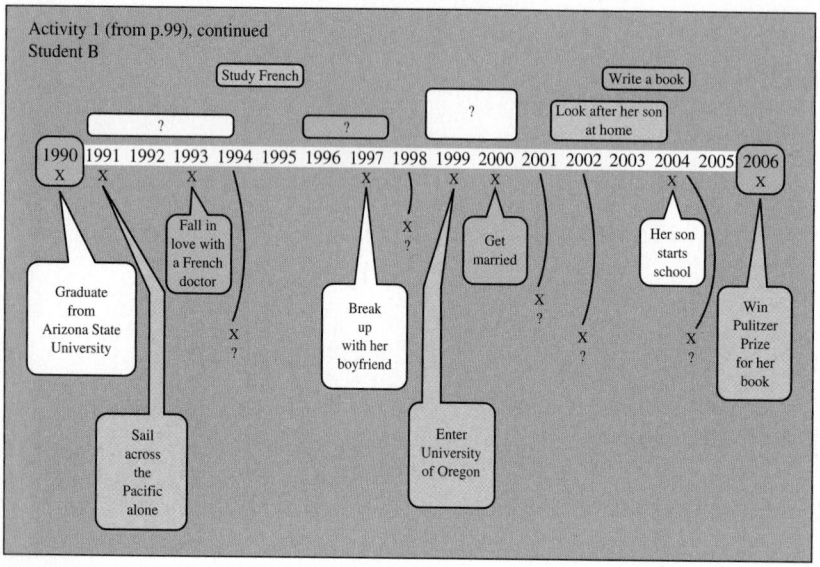

UNIT 7

Solution to the Opening Task (pages 104–105)

Linda
Susan

Bob
Diana
Carla

George
Frank

UNIT 9

Solution to Opening Task (page 137)

a. 2, b. 1, c. 4, d. 3

MEDICAL HISTORY					
Name	*Micheal Menendez*				
Date of birth _/_/ 75	Cigarettes? Yes/No	Alcohol Yes/No	Glasses? Yes/No	Serious Injuries ? _____	Health problems? *Headaches*
Height _____ **Weight** 185 lbs	**How long?** *For 5 years* *Started 1995* *Stopped 2000*	**How much?**	**How long?** *Since 2003*	**When?** *In* _____	**How long?** *For 2 months*

UNIT 10

Solution to Exercise 7 (page 159)

First, the woman should take the mouse to the car, leaving the cat with the cheese. Next, she should return and pick up the cat and take it to the car. As soon as she gets to the car with the cat, she should remove the mouse and take it with her, leaving the cat in the car. When she gets back to the shopping area, she should pick up the cheese and leave the mouse. Then she should take the cheese to the car and leave it there with the cat. Finally, she should return to collect the mouse and bring it with her to the car.

UNIT 13

Student B Opening Task (page 197)

Student B: Complete the information on the medical history form by asking your partner questions about Michael Menendez. Your partner will answer your questions by looking at page 197. Use complete questions.

Example: Student A: *Does he smoke?*
Student B: *Yes, he does.*
Student A: *How long has he smoked?*

UNIT 22

Student B Solution to Exercise 4 (page 317)

Picture B

UNIT 23

Student B Opening Task (page 329)

						7 W		
				4 C	R	O	S	8 S
						R		T
	2 H		3 L	O	O	K		A
1 M	A	K	E					N
	N		A		6 F	I	N	D
	D		V		I			
			E		L			
				5 C	L	E	A	N

UNIT 24

Solution to the Opening Task (page 349)

The person *who* loves Lee is *Sid*. The person *who* loves Kit is *Tracy*.
The person *whom* Sid loves is *Lee*. The person *whom* Tracy loves is *Kit.*

Unit 25

Opening Task (page 364) Possible answers

- If I had a knife, I would use it to cut wood for a fire.
- If I saw a ship, I would try to make a fire so they would see the smoke.
- If I found human footprints, I would follow them to find out who it was.
- If I didn't have any water, I would get juice from fruit or plants.
- If I met another survivor, I would work with him or her to make a plan / escape / build a shelter / get help.

CREDITS

Text Credits

p. 88: From *Crime and Puzzlement* by Lawrence Treat, Illustration by Leslie Cabarga. Reprinted by permission of David R. Gordine, Publisher Inc. Copyright 1981 by Lawrence Treat, Illustrations by Leslie Cabarga.

p. 176: Adapted with permission from "How not to collide with local road laws," *The European* (Magazine section) June 9, 1985.

p. 298: Adapted with permission from "Volunteers Head South to Help Victims of Hurricane Katrina" *Los Angeles Business Journal*, Sept 12, 2005 v27 i37 p.10(1).

p. 306: Adapted with permission from "Burma: A Travel Survival Kit" by Tony Wheeler. Lonely Planet Publications 1982.

Photo Credits

Page 0: Top: © Photos.com/RF, Bottom: © Photos.com/RF
Page 5: Top Left: © ImageState/Alamy, Bottom Left: © Design Pics Inc./Alamy/RF, Top Right: ©Henning von Holleben/Photonica/Getty, Bottom Right: © Erik Dreyer/Stone/Getty
Page 11: Photos.com/RF
Page 15: © Stockbyte Platinum/Alamy/RF
Page 18: © Photos.com/RF
Page 25: © Nick Koudis/Photodisc Red/Getty/RF
Page 34: © A. Inden/zefa/Corbis
Page 43: © IndexOpen/RF
Page 48: © Julia Fullerton-Batten/Stone+/Getty
Page 49: © Photos.com/RF
Page 59: © BananaStock /Alamy/RF
Page 62: Left: © Jon Feingersh/zefa/Corbis, Right: © Rick Gomez/Corbis
Page 70: © Photos.com/RF
Page 76: © Marsi/Photodisc Red/Getty/RF
Page 86: Left: © Andrew Holt /Alamy, Left Center: © Charles Gullung/Photonica/Getty, Right Center: © Comstock Premium / Alamy/RF, Right: © NASA / Photo Researchers, Inc
Page 96: © Getty Images
Page 98: © Charlotte Thege / Peter Arnold, Inc.
Page 99: © Photos.com/RF

Page 127: © Profimedia.CZ s.r.o./Alamy
Page 139: © Photos.com/RF
Page 144: © Chris Craymer/Stone/Getty
Page 153: © Don Mason/CORBIS
Page 154: © Jose Luis Pelaez Inc/Blend Images/Getty
Page 166: © Boris Roessler/Corbis
Page 171: © Ryan McVay/Photodisc Green/Getty/RF
Page 177: © David Levenson /Alamy
Page 184: © PhotoObjects.net/RF
Page 196: © Jeff Kaufman/Taxi/Getty
Page 198: © Jim Arbogast/Photographer's Choice/Getty/RF
Page 212: Top: © IndexOpen/RF, Bottom Left: © Jon Arnold/Digital Vision/Getty/RF, Bottom Right: © IndexOpen/RF
Page 226: © IndexOpen/RF
Page 238: © Royalty-Free/Corbis
Page 248: © BananaStock / Alamy
Page 252: © Walter Lockwood/Corbis
Page 253: © D. Hurst / Alamy
Page 262: Top Left: © Alex Oliveira/Reuters/Corbis, Top Right: © Mike Finn-Kelcey/Reuters/Corbis, Middle Left: © Ken James/Corbis, Middle Right: © Eddie Keogh/Reuters/Corbis, Bottom Left: © Frank Trapper/Corbis, Bottom Right: © Mario Anzuoni/Reuters/Corbis
Page 263: Top Left: © Getty Images, Top Center: © Getty Images, Top Right: © Time Life Pictures/Getty Images, Bottom Left: © Getty Images, Bottom Center: © Neal Preston/CORBIS, Bottom Right: © Time Life Pictures/Getty Images
Page 284: © David Buffington/PhotoDisc Green/Getty/RF
Page 297: © Associated Press, AP
Page 302: Top Left: © John Van Hasselt/Corbis, Top Middle: © MedioImages/Getty/RF, Top Right: © Daniele Pellegrini/Stone/Getty, Bottom Left: © Digital Vision/Getty/RF, Bottom Center: © NASA/Corbis, Bottom Right: © NASA/Roger Ressmeyer/CORBIS
Page 323: © SuperStock, Inc./SuperStock
Page 328: Top: © GIRY DANIEL/CORBIS SYGMA, Bottom: © Digital Vision/Getty/RF
Page 330: © Yashuhide Fumoto/Photodisc Red/Getty/RF
Page 338: Top Left: © archivberlin Fotoagentur GmbH/Alamy, Top Right: © Royalty-Free/Corbis, Bottom Left: © Royalty-Free/Corbis,
Page 348: © Royalty-Free/Corbis, Bottom Right: © Erik Dreyer/Stone/Getty
Page 362: © Photos.com/RF
Page 365: © Ingram Publishing/Getty/RF

INDEX

Ø (*See* no article)

A

a couple (of), 130
a few/a little, 130
a great deal of, 129
a lot of, 129
a/an, 284–301
actions
  nonprogressive or stative verbs to describe, 26–27
  present progressive tense to describe, 20
active verbs, *vs.* passive, 314
adjective clauses, 348–361
  –ed to form participles for, 355–358
  –ing to form participles for, 355–358
  participles as adjectives in, 355–358
  that used in, 350–355
  which used in, *vs. that,* 352–355
  who used in, 350–352
adjectives
  adjective clauses and (*See* adjective clauses)
  as...as and *not as...as* used with, 110
  comparatives and superlatives used with, 106
  –ed to form participles for, 355–358
  –ing to form participles for, 355–358
  participles used as, 355–358
  the used with, 295–298
adverbs
  as...as and *not as...as* used with, 110
  comparatives and superlatives used with, 106
  of frequency, 4–10, 268
advice, 150–165
  could used to express, 157–159, 160
  had better used to express, 160
  had better vs. should and *ought to,* 155–157
  imperatives used to express, 153
  might used to express, 157–159, 160
  must used to express, 160
  must vs. should and *ought to,* 154
  need to used to express, 153, 160
  ought to used to express, 152, 154, 161
  should used to express, 152, 154, 157, 161
  shouldn't used to express, 152
afraid that, refusing requests using, 251
after, 94–98
  past perfect tense using, 277–278
agreement with likes and dislikes, using short phrases, 188–189
all, 129
almost, 108, 129
already, 219–220
always, 4, 268
anymore
  negative form of, 265
  used to used with, 265
anywhere, 108
anywhere near, 108
appear, 26
appreciate, 26
articles, 284–301
  a/an used as, 286–287
  adjectives and, 295–298
  count nouns using, 286–298
  definite, 286–287
  first and second mention using, 287–288
  general statements expressed using no article, 292–293
  indefinite, 286–287, 289
  institutions using, 307–308
  no article use and, 286–287
  noncount nouns using, 286–287, 291–292
  nouns and, 286–287, 289, 291–292
  place names using, 304–306
  plural nouns using, 289, 291–292
  singular nouns using, 289, 291–292
  some instead of no article in, 290
  some used as, 286–287
  superlatives and, 295
  unique nouns using, 293–295
  the used as, 286–287
  the used as, adjectives and, 295–298
  the used as, second or related mention of, 295–298
as soon as, 92–98
as...as to express similarity or difference, 108–112
asking questions (*See* questions)
at present, 20
at the moment, 20

B

be, 4, 26, 28
  modals using, 74, 77
  passive forms of, 215–216, 322–323
  present progressive tense using, 21
  wh- questions with, 52
  yes/no questions using, 50
be going to, 37
  future tense use of, 36–40
before, 94–98
  past perfect tense using, 277–278

beliefs (*See* opinions and beliefs)
believe, 26
belong, 26
best, 295
break down, 341
by
passive verbs using, 318–319
past perfect tense using, 277–278
by the time, past perfect tense using, 277–278

C

call off, 333
can/could, 248–256
permission expressed using, 168
requests using, 256
cannot/can't
used to express probability, 72–73
used to express prohibition, 168, 173–174
catch on, 341
certainly, 190
certainty about a situation expressed using modals, 72–73
choice questions, 58–59
clauses, *as...as* and *not as...as* used with, 110
clean up, 335
come across, 337
come back, 341
come to, 341
comma
after clause with *before* or *after,* 277
used with dependent clauses, 94–98
comparatives, 104–119 (*See also* similarities and differences)
conditionals, 362–381
factual, 375
future, 371–372
future *vs.* hypothetical, 373–374
hypothetical, 364–365
if clauses used in, 364–377
may used in, 376–377
might used in, 376–377
past hypothetical, 367–370
past perfect tense and
will used in, 376–377
word order for, 366–367
would used as, 376–377
connecting events, present perfect tense to express, 278–279
containers for food, 122
continuing actions, *still* to express, 262–271
contrast, past perfect tense to express, 278–279
cost, 26
could, 72, 81, 248–256
advice expressed using, 157–160
in permissions, 255
in polite requests, 250
requests using, 256
could not/couldn't used to express prohibition, 186
couldn't/can't, 72–63
count nouns
articles used with, 286–298
degree complements using, 142
measure words and, 125–128
quantifiers and, 129–130
some used with, 286, 290
couple, 130

D

decisions, *will* when making, 41–43
definite articles, 286–287
degree complements, 136–149
count nouns and, 142
enough used with adjective/adverb + infinitive, 140
enough used with noun/verb + infinitive, 140
enough/not enough as, 138–141
noncount nouns and, 142
too as, 138–141
too little/too few as, 142–143
too much/too many as, 142–143
too placed before adjectives/adverbs, 140
too vs. very in, 143–145
dependent clauses
comma used with, 94–98
time clauses as, 94–98
differences (*See* similarities and differences)
dislike, 26
dislikes (*See* likes and dislikes)
do
as...as and *not as...as* used with, 110
emphatic, 190–191
do not have to
future tense and, 178–180
lack of necessity expressed using, 175–177
past tense and, 178–180
permission expressed using, 168
present tense and, 178–180
do you mind
permissions expressed using, 255
requests using, 256
do you want used in making offers, 238–247

E

eat out, 341
–ed to form participles, 355–358
either used to express similarity in likes and dislikes, 186
emotions and feelings, nonprogressive or stative verbs to describe, 26
emphatic *do,* 190–191
enough
as degree complement, 138–141
used with adjective/adverb + infinitive, 140
used with noun/verb + infinitive, 140
ever used in questions, 217
everyone, 129

everything, 129
exactly, 108
exist, 26

F

facts, simple present tense verbs to describe, 11–12
factual conditionals, 375
feel, 322
few, 130
first, 295
food, 120–125
  containers for, 122
  measurements of, 120–125
  portions of, 123
food shapes and states of food, 124
for
  present perfect tense used with, 196–211
  showing length of time with, 202–203
  verbs not used in present perfect with, 204–206
frequency, adverbs of, 268
future perfect tense, passive verbs using, 315
future tense, 34–47
  be going to used in, 36
  conditionals using, 371–372
  do not have/will not have to used with, 178–180
  future plans and intentions with *be going to* and *will,* 39–40
  have to/will have to used with, 178–180
  modals of probability and possibility in, 81–83
  must used with, 178–180
  passive verbs using, 315
  predicting the future with *be going to* and *will,* 38–39
  quick decisions using *will,* 41–43
  serious promises using *will,* 41–43
  subject/verb agreement when using *be going to* and *will,* 37–39
  will used in, 36

G

gerunds, likes and dislikes expressed using, 192
get by, 341
get off/on, 337
get over, 337
get– passive verbs, 319–320, 322–323
go over, 337
good/better/best, 106
great deal of, 129
grow up, 341

H

habits and habitual actions
  present perfect progressive to express, 231–232
  simple present tense verbs to describe, 2
had better used to express advice, 155–157, 160
happiest, 295
hardest, 295
hardly ever, 4
hate, 26, 192, 322
have got to used to express necessity, 168
have to/has to
  future tense and, 178–180
  necessity expressed using, 168, 175–177
  nonprogressive or stative verbs using, 27
  obligation expressed using, 172–173
  past tense and, 178–180
  phrasal modal use of, 169–171
  present tense and, 178–180
have/had/has, 26
  nonprogressive or stative verbs using, 27
  past participle used with, to form present perfect tense, 200–201
  past perfect tense using, 274–276
  present perfect progressive formed using *been* + verb + *-ing,* 229
hear, 26
hedge phrases to express likes and dislikes, 190–191
how, 52
hypothetical conditionals, 364–365, 373–374

I

I can't either to express similarity in likes and dislikes, 188–189
I do too to express similarity in likes and dislikes, 188–189
if clause
  factual conditionals using, 375
  future conditionals using, 371–373
  hypothetical conditional use of, 364–365, 373
  past/past perfect conditionals using, 367–370
imaginary situations, hypothetical conditionals to express, 364–366
imperatives used to express advice, 153
in, 330
in general, 292–293
incomplete actions, present perfect progressive to express, 230–231
indefinite articles, 286–287, 289
independent clauses, time clauses as, 94–98
infinitives, likes and dislikes expressed using, 192
–ing to form participles, 355–358
institutions, articles used with, 307–308
interesting, 355

J

just, recent activities in present perfect progressive using, 228
just about, 108

K

kind of, to express partial similarity in, 190–191
know, 26, 322
knowledge, opinions, beliefs (*See* opinions and beliefs)
knows, 27

L

last, 295
like, 26, 192, 322
like to, refusing requests using, 251
likes and dislikes, 184–195
  agreement with, using short phrases, 188–189
  either used to express similarity in, 186
  gerunds (verb + *–ing*) used to express, 192
  hedges to express partial, 190–191
  I can't either to express similarity in, 188–189
  I do too to express similarity in, 188–189
  infinitives (*to* + verb) used to express, 192
  neither do I to express similarity in, 188–189
  neither used to express similarity in, 186–187
  similarity of, 186
  so do I to express similarity in, 188–189
  so used to express similarity in, 186–188
  sort of/kind of to express partial similarity in, 190–191
  too used to express similarity in, 186
little, 130
live used as present perfect progressive, 232
look after, 331
look out, 331
look over, 331
lots of, 129
love, 26, 192, 322

M

many, 129
may, 72, 74, 77, 79, 248–256
  conditionals using, 376–377
  in permissions, 255
  requests using, 256
measure words, 120–136
  containers for food, 122
  count nouns and, 125–126
  food described using, 120–125
  measurements of quantity, 123
  noncount nouns and, 125–126
  portions of food, 123
  shapes and states of food, 124
  singular *vs.* plural nouns and, 126
might, 72, 74, 77, 79
  advice expressed using, 157–160
  used in conditionals, 376–377
modal auxiliaries, *should/ought to* as, 152
modals (*See also* phrasal modals)
  affirmative statements using, 74, 77
  be used with, 74, 77
  certainty about a situation expressed using, 72–73
  future tense, probability and possibility, 81–83
  guessing or drawing conclusion using, 79
  have to/have got to as phrasal modals, 169–173
  must as, 169–171
  necessity expressed using, 166–183
  negative statements (*not*) using, 74, 77
  past tense, probability and possibility, 77–78
  permission expressed using, 168
  phrasal modals, 169–171
  probability and possibility expressed using, 70–87
  progressive tense and, probability and possibility, 79–83
  prohibition expressed using, 166–183
  questions using, 74, 77
  wh- questions using, 52
  yes/no questions using, 51
most, 129
much, 129
must, 72, 74, 77, 79
  advice expressed using, 160
  future tense and, 178–180
  modal use of, 169–171
  necessity expressed using, 168, 175–177
  past tense and, 178–180
  present tense and, 178–180
  should and *ought to vs.,* 154
must not/mustn't used to express prohibition, 168, 173–177

N

nearly, 108
necessity
  do not have to used to express lack of, 175–177
  have to/have got to to express, 169, 172–173, 175–177
  modals to express, 166–183
  must used to express, 169, 175–177
need, 26
need to used to express advice, 153, 160
negatives
  anymore used in, 265
  had better and, 155–157
  ought to used with, 152
  passive verbs used in, 320
  used to in, 265
neither do I to express similarity in likes and dislikes, 188–189
neither used to express similarity in likes and dislikes, 186–187
never, 4, 268
  used in questions, 217
next, 295
no, 130, 217
no article (Ø), 284–298
  general statements expressed using, 292–293
  place names using, 304–308
no thanks/no thank you, 242–244
noncount nouns
  articles used with, 286–287, 289
  as...as and *not as...as* used with, 110
  degree complements using, 142
  measure words and, 125–128
  quantifiers and, 129–130
  some used with, 286, 290
  the used with, 291–292